MW01137710

OPPENHEIMER

AND THE ATOMIC BOMB

OPPEN

HEIMER
AND THE ATOMIC BOMB

Young Readers Edition of *American Prometheus:
The Triumph and Tragedy of J. Robert Oppenheimer*

BY **KAI BIRD** AND **MARTIN J. SHERWIN**
ADAPTED BY **ERIC S. SINGER**

G. P. PUTNAM'S SONS

OPPENHEIMER

AND THE ATOMIC BOMB

For Susan Goldmark and Susan Sherwin
and in the memory of
Angus Cameron
and
Jean Mayer

dedication from

American Prometheus: The Triumph and Tragedy of J. Robert Oppenheimer

G. P. Putnam's Sons
An imprint of Penguin Random House LLC
1745 Broadway, New York, New York 10019

First published in the United States of America by G. P. Putnam's Sons,
an imprint of Penguin Random House LLC, 2025

Adapted from *American Prometheus: The Triumph and Tragedy of J. Robert Oppenheimer*, copyright © 2005 by Kai Bird and Martin J. Sherwin
Copyright © 2025 by Kai Bird and Susan Sherwin
"Our Ride-Along with Marty" © 2025 by Alex Sherwin

Photo credits on page 301

Penguin Random House values and supports copyright. Copyright fuels creativity, encourages diverse voices, promotes free speech, and creates a vibrant culture. Thank you for buying an authorized edition of this book and for complying with copyright laws by not reproducing, scanning, or distributing any part of it in any form without permission. You are supporting writers and allowing Penguin Random House to continue to publish books for every reader. Please note that no part of this book may be used or reproduced in any manner for the purpose of training artificial intelligence technologies or systems.

G. P. Putnam's Sons is a registered trademark of Penguin Random House LLC. The Penguin colophon is a registered trademark of Penguin Books Limited.

Visit us online at PenguinRandomHouse.com.

Library of Congress Cataloging-in-Publication Data is available.

ISBN 9780593856451

1 3 5 7 9 10 8 6 4 2

Printed in the United States of America

BVG

Design by Alex Campbell | Text set in Adobe Devanagari

The publisher does not have any control over and does not assume any responsibility for author or third-party websites or their content.

The authorized representative in the EU for product safety and compliance is Penguin Random House Ireland, Morrison Chambers, 32 Nassau Street, Dublin D02 YH68, Ireland, https://eu-contact.penguin.ie.

for Marty

Prometheus stole fire from the gods and gave it to man.
For this he was chained to a rock and tortured for eternity.[1]

CONTENTS

PART TWO: LOS ALAMOS

PART THREE: FALLOUT

PART FOUR: AMERICAN INQUISITION

J. Robert Oppenheimer, circa 1928

OUR RIDE-ALONG WITH MARTY

by Alex Sherwin

When I was ten years old, I had a conversation with my dad that I remember clearly. We were walking our dog Biscuit on Knoll Drive in Princeton, New Jersey, and he asked me if I ever worried about nuclear war. I'd been around more conversations about the proliferation of atomic weapons than the average ten-year-old, and I'd already seen *Dr. Strangelove* a few times, so the question wasn't out of the blue, nor did it feel foreboding. "No," I said. And then I added something along the lines of "I just think people couldn't actually *do that* to each other."

This book is an origin story for how humans *could*. And did.

My father was Martin J. Sherwin, the co-writer of *American Prometheus* with Kai Bird. He was a profoundly wise and grounded person—not at all like J. Robert Oppenheimer, the tortured brilliant doula of the nuclear era. Marty was warm and jovial, rarely brooding and never distant. Some of the best memories of my childhood are watching my dad laugh to the point of tears at slapstick comedy, observed both on-screen and in our family life. So it was somewhat of a strange pairing, my nice dad and Oppenheimer's complex "triumph and tragedy"—a pairing that would endure for most of his adult life. According to my mom, it was a pairing that he entered into reluctantly. "Biography is written by older, wiser people," she recalls him saying at age forty. He feared that to do the subject justice, he would need to get obsessed, and being obsessed didn't sync with his plans as a husband, a father, and a teacher. But the pull of the Father of the Atomic Bomb was strong, as were the persuasive talents of his Knopf editor, Angus Cameron. He signed on.

In pursuit of early research, my dad took our family on the first big trip I remember in my life—to New Mexico, where he interviewed physicists who'd remained in the Los Alamos area and led us on a horseback-riding adventure to find Robert's son, Peter Oppenheimer. We camped near the Oppenheimer ranch, Perro Caliente, and rode the same trails that Robert and his brother Frank had. Later, on that same trip, we found our way to Giovanni Rossi Lomanitz, the physicist who had been a student of Oppenheimer's in Berkeley but who'd been denied a role in the Manhattan Project because of suspected communist affiliation and hounded by the FBI well into the 1950s. We helped him build adobe bricks for his house.

For twenty years, Marty forged on, compiling fifty thousand pages of research on the book while flourishing as a professor at Tufts University and Dartmouth College. It wasn't until he recruited Kai Bird to join as co-writer in 2000 that completing the project became a reality. Marty and Kai were a perfect pair, with deep respect and admiration for each other's talent, and a productive and spirited dynamic. The collaboration cemented a close friendship, and the result was a 2006 Pulitzer Prize–winning biography.

The author's note written by my dad at the end of *American Prometheus* (an abridged version of which appears at the end of this book) is titled "My Long Ride with Oppie"—an homage to Robert's lifelong love of horses and a nod to our 1979 family vacation.

The ride has continued for our family. In 2024, Christopher Nolan's film *Oppenheimer* was an Oscar-winning astonishing success. And now we have Eric Singer's young readers adaptation, *Oppenheimer and the Atomic Bomb*. Marty would have loved that his work was reaching a new generation of readers, and my youngest daughter eagerly dug into Eric's manuscript. She's roughly the same age I was for the dog-walking/nuclear-worries talk I had with her grandfather. Conversations about atomic weapons are less a part of her childhood than mine, but the other day I asked her the same question my dad asked me forty-five years earlier: "Are you worried about nuclear war?"

"Not really," she answered. I thought of my father standing on Knoll Drive, our dog at the end of the leash. Then she offered this: "I think there are things that we can't really think of. We can't comprehend that the world would just . . . vanish. Why would anyone do that?"

Family Journey.
The Sherwins ride along to Perro Caliente, Oppenheimer's New Mexico ranch.

PROLOGUE

Ten-year-old Toshio Nakamura woke from a short night's sleep. He was home in Hiroshima, Japan, eating peanuts as he sat on his bedroll. Suddenly, without warning, an enormous FLASH bathed the space around him in a blinding white light. Before he knew it, he and his two younger sisters, Myeko and Yaeko, were in the air—a violent blast blew them clear across the room. Toshio landed on top of Myeko, whose legs were pinned under a piece of fallen timber. She was crying, "Mother, help me!"

With a mother's reflex, Mrs. Hatsuyo Nakamura ran to her children, desperate to dig them out of the debris. Toshio was unharmed, but Myeko was buried up to her chest. Yaeko was still below—silent. Frantically, Mrs. Nakamura threw aside shards of broken tile and lifted the heavy pieces of timber pinning her two daughters. She quickly freed Myeko. Then she saw Yaeko's arm. She tugged.

"*Itai!* It hurts!" Yaeko wailed.

Relieved that her children were unharmed, Mrs. Nakamura yelled back, "There's no time now to say whether it hurts or not." Then she jerked Yaeko up, freeing her from the remains of their collapsed house.

The Nakamuras went out to the street. They gasped in disbelief, for in front of them lay a scene of utter destruction. All the houses on their block had been reduced to piles of rubble, just like theirs.

As they would later find out, the four-engined American B-29 Superfortress *Enola Gay* had just dropped on their city the first atomic bomb ever used in war. The bomb exploded two thousand feet over Hiroshima's main shopping district, and in less than a second, the temperature at ground zero reached seven thousand degrees Fahrenheit. People as far away as one half mile instantly turned to water vapor. Statues melted, roof tiles fused together, and buildings caught fire or exploded with unimaginable ferocity. At least eighty thousand people died immediately. The Nakamuras' house was about three-quarters of a mile from the center of the explosion, sparing them that fate.

"The neighbors were walking around burned and bleeding," Toshio later recalled. "We went to the park. A whirlwind came. At night a gas tank burned, and I saw the reflection in the river. We stayed in the park [that] night. Next day I went to Taiko Bridge and met my girlfriends Kikuki and Murakami. They were looking

 for their mothers. But Kikuki's mother was wounded, and Murakami's mother, alas, was dead."[2]

Hiroshima, Japan,
after the bomb

Three Days Later
Nagasaki, Japan

Shortly after 11:00 in the morning, twelve-year-old Hiroyasu Tagawa heard the distant whir of a plane flying high over his aunt's house, where he was staying with his sister. Four months earlier, an evacuation forced the family to leave their home in downtown Nagasaki. So that the kids could remain close to school, they agreed to temporarily split up. Hiroyasu and his sister moved in with their aunt, who lived a short distance from town, while their parents moved to Urakami, a neighborhood farther up the Urakami River on the city's northern fringe.

Hiroyasu ran out to the garden. He looked up to the sky. Sure enough, a plane sailed high over the mountaintop, the sun glinting off the metal of its fuselage.

Suddenly, everything turned orange. Hiroyasu quickly covered his eyes and ears and dropped to the ground. This was the position he practiced daily at school for times like this. "Soon dust and debris and pieces of glass were flying everywhere," he recalled. "After that, silence."

At 11:02 a.m. on August 9, 1945, another American B-29 Superfortress named *Bockscar* had dropped a second atomic bomb on Nagasaki. But unlike in Hiroshima, this bomb missed its downtown target—this one exploded directly over Urakami.

After three days went by with no word from his parents, Hiroyasu traveled to Urakami to search for them. When he arrived, he saw piles of bodies all around. So many others were, like him, looking for their families. "Using long bamboo sticks, they were turning over one corpse after the other as they floated down the river. There was an eerie silence and an overwhelming stench."

Hiroyasu heard his mom's voice. She was alive! So was his dad. But they were both hurt so severely they couldn't move. His dad was in the worst shape. He had been handling toxic chemicals at the factory where he worked when the bomb exploded. The chemicals fell on his feet, burning them terribly.

Hiroyasu knew he needed to help his dad immediately. He enlisted a few neighbors to help move him to a makeshift hospital. There, doctors amputated his dad's feet with a wood saw.

But it was no use—his father died a few days later. Heartbroken, Hiroyasu lived with the uncertainty of whether he'd done right by taking his dad to the hospital. "I wondered if I had done the wrong thing by taking him over there. Had I not brought him to have the surgery, maybe he would have lived longer. Such regrets felt like thorns in my heart."

When Hiroyasu finally made it home, he learned that his mom was in critical condition, suffering from the effects of a mysterious illness. He raced back to her on his bike, arriving just in time to say goodbye: "My aunt said, 'Your mother almost died last night, but she wanted to see you one last time. So she gave it her best to live one more day.' My mother looked at me and whispered, 'Hiro-chan, my dear child, grow up fast, okay?' And with these words, she drew her last breath."[3]

Mother and son hold rice balls with no energy to eat, 1.5 kilometers south of hypocenter, Nagasaki, August 10, 1945.

INTRODUCTION

This is the story of J. Robert Oppenheimer, the physicist who led the project to build the atomic bombs that destroyed Hiroshima and Nagasaki, adapted from the Pulitzer Prize–winning book *American Prometheus*. The award-winning film *Oppenheimer* was based upon the same book. It is also a story about what happens when scientists invent technologies they believe will make lives better, only to cede their control to others who use them in unintended ways.

Over the past two hundred years, rapidly changing technologies have dramatically altered life on Earth. Stunning new inventions have made many lives easier, while others have become tools of terrible destruction. Some of them have done both.

Fossil fuels and engines that burn them transformed nations on horseback into global empires. Automobile travel, the jet engine, factory farming, food preservatives, plastics, computers, and smartphones enrich the lives of those who can afford them, but the emissions they produce, the materials they demand, the pollution they create, and the social changes they bring about force us to weigh their benefits against their risks.

In 1939, the world gasped in awe when scientists figured out how to split the uranium atom. They knew the reaction would produce unimaginable amounts of energy. Many hoped such "atomic energy" could be used to power the engines of the future. But they also feared it could be used to build "atomic" bombs capable of killing people on an unimaginable scale—and that they might not have the power to stop it.

During World War II, the United States government asked Oppenheimer to wrest from the atom its awesome power for his country. A brilliant physicist, a passionate advocate for social justice, and a Jew, Robert deeply feared what might happen if Nazi Germany got its hands on such a weapon first. He dived into the project with youthful vigor, idealistic optimism, and a patriotic duty to the country his parents had immigrated to. But he quickly understood that the power he was unleashing, if not controlled together by all nations on Earth, could very well threaten millions of lives and the existence of entire species.

Unlike other scientists who tried to prevent the bomb from being built, Robert believed it *had* to be built—because once an idea enters the scientific mind, it becomes almost unstoppable. He believed that humans should see what horrific things they had the power to create so they might work together to safely control them.

At every stage, Robert tried to advise those who would listen about the dangers of what he helped birth, and warn that future bomb-building had to be contained. He found himself increasingly ignored by a government that prioritized national security and secrecy over global cooperation. That didn't stop him from speaking his mind—first within government, then to the public. He knew the bombs would keep getting bigger and bigger. He knew other countries would get them, putting the world at grave risk of nuclear war. No one else should have to suffer the same fate as those incinerated at Hiroshima and Nagasaki.

But his willingness to warn the world destroyed him. The very government that commissioned his service accused him of disloyalty and put him on trial, then stripped him of his ability to speak within the corridors of power. Like that rebellious Greek god Prometheus—who stole fire from Zeus and gave it to humankind—J. Robert Oppenheimer gave the world atomic fire. But then, when he sought to make us aware of its terrible dangers, the powers that be, like Zeus, rose in anger to punish him.

PART ONE

A WORLD OF PROMISE

CHAPTER ONE

"My life as a child did not prepare me for the fact that the world is full of cruel and bitter things."

At the turn of the twentieth century, people around the world celebrated scientists as heroes. Many looked to science to free them from the people and systems that controlled their lives. They wanted to understand exactly how the amazing machines around them worked. They wanted to find for themselves the answers to the universe's most vexing questions without having to rely on priests or kings or demagogues. Movements for change challenged the church, the crown, and other systems of authority. American president Theodore Roosevelt used his bully pulpit to argue that government, together with science and technology, could launch a new era of progressive reform.

On April 22, 1904, J. Robert Oppenheimer was born into that world of promise. He came from a family of German Jewish immigrants striving to be American. His father, Julius Oppenheimer, immigrated to New York City in 1888. Julius had a keen eye for color and style, and over time became one of the most knowledgeable "fabrics" men in the city. Robert's mother, Ella Friedman, was born in Baltimore in 1869. She was "an exquisitely beautiful" brunette with finely chiseled features. By the time she met Julius, she was a good enough painter to have her own students and a private rooftop studio in a New York apartment building—incredibly uncommon for a woman at the time.

Julius wanted to call his son Robert. But at the last moment, he decided to name the child after himself. He added a "J" before Robert's name, so that the birth certificate read "Julius Robert Oppenheimer." This, too, was uncommon. Naming babies after living relatives wasn't in line with European Jewish tradition. But regardless of what the birth certificate said, the boy would always be called Robert.

The Oppenheimers were wealthy. Robert and his parents lived in a spacious eleventh-floor apartment on Manhattan's Upper West Side, overlooking the Hudson River. His mother decorated the rooms with fine furniture and the walls with an exquisite collection of art, which she chose herself. Live-in maids kept the place spotless. His mother always told Robert that he needed to live his life with "excellence and purpose."

Robert's parents loved him and doted on him. He grew up in luxury and had everything he wanted. Despite his affluence, he didn't show it. Rather, his friends viewed him as thoughtful and kind. One of them later recalled, "[Robert] was extremely generous . . . He was not a spoiled child in any sense."

When Robert was only four years old, his brother Lewis died shortly after birth. From then on, his mother became overly protective of her surviving son. It would be four more years before she gave birth again to Robert's youngest brother, Frank.

As a kid, Robert was often sick. Fearing germs and not wanting her firstborn to suffer the same fate as her second, his mom kept him apart from other kids—and from the wider world. She didn't allow him to buy food from street vendors. Instead of taking him to get haircuts in a barbershop, she had a barber come to the apartment. So, Robert spent his early childhood in his mother's comfortable but lonely nest on Riverside Drive.

Robert was an introvert. He wasn't athletic. But he was artistic like his mother. With her encouragement, he learned how to paint. She also insisted, when he was age five or six, that he take piano lessons. Dutifully, he practiced playing every day. But he hated it the whole time.

After about a year of piano lessons, Robert became terribly sick. His mother expected the worst. She worried he might become paralyzed. Nursing him back to health, she kept asking him over and over, "Robert, how do you feel?" One day, Robert finally had enough. He looked up from his sickbed into her eyes and grumbled defiantly, "Just as I do when I have to take piano." He didn't take another lesson after that.

Robert, born in 1904, sits on his father's lap.

Robert and his mother

Robert holding a teddy bear, circa 1907

Young Robert on a rocking horse

Future sailor

Robert, age three or four

Robert takes a break from playing outdoors to look at the camera.

Julius and Robert

Robert appreciated music from an early age.

Robert and his younger brother Frank

As a young child, he (right, with a friend) had a passion for blocks and collecting rock specimens.

When Robert recovered, his father took him on the first of four trips across the Atlantic to visit his grandfather Benjamin in Germany. Benjamin made a strong impression on him. "It was clear," Robert recalled, "that one of the great joys in life for him was reading, but he had probably hardly been to school." One day, while Robert played with wooden blocks, Benjamin surprised him with an encyclopedia of architecture. He also gave his grandson an ordinary rock collection, which consisted of a box with about two dozen rock samples labeled in German. From that moment on, Robert was a devoted mineral collector.

Back in New York, Robert pleaded with his father to take him on rock-hunting expeditions along the Hudson River. The apartment quickly became crammed with rocks. Robert neatly labeled each one with its scientific name. His father encouraged his son's solitary hobby by buying him books on the subject, but Robert wasn't actually interested in where the rocks came from or how they were formed. Instead, he was fascinated by crystals and how they changed colors so radically in different shades of light.

Robert's father and grandfather lit a spark that ignited a lifelong passion for science. And eventually that spark, together with his natural drive and curiosity, would propel Robert to become one of the most famous, consequential, and controversial scientists in the history of the modern world.

CHAPTER TWO

"Ask me a question in Latin, and I will answer you in Greek."

Robert was an awkward child, but he was never shy when it came to sharing his knowledge with others. When he was twelve, he used the family typewriter to write letters to well-known geologists about rock formations he observed in Central Park. One of the geologists, fascinated by what he had discovered, nominated Robert for membership in the New York Mineralogical Club, which invited him to speak at one of its meetings. The geologists had no idea they were communicating with a kid.

Robert dreaded the thought of having to talk to an audience of adults. He begged his father to tell them that they had invited a twelve-year-old. Greatly amused, Julius encouraged his son to accept the honor.

On the night of the event, Robert showed up at the club with his parents. They proudly introduced their son as "J. Robert Oppenheimer." The startled audience of geologists and amateur rock collectors burst out laughing when he stepped up to the podium. Someone found a wooden box for him to stand on so the audience could see more than a shock of his wiry black hair sticking up above the lectern. Robert nevertheless rose to the occasion and read a speech he had prepared. The crowd gave him a hearty round of applause.

Robert's father actively encouraged him to engage in adult pursuits. Both of his parents knew by that point that they had a "genius" on their hands. One day, his dad gave him a professional-quality microscope. It quickly became his favorite toy. "I think that my father was one of the most tolerant and human of men," Robert remarked later in life. "His idea of what to do for people was to let them find out what they wanted." There was no doubt what Robert wanted—from an early age, he lived within the world of books and science.

"I was an unctuous, repulsively good little boy," Oppenheimer later said. "My life as a child did not prepare me for the fact that the world is full of cruel and bitter things."

Robert was a dreamer. He wasn't interested in the rough-and-tumble lives of other kids his age. As a result, they often teased and ridiculed him. His mother worried about that. She tried whatever she could to get Robert to be like the other children, but nothing seemed to work. He remembered, "I was an unctuous, repulsively good little boy. My life as a child did not prepare me for the fact that the world is full of cruel and bitter things." But Robert's sheltered home life fostered an emotional and even physical toughness that would always stay with him.

Robert was his own unique person, so it was fitting that in 1911, his parents enrolled him in a unique school—the Ethical Culture

School. Founded in 1880 as the Workingman's School for the children of industrial workers, the school insisted that in addition to the usual subjects of math, reading, and history, students would learn art, drama, dance, and technical skills that would help them thrive in an industrial society. The school's founder, Felix Adler, believed that each child had a special talent. Those who had no talent for math might have other extraordinary "artistic gifts to make things with their hands." Adler encouraged kids to expand their talents and use them to create a better world.

Adler sympathized with the hard lives of working-class immigrants. He believed that workers deserved fair pay, guaranteed jobs, and society's respect. He believed all Americans had a moral responsibility to improve the lives of those who toiled in back-breaking conditions to build the bridges they crossed, the railroads they used, and the streets they walked upon.

Like the Oppenheimers, Adler was also a Jew of German origin. His father was the rabbi of Temple Emanu-El, one of the largest synagogues in the United States. Adler believed that Jews shouldn't see themselves as separate from or better than others. Instead, rather than continue to refer to themselves as the Chosen People as the Bible did, Jews should focus on helping all people in the communities they lived in. They should pay most attention to helping those with the least. For Adler, the future for Jews lay not in Palestine, as Zionists believed it should, but in America:

"I fix my gaze steadfastly on the glimmering of a fresh morning that shines over the Alleghenies and the Rockies, not on the evening glow, however tenderly beautiful, that broods and lingers over the Jerusalem hills."

At a time when many elite private schools were closing their doors to Jews because of antisemitism, many wealthy Jewish families like Robert's clamored to have their kids go to the Ethical Culture School—so much so that by 1911, only 10 percent of the student body came from a working-class background. But the school remained devoted to social justice for all. Students graduated with a mission to change the world for the better. They would help those less fortunate improve their lives. They would also consider how their decisions and actions would affect others—for the better, and the worse.

> At the Ethical Culture School, Robert learned to think of himself as a catalyst for a better world—to see things not as they were but as they should be.

Some members of Adler's Ethical Culture Society, which ran the school, modeled political activism for students by serving as change agents for race relations, workers' rights, civil liberties, and environmentalism. They helped found the National Association for the Advancement of Colored People (NAACP), aided young female garment workers when they went on strike for better wages and conditions, and helped found the National Civil Liberties Bureau, which became the American Civil Liberties Union (ACLU).

Robert was a star student. As early as third grade, he was doing lab experiments. By the time he was ten, he was studying physics and chemistry. He skipped several grades. He mastered multiple languages. When he was nine, he told one of his older cousins, "Ask me a question in Latin, and I will answer you in Greek."

His peers thought of him as distant. "We were thrown together a lot," said one of them, "and yet we were never close. He was usually preoccupied with what he was doing or thinking." Another classmate recalled him sitting silently in class, "exactly as though he weren't getting enough to eat or drink." Some of his peers thought of him as "rather gauche . . . he didn't really know how to get along with other children." He had an abrupt, jerky way of walking and possessed a slight arrogance about how much more he knew than his classmates. "It's no fun," he once told a friend, "to turn the pages of a book and say, 'Yes, yes, of course, I know that.'"

Robert's homeroom teacher in high school was Herbert Winslow Smith. Smith was well on his way to obtaining a doctorate from Harvard when he started teaching but was so taken by his experience at the Ethical Culture School that he never went back to finish his degree.

As a teacher, Smith was warm and gentle. He somehow always managed to find out what each student was most curious about and relate it to the topic of the day. After every class, students lingered around his desk, trying to squeeze more conversation out of him. Though Robert's first passion was clearly science, Smith stoked his literary interests. Once, after Robert wrote an entertaining essay on oxygen, Smith suggested, "I think your vocation is to be a science writer." Smith became Robert's friend and counselor. Their relationship endured. Later in life, Robert would turn to Smith for advice and consolation.

Robert had a breakthrough year as a junior when he took a

course in physics with teacher Augustus Klock. "He was marvelous," Robert said. "I got so excited after the first year, I arranged to spend the summer working with him setting up equipment for the following year, when I would then take chemistry. We must have spent five days a week together." Sometimes after school the teacher and student would go hunting around the city for minerals.

Klock stirred up such excitement and wonder in Robert. In his class, Robert began experimenting with electrolytes and conduction. "I loved chemistry so deeply . . . Compared to physics, it starts right in the heart of things, and very soon you have that connection between what you see and a really very sweeping set of ideas which could exist in physics but is very much less likely to be accessible."

When he was a senior, Robert's ethical studies teacher John Lovejoy Elliott asked his students to consider: If they had a choice between a job teaching or a job that paid more money working in Wrigley's chewing gum factory—which would they choose? He asked them to think about the proper roles of government, and the ethics of loyalty and treason. What if the government did things that weren't in the best interest of its citizens? That hurt innocent people in other countries? Or that took advantage of its power to limit the power of others? Should citizens remain loyal to such a government? Should they speak out against it? And if they spoke out against it, and the government accused them of treason, would it be justified? Would it be worth it?

The Ethical Culture School's sheltered atmosphere was perfect for an unusually awkward but brilliant teenager. Robert could shine where he wanted while being protected from social situations that he couldn't yet cope with. The school allowed him to remain a curious child long after other schools might have beaten that curiosity out of him.

After Robert and his brother Frank graduated, John Elliott wrote Julius: "I did not know how close I could get to your boys. Along with you, I am glad and grateful for them." The school planted deep moral roots in Robert's psyche. He graduated as class valedictorian—determined to help people less fortunate than him and make a positive difference in the world.

ROBERT HAD BEEN "TORTURED" THAT NIGHT.

Robert was a sheltered kid, so when he was fourteen his dad sent him to summer camp to get him outdoors and playing with boys his age. For most of the other boys there, Camp Koenig was a mountain paradise full of fun and friendship. For Robert, it was just stressful. Everything about him—his shyness, his sensitivity, his unique interests—made him the target of bullying. The other boys called him "Cutie" and teased him mercilessly. Robert refused to fight back. Instead, he avoided activities that required him to interact with others. He walked the trails by himself. He collected rocks. He wrote poetry and read a lot.

One day, Robert made the great mistake of writing his parents that he was glad he had come to camp because the other boys were teaching him the facts of life. Outraged, his parents drove to the camp to meet with the director. They thought Robert was way too young to be talking so freely about sex. After they left, the camp directors cracked down on the telling of salacious stories.

Robert was branded a tattler. One night, a group of boys dragged him out of bed and carried him off to the camp icehouse. They stripped him of his clothes and pushed him and shoved him. Then they sprayed his buttocks and genitals with green paint. They left him naked and locked inside the icehouse for the whole night. The one friend he had at camp later explained that Robert had been "tortured" that night.

Robert suffered this horrible treatment in stoic, stubborn, determined silence. He didn't tell anyone about it. He didn't complain. He didn't ask his parents to pick him up. "I don't know how Robert stuck out those remaining weeks," said his friend. "Not many boys would have—or could have—but Robert did. It must have been hell for him."

"ROBERTY, ROBERTY . . ."

To escape his challenging social life, Robert turned to the water. By age sixteen, he was an expert sailor who pushed his boat to the edge. His father bought him a twenty-eight-foot sloop, which Robert named the *Trimethy* after the chemical compound trimethylene dioxide. He loved sailing in summer storms. Fearlessly, he raced his boat against the tides through the Fire Island inlet and straight out into the Atlantic. With his little brother Frank hunkered down in the cockpit, Robert stood with the tiller between his legs, screaming gleefully into the wind as he tacked the boat back into Long Island's Great South Bay.

His parents couldn't understand how a kid so shy on land could become so headstrong and devil-may-care on the sea. Time after time, his mother stood at the window of their Bay Shore summer home, frantically searching for a trace of the *Trimethy* on the horizon. More than once, his father had to ride out into the ocean on his motorboat to chase Robert back to shore. He warned Robert about the risks he was taking with his own and others' lives. "Roberty, Roberty . . ." he would say, shaking his head. But Robert wasn't ashamed. He had complete mastery over wind and sea and knew no fear. It could have been deeply ingrained arrogance or inner resiliency, but Robert had an irresistible urge to flirt with danger. He saw no reason to cheat himself of the thing that brought him such complete joy and excitement.

In the summer of 1921, Robert's parents took him and nine-year-old Frank to Germany for the summer. Robert had recently graduated from high school, ready to spread his wings. After he traveled for some time with his family, his parents allowed him to strike out on his own. Robert decided to go mineral prospecting among some old mines not far from Berlin. There, the physically delicate seventeen-year-old camped out by himself in rugged conditions.

He came back to his family with a suitcase full of rock specimens and a near-fatal

Robert takes a swim lesson.

case of trench dysentery, a terrible bowel disease caused by contaminated water. He returned to New York on a stretcher. Sick and bedridden, Robert had to postpone his arrival to Harvard, where he had been accepted earlier that year. Instead, his parents pressured him to remain at home to recuperate.

CHAPTER THREE

The Canyon's Name Was Los Alamos

Robert spent the long winter of 1921–22 cooped up in the New York apartment. He was a terrible patient. He acted boorishly, locking himself in his room and brushing aside his mother's efforts to help ease his discomfort.

By spring, Julius decided Robert was well enough to get him out of the house. He called Robert's old teacher Herbert Smith and urged him to take Robert with him on a trip to the Southwest that summer. Smith had made a similar trip with another student the previous year. Perhaps a Western adventure would help toughen Robert up. Smith agreed to take him.

The student and his teacher started out in the South. They gradually made their way across the mesas of New Mexico to Albuquerque. There, they stayed with the family of Robert's only real friend, Francis Fergusson, who had attended the Ethical Culture School on scholarship.

The two boys had become close during their senior year, but it was this visit that would cement a lifelong friendship. Francis introduced Robert to another Albuquerque boy their age, Paul Horgan. Paul's first impressions of Robert were striking: "He combined incredibly good wit and gaiety and high spirits . . . He had this lovely social quality that permitted him to enter into the moment very strongly, wherever it was and whenever it was." Like Robert and Francis, Paul was very bright. All three were headed for Harvard in the fall.

From Albuquerque, Smith led Robert—and Paul and Francis— twenty-five miles northeast of Santa Fe to a dude ranch called Los Pinos. The ranch was run by twenty-eight-year-old Katherine Chaves Page. Katherine was a charming and headstrong young woman. Robert found himself instantly attracted to her. But any hopes he may have had for a romance with her were dashed—she had just married Winthrop Page, a man old enough to be her father. The ranch boasted a spectacular view of the Pecos River as it twisted north toward the snowcapped Sangre de Cristos. This was to be Robert's stomping ground for the summer.

Romantic feelings aside, Katherine and Robert became very good friends. Katherine taught Robert how to ride a horse. Soon, as Paleo-Indians and Ancestral Pueblo people had done for thousands of years before them, Robert and his adventurous companions set out to explore the breathtakingly beautiful wilderness on rides that sometimes lasted five or six days.

Despite his lingering illness and fragile appearance, Robert relished the physical challenges of horseback riding. One day, while riding back from Colorado, Robert insisted they take a snow-covered trail over the highest pass in the mountains. Smith was certain that trail could easily expose them to death. Robert was set on going anyway. Slightly panicked, Smith suggested they toss a coin to decide which route they would take. "Thank God I won," he remembered. "I don't know how I'd have got out of it if I hadn't."

> Smith knew from that moment on that Robert wouldn't allow fear to limit his actions.

That summer at Los Pinos, Robert evolved from a shy and emotionally vulnerable young boy into a much more self-confident young man—one who seemed more in control of his own destiny. Katherine motivated him and emboldened him to take risks. She approved of him the way he was. "[For] the first time in his life," Smith recalled, Robert "found himself loved, admired, sought after."

Oppenheimer (right) riding in Central Park

One day Robert, Katherine, and a few others grabbed horses and rode south from the village of Frijoles. They ascended the Pajarito Plateau, rising to a height of over ten thousand feet. From there, they traversed the Valle Grande, a canyon inside the Jemez Caldera, a bowl-shaped volcanic crater twelve miles wide. Turning northeast, they rode four miles and came upon another canyon, which took its Spanish name from the cottonwood trees that bordered a stream trickling through the valley. The canyon's name was Los Alamos.

Patches of grazing meadows broke up dense pine and juniper forests. Atop a two-mile-long mesa bounded on both the north and south by steep canyons stood a spartan boys' school, the Los Alamos Ranch School. The school enrolled only twenty-five boys, most of them the sons of wealthy Detroit car manufacturers. Throughout the year, they wore shorts and slept on unheated porches. Each boy was responsible for tending a horse. Frequently, they packed up their horses with food and clothing and rode off into the nearby Jemez Mountains. It was a completely different kind of education from what Robert was used to at the Ethical Culture School in New York City.

Robert immediately connected with the rugged landscape. His experience there changed his life. It opened his personality and gave him a much wider perspective on the beauty of the earth. He later wrote a friend, "My two great loves are physics and New Mexico. It's a pity they can't be combined."

Dense pine and juniper forests near Los Alamos

On later trips, Robert and his horse Crisis went for long rides with his brother Frank and other friends.

Robert didn't know it then, but that very same New Mexico plateau would shortly become ground zero for a project that would impact hundreds of thousands of people and forever change the course of human history. And he would be the one to lead it.

CHAPTER FOUR

"He knew enough to ask questions."

Autumn inevitably rolled around, and Robert arrived at Harvard. The college assigned him a single room in Standish Hall, a dormitory facing the Charles River. Now nineteen, Robert was oddly handsome. Every feature of his body seemed to be exaggerated. His fine pale skin drew taut across high cheekbones. His eyes were the brightest pale blue, but his eyebrows were glossy black. He wore his coarse, kinky black hair long on top but short on the sides—so he seemed even taller than his lanky five-feet-ten-inch frame. He weighed so little—never more than 130 pounds—that he gave an impression of flimsiness. His straight nose, thin lips, and large, almost pointed ears made him seem even more delicate. He spoke in grammatically correct sentences with the kind of European politeness his mother had taught him. But as he talked, his long, thin hands made his gestures seem somehow crooked. His appearance was striking and slightly bizarre.

As a young man, Robert appeared immature, socially awkward, and studious. His personality that had bloomed so intensely on the waters off Long Island and in the desert of New Mexico became stifled once again in the storied corridors of Harvard. He thrived in the university's intellectual environment but struggled mightily to make new friends besides Paul and Francis. He was on his own much of the time. So, he retreated to the security of dark-spirited writers like Anton Chekhov and Katherine Mansfield. Most days he consumed little more than chocolate, beer, and artichokes. For lunch, he often ate just a "black and tan"—a piece of toast slathered with peanut butter and topped with chocolate syrup.

His friend Paul remembered that Robert had bouts of "deep, deep depressions as a youngster." He held his emotions close to his chest, often refusing to talk about what he was feeling for days at a time. His sophomore year, he decorated his dorm room with an Oriental rug, oil paintings, and etchings he brought from home, and insisted on making tea from a charcoal-fired Russian urn. His roommate Frederick Bernheim recalled, Robert "wasn't a comfortable person to be around, in a way, because he always gave the impression that he was thinking very deeply about things. When we roomed together he would spend evenings locked in his room," pondering scientific problems. "I had visions of him suddenly bursting forth as a great physicist, and here I was just trying to get through Harvard."

Fred thought Robert was a hypochondriac, and that he had other strange habits. "He went to bed with an electric pad every night, and one day it started to smoke." Robert woke up and ran to the bathroom with the burning pad. He then fell back asleep, unaware that the pad was still burning. Fred had to extinguish it himself before it burned the house down. He was a tough guy to live with, Fred recalled, "because you had to more or less adjust to his standards or moods—he was really the dominant one."

William Clouser Boyd met Robert in chemistry class one day. He liked him immediately. "We had lots of interests in common aside from science," William recalled. They both tried to write poetry, sometimes in French, and short stories inspired by Russian playwright Anton Chekhov. Robert always called him "Clowser," purposely misspelling his middle name. Clowser often joined Robert and Fred on weekend trips to Cape Ann, Massachusetts, about an hour's drive northeast of Harvard. Robert didn't know how to drive yet, so Fred drove them in his Willys-Overland. They spent the night at an inn in Folly Cove outside of Gloucester where the food was particularly good.

Back on campus, Robert had almost no social life. He spent many long hours in his room studying and writing poetry that channeled his sad and lonely feelings. He read works of French literature and devoured all three thousand pages of Edward Gibbon's *The History of the Decline and Fall of the Roman Empire*. Clowser knew Robert could run circles around him intellectually. "He had a very quick mind. For instance, when someone would propose a problem, he would give two or three wrong answers, followed by the right one, before I could think of a single answer."

Robert's depression came on particularly strong after his family's visits. After they left, he would drag Francis or Fred with him on long walks, talking all the while in his quiet, even voice about some scientific topic or other. Walking was Robert's only therapy. One winter night he, Fred, and some others were out hiking at 3:00 a.m. Suddenly, one of the boys dared the others to jump into the Charles River. Robert didn't think twice. He immediately stripped down to his underwear and plunged into the icy water.

When he was depressed, Robert turned to his old teacher Herbert Smith for help. In the late winter of 1924, he wrote him a letter in the throes of an emotional crisis. Smith wrote back, reassuring Robert that everything would be okay. Robert replied to him, "What has soothed me most, I think, is that you perceived in my distress a certain similarity to that from which you had suffered." Robert took comfort in knowing that there was at least one other human being in the world who had felt pain similar to what he was feeling.

> The empathy Smith showed Robert stuck with him throughout his life. It shaped his perspectives toward others who suffered the horrors of what he would help create.

When Robert started at Harvard, he wasn't sure what he should major in. He took philosophy, French literature, English, calculus, history, and three chemistry courses. Maybe he should study architecture? Greek classics? Maybe he should write poetry? Or even paint?

Within months he settled on his first passion—chemistry. Determined to graduate in three years, he took the maximum of six courses per semester. He somehow managed to sit in on two or three more. But by the end of his freshman year, he decided that picking chemistry had been a mistake. "I can't recall how it came over me that what I liked in chemistry was very close to physics," he said.

Robert had never taken even a basic physics course. But he pleaded with the physics professors to accept him into the most advanced classes. In response, they asked him to demonstrate that he knew something about the subject. He responded with a list of fifteen books that he claimed to have read. One of the professors,

George Washington Pierce, quipped, "Obviously, if he says he's read these books, he's a liar, but he should get a PhD for knowing their titles." They approved his petition.

Robert's physics tutor was Percy Bridgman, who later won a Nobel Prize. "I found Bridgman a wonderful teacher," recalled Robert. He admired his tutor because he was always thoughtful and willing to think outside the box. And Bridgman admired his student's curiosity. "He knew enough to ask questions." But when Bridgman assigned Robert a lab experiment that required him to make a copper-nickel alloy in a self-built furnace, Robert "didn't know one end of the soldering iron from the other." Years later, he admitted that he had been very insecure about how little he knew about physics. "To this day," he told an interviewer later in life, "I get panicky when I think about a smoke ring or elastic vibrations. There's nothing there—just a little skin over a hole."

Robert didn't know it then, but he had entered the world of physics at an incredibly exciting time. The field was in the earliest stages of a radical revolution. For most of the nineteenth century and human history before it, physicists used "classical mechanics" theory to study how objects interacted with other things to cause reactions. A ball hits a wall. It bounces. It comes back to you, and you catch it. The ball doesn't go through the wall, or disappear. Those reactions were understood, predictable, and measured.

But by the time Robert arrived at Harvard, physicists were just starting to understand how physical substances around them were actually made up of tiny "subatomic" particles—electrons, protons, and neutrons—that behaved like waves. When those particles or waves interacted with each other, they caused very different reactions from what classical mechanics theory may have

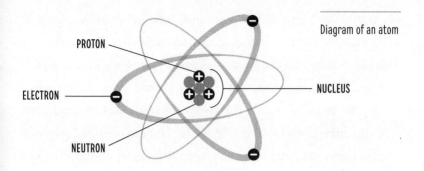

PROTON

ELECTRON

NUCLEUS

NEUTRON

Diagram of an atom

predicted. The world at the atomic and subatomic levels was much stranger, more unpredictable, more unstable, and much more exciting than the world most people thought they knew. Physicists theorized that subatomic particles could move through walls or rock or entire planets. They also learned more about how matter could be transformed, releasing incredible amounts of energy in the process. They called the theory that described what happened in that new subatomic world "quantum mechanics."[4]

When Robert was a sophomore, one of the stars of quantum mechanics, Danish physicist Niels Bohr, visited Harvard. The year before, Bohr had won his Nobel Prize for helping the world better understand the structure of the atom. A wave of excitement washed over campus.

Robert respected Bohr deeply and was captivated when he got his first glimpse of the thick-haired, wide-eyed scientist. Bridgman reflected that "the impression [Bohr] made on everyone who met him was a singularly pleasant

Niels Bohr

one personally. I have seldom met a man with such evident singleness of purpose . . . he is now idolized as a scientific god through most of Europe." In Bohr's hands, physics became a joyous celebration of life.

From that moment on, Robert knew he had found his calling.

In June 1925, after only three years of study, Robert graduated Harvard summa cum laude. He made the dean's list and was one of only thirty students to be selected for membership in Phi Beta Kappa, America's most respected honor society. Though he had spent so many hours studying alone in his room, he confessed that he could have worked much harder: "Although I liked to work, I spread myself very thin and got by with murder; I got A's in all these courses which I don't think I should have."

Robert, Clowser, and Fred skipped their graduation ceremony. Instead, they celebrated privately in one of their dorm rooms. Later that weekend, Robert took Clowser to the summer house in Bay Shore and sailed his beloved *Trimethy* to Fire Island. "We took off our clothes," Clowser remembered, "and walked up and down the beach getting a sunburn."

Robert could have stayed at Harvard—he was offered a graduate fellowship. But he had bigger ambitions. The center of the physics world at the time wasn't in Cambridge, Massachusetts, but rather in Cambridge, England. There, Robert hoped he might be able to study with the eminent physicist Ernest Rutherford, who was celebrated as the man who had first developed a model of the nuclear atom in 1911.

He asked Bridgman to write him a letter of recommendation. In his letter, Bridgman wrote honestly, telling Rutherford that though Robert had a powerfully analytical mind, "his weakness is on the experimental side . . . he is not at home in the manipulations of the laboratory . . . It appears to me that it is a bit of a gamble as to whether Oppenheimer will ever make any real contributions of an important character, but if he does make good at all, I believe he will be a very unusual success."

Bridgman then commented on Robert's Jewish background, not unusual for a time rife with antisemitism: "As appears from his name, Oppenheimer is a Jew, but entirely without the usual qualifications of his race. He is a tall, well set-up young man, with a rather engaging diffidence of manner, and I think you need have no hesitation whatever for any reason of this sort in considering his application."

His heart and mind full of anticipation and hope, Robert took off for his beloved New Mexico. This time he brought his parents with him. He showed them his few acres of heaven at Katherine's Los Pinos ranch. "The parents are quite pleased with the place," Robert wrote with obvious pride to Herbert Smith, "and are starting to ride a little."

Together with Paul Horgan and Robert's brother Frank, now thirteen, the boys went for long horseback rides in the mountains. They rode on the Lake Peak trail across the Sangre de Cristo Mountains and down to the village of Cowles. Paul recalled, "We hit the divide at the very top of that mountain in a tremendous thunderstorm . . . immense, huge pounding rain. We sat under our horses for lunch and ate oranges, [and we] were drenched . . . I was looking at Robert and all of a sudden I noticed his hair was standing straight up, responding to the static. Marvelous." When they finally rode into Los Pinos that night after dark, Katherine's windows were lit. "It was a very welcome sight," Paul said. "She received us and we had a beautiful time for several days there."

Katherine taught them to ride light and pack the bare minimum. One night on the trail Robert ran out of food. Someone offered him a pipe to quell his pangs of hunger. Pipe tobacco and cigarettes quickly became a lifelong addiction.

While Robert's mom sat on the shaded, wraparound porch of the ranch house, Katherine and the boys rode every day into the surrounding mountains. On one of their expeditions, Robert found a small, uncharted lake on the eastern slopes of the Santa Fe Baldy. He named it Lake Katherine.

At the end of August, Robert returned to New York. In his mailbox was the letter he had anticipated all summer. He took a deep breath and opened it. The news was not what he had hoped. Ernest Rutherford had turned him down. "Rutherford wouldn't have me," Robert recalled. "He didn't think much of Bridgman and my credentials were peculiar."

But Rutherford had forwarded Robert's application to J. J. Thomson, the former director of the University of Cambridge's Cavendish Laboratory. At sixty-nine years old, Thomson, who had won the 1906 Nobel Prize in Physics for his detection of the electron, was well past his prime as a working physicist. He only came into the lab from time to time to tutor just a few students. Robert, to his great relief, learned that he would be one of them. Brimming with excitement and savoring his good fortune, Robert packed his bags and boarded a ship bound for England and the exciting new world of quantum mechanics.

CHAPTER FIVE

"I am having a pretty bad time."

When he arrived in Cambridge, Robert settled into a dreary apartment that he called a "miserable hole." He spent his days in a corner of Thomson's basement laboratory, suffering through the work his new mentor gave him. After a few months, he wrote Francis Fergusson in anguish, "I am having a pretty bad time. The lab work is a terrible bore, and I am so bad at it that it is impossible to feel that I am learning anything . . . the lectures are vile." Even though he hated the lab, being in Cambridge gave Robert the opportunity to meet world-renowned physicists like Rutherford, James Chadwick, C. F. Powell, and P. M. S. Blackett, who soon became one of his tutors.

Robert's depression only deepened on the other side of the Atlantic. One day he stood in front of an empty blackboard with a piece of chalk in his hand, muttering over and over, "The point is, the point is . . . the point is." His friend Jeffries Wyman became worried. Walking into his room on one occasion, Jeffries found Robert lying on the floor, groaning and rolling from side to side because he felt so miserable. On another occasion, Rutherford witnessed him collapse in a heap on the lab floor.

Adulthood had come for Robert while he wasn't looking. An

ocean away from his family and unmoored from the lives of his few friends, the world seemed to be moving on without him. Fred Bernheim, Robert's roommate and partner in crime at Harvard, had met a woman and fallen in love. Robert sensed that things would never be the same between them. Stubbornly, he tried to revive the friendship, but Fred finally told him that he was going to marry and that "we couldn't re-establish what we'd had at Harvard." Robert couldn't understand how someone he had known so well could decide so suddenly to spin out of his orbit. He was also astonished when he learned that Jane Didisheim, one of his old classmates from the Ethical Culture School, had gotten married young and was already pregnant with her first child.

After just a few months at Cavendish, Robert was unraveling emotionally. He was losing control.

Would he ever find someone himself? Would he ever fall in love? Would that person love him back? Would his career take off? Or did his difficulty in the lab signal more difficulty to come? Would he ever make one bit of difference in the world?

Francis declared that Robert had a "first class case of depression." From his letters, his parents could tell that their son was in crisis. They raced across the Atlantic to be with him.

Robert jumped on a train to Southampton to meet them as their ship docked. But the first person he saw way up on the gangplank wasn't his mother or father but Inez Pollak, another of his classmates from the Ethical Culture School. His mother decided to bring Inez with them to set her up with Robert, or at least distract him from his anguish. Robert's first instinct was to turn and run. He was terrified. Inez may have been too. But by that point there was no other choice—they all traveled together back to Cambridge.

In the mornings, Robert busied himself with physics. But in the afternoons, he took Inez on long walks around town. They went through the motions of dating. They even got informally engaged. Francis recalled that Robert "did a very good . . . imitation of being in love with her. She responded in kind."

But it didn't work out. In the end, the pair didn't have much chemistry. Over time, Robert's mother began to view Inez as "ridiculously unworthy" of him and regretted bringing her to England. Finally, fed up with the awkwardness of her relationship with Robert and annoyed at Ella's attitude, Inez packed her things and left for Italy.

Breaking up with Inez only made Robert's depression worse. He became even more unsure of himself and stubbornly ill-tempered. His relationship with his new tutor, P. M. S. Blackett, also began to deteriorate. Robert liked Blackett, but Blackett loved to perform hands-on experiments in the lab, and Robert wasn't good at lab work, so he hated it. Their relationship made Robert extremely anxious.

When faced with such anxiety, Robert had a tendency to sabotage himself. Late that autumn of 1925, consumed by feelings of inadequacy and intense jealousy, he poisoned an apple with chemicals from the lab. Then he left the apple on Blackett's desk. Luckily, Blackett didn't eat it. But university officials found out what Robert had done. Two months later, he confessed to Francis, who recalled, "[Robert] had kind of poisoned the head steward. It seemed incredible, but that was what he said. And he had actually used cyanide or something . . . and fortunately [Blackett] discovered it. Of course there was hell to pay with Cambridge."

If the poison was deadly, Robert could have been charged with attempted murder. But it is more likely that he laced the apple with something that would have only made Blackett sick instead of cyanide. One way or another, it was an incredibly serious offense—and grounds for expulsion.

Julius and Ella were still in Cambridge. The university immediately told them about what their son had done. Julius frantically raced to campus and pleaded with the administration not to press charges. Reluctantly, they agreed. But Robert was now on probation. He would have to see a psychiatrist in London. If he didn't, he would be kicked out of school.

"HE JUMPED ON ME FROM BEHIND WITH A TRUNK STRAP AND WOUND IT AROUND MY NECK."

Concerned about Robert, Francis went to visit his troubled friend in London. The two met up just after Robert came out of a meeting with the psychiatrist. "I saw him standing on the corner, waiting for me, with his hat on one side of his head, looking absolutely weird . . . He was sort of standing around, looking like he might run or do something drastic."

They took off together at a brisk pace, Robert walking his peculiar walk with his feet turned out at a severe angle. Francis asked him how the sessions had been going so far. Robert responded that the psychiatrist was "too stupid to follow him and that he knew more about his troubles than the doctor did." Francis knew his friend well enough to know he would be able to move past this terrible time in his life. But Robert's crisis was far from over.

Robert was getting very little sleep. His strange behavior kept getting stranger. While on holiday with his parents in France, he locked his mother in her hotel room. She became infuriated and forced him to see a French psychotherapist, who declared that he was having a moral crisis.

One evening, in an unstable mood, Robert went to visit Francis, who had traveled to Paris and was staying in a hotel there. Francis tried to calm his friend with some poetry that his girlfriend, Frances Keeley, had written. Francis then told Robert that he and Keeley were going to get married. Stunned at the news, Robert snapped. "I leaned over to pick up a book," Francis recalled, "and he jumped on me from behind with a trunk strap and wound it around my neck . . . And then I managed to pull aside, and he fell on the ground weeping."

Robert had already lost one good friend, Fred Bernheim, to marriage. The thought of losing another was too much for him to bear. Even though Robert had tried to choke him, Francis understood what he was going through and stood by him.

Francis, Jeffries Wyman, and John Edsall knew that Robert needed his friends more than ever. They persuaded him to go on vacation with them to the beautiful Mediterranean island of Corsica. For ten days, the four friends bicycled the length of the island. Some nights, they slept in small village inns. Other nights, they camped out under the stars. Corsica's craggy mountains and lightly forested high mesas reminded Robert of his beloved New Mexico.

Though he was beginning to break the cycle of his depression, Robert occasionally felt dark moods descend. When they did, he found comfort in literature like he always had. In the evenings by flashlight, he devoured Marcel Proust's *À la recherche du temps perdu* (*In Search of Lost Time*), a book Proust wrote about his life and his search for meaning in the world. Later, Robert said reading it was one of the great experiences of his life.

One night, after a sudden thunderstorm drenched them to the bone, Robert and his three friends took refuge at a local hotel. As they hung their wet clothes by the fire and huddled in blankets, John and Robert began arguing about who they thought was the best Russian writer, Leo Tolstoy or Fyodor Dostoyevsky. "Tolstoy is the writer I most enjoy," argued John. "No, no, Dostoyevsky is superior," Robert shot back. "He gets to the soul and torment of man."

Reading gave Robert a lens into how others dealt with similar feelings. It made him realize that he needed to care more about others' pain and suffering. He also began to understand that he wasn't alone—that Proust and so many other great minds were struggling to make sense of a strange and senseless world. He no longer had to blame himself for feeling so lost in it.

As they hiked through the Corsican mountains, Robert began to feel better. The trip stirred an awakening within him. His friends noticed it too. Corsica's dramatic beauty, great food and wine, and the rich books he devoured wrenched him from the black hole of his depression and inspired him to take his first steps on the bridge to adulthood.

"OPPENHEIMER SEEMED TO ME RIGHT FROM THE BEGINNING A VERY GIFTED MAN."

When he returned to Cambridge, an invigorated Robert threw himself into the exciting world of quantum mechanics. All around him, budding scientists experimented with the little-known or the unknown. Werner Heisenberg was trying to figure out how electrons behaved. Erwin Schrödinger answered that they behaved like waves curving around the nucleus of an atom. Paul Dirac was doing something or other that Robert didn't understand.

In the spring of 1926, Robert met the man who first inspired him to enter the world of quantum mechanics—the great Danish physicist Niels Bohr. Robert had a great deal in common with Bohr. Nineteen years older, Bohr had also been born into an upper-class Jewish family surrounded by books, music, and learning. He became one of Robert's most important role models.

It was one thing to hear Bohr address an audience as he had years before at Harvard. It was quite another to encounter the Nobel Prize winner face-to-face. Tall and athletic, Bohr had a warm and gentle soul, and a wry sense of humor. He always spoke softly and with humility. "Not often in life," Albert Einstein wrote to Bohr, "has a human being caused me such joy by his mere presence as you did."

Robert had been working very hard on what would become his first major paper in theoretical physics. One day, he walked into Rutherford's office. He saw Bohr sitting in a chair. Rutherford rose from behind his desk and introduced the two men. Bohr asked Robert politely, "How is it going?" Robert replied bluntly, "I'm in difficulties." Bohr responded, "Are the difficulties mathematical or physical?" When Robert replied, "I don't know," Bohr responded, "That's bad." Bohr couldn't help thinking how young Robert looked. After he left the room, Rutherford turned to Bohr and remarked that he had high expectations for the young man. After a while, Robert came to speak of Bohr as "his God."

Soon after meeting Bohr, Robert met Max Born, the physicist

who had coined the term "quantum mechanics." Born was visiting from the Institute of Theoretical Physics at the University of Göttingen in Germany, which he directed. There, he nurtured the work of Heisenberg, Eugene Wigner, Wolfgang Pauli, and Enrico Fermi. Born was a pacifist and a Jew. His students thought of him as an unusually warm and patient teacher.

Immediately, Born admired Robert's curiosity and realized how smart he was. "Oppenheimer seemed to me," Born said, "right from the beginning a very gifted man." He was the perfect mentor for a young student with Robert's delicate personality. Born invited Robert to study with him in Göttingen after he completed his studies at Cambridge.

In many ways, Robert's year at Cambridge had been a disaster. He had narrowly avoided being expelled for the "poison apple" incident. His closest friends witnessed him fall into the worst depression of his life. At some of his lowest points, he had convinced himself that he would never make a difference in the world or find anyone to share his life with. But his mentors taught him that it was okay to not have the answers to difficult questions—both in physics and in life. When Bohr asked Robert whether his problems were mathematical or physical, he was telling Robert that he shouldn't let life's confusing details distract him from his great ideas—and from his deep yearning to serve a meaningful purpose in the world.

CHAPTER SIX

"I find the work hard, thank God, & almost pleasant."

Late in the summer of 1926, Robert arrived in Göttingen, a small medieval town that boasted a city hall and several churches dating back to the fourteenth century. At the corner of Barfüsserstrasse and Jüdenstrasse (Barefoot Street and Street of the Jews), he dined on Wiener schnitzel at the four-hundred-year-old Junkers' Hall, sitting beneath a steel engraving of Otto von Bismarck and surrounded by three stories of stained glass.

Quaint half-timbered houses were scattered about the town's narrow, winding streets. Nestled on the banks of the Leine Canal, Göttingen's main attraction was Georgia Augusta University, founded in the 1730s. By tradition, graduates of the university had to wade into the fountain in front of the ancient city hall and kiss the Goose Girl, a bronze maiden in the fountain's center. Robert had arrived in the global epicenter of theoretical physics.

There, he found himself surrounded by an extraordinary collection of scientists. James Franck had won the Nobel Prize the year earlier for his work on the impact electrons had on atoms. Otto Hahn was working on what would become nuclear fission—the science behind the atomic bomb. Pascual Jordan was working with Born and Heisenberg on matrix mechanics. George Eugene Uhlenbeck and Samuel Abraham Goudsmit discovered the electron spin. Paul Dirac, who would later win his Nobel in 1933 (shared with Erwin Schrödinger), was experimenting with other tough problems that quantum theory might solve.

Robert quickly drew the attention of these men. "We got along very well immediately," recalled Uhlenbeck. He fit in so easily that it seemed to Uhlenbeck "as if we were old friends."

Unlike at Cambridge, Robert felt a pleasant camaraderie with his fellow students. "I was part of a little community of people who had some common interests and tastes." At Harvard and Cambridge, Robert had buried himself in books because he saw them as the only sources of knowledge. But at Göttingen, for the first time, he realized he could learn from others: "I began to have some conversations. Gradually, I guess, they gave me some sense . . . something that I probably would not have ever gotten to if I'd been locked up in a room."

In the evenings, Robert and his new friends strolled down to the fifteenth-century Zum Schwarzen Bären—the Black Bear Pub—to drink beer; or sip coffee at the Cron & Lanz coffee shop. Realizing that he had more money than most of them, Robert often paid for his friends. He was transformed; he was now confident, excited, and focused. He was, said Uhlenbeck, "clearly a center of all the younger students . . . he was really a kind of oracle. He knew very much. He was very difficult to understand, but very quick." Soon, Robert had "a whole group of admirers" trailing around after him.

The admiration did wonders for Robert's self-confidence. It also helped that his reputation preceded him. At Cambridge, he had written and presented two papers on quantum theory. Both papers represented small but important contributions to the field, and Robert was happy to find out that the Cambridge Philosophical Society had published them before he arrived in Göttingen.

The publications emboldened Robert to participate more enthusiastically in class. He settled in nicely. For the first time in a long time, he began enjoying himself. He wrote Francis, "You would like [it here], I think. Like Cambridge, it is almost exclusively scientific . . . [but] the science is much better than at Cambridge, & on the whole, probably the best to be found . . . I find the work hard, thank God, & almost pleasant."

Sometimes he became a little too enthusiastic—and a little too arrogant. "He was a man of great talent," Born later wrote, "and he was conscious of his superiority in a way which was embarrassing and led to trouble."

In one quantum mechanics class, Robert routinely interrupted whoever was speaking, including Born. He would step to the blackboard with chalk in hand and declare in his American-accented German, "This can be done much better in the following manner . . ." His classmates complained about the interruptions. The mild-mannered Born tried to politely change Robert's behavior, but Robert didn't seem to get that he was being annoying.

One day, one of his classmates, Maria Göppert—a future Nobelist—wrote a petition on thick parchment paper and got most of the others to sign it. Unless Born shut Robert down, his fellow students would boycott the class. But still, Born wouldn't confront Robert directly about his behavior. Instead, Born left the petition on his desk in a place he knew Robert would see it. Then he arranged to be called out of the room for a few minutes. "This plot worked," Born recalled. "When I returned I found him rather pale." Robert was sufficiently embarrassed. After that, he stopped interrupting the class.

But that didn't tame him entirely. He startled his classmates and professors alike with his brutal honesty. Born was a brilliant physicist. But sometimes, he made small mistakes in his math and asked his students to recheck him. One time, he asked Robert to do the rechecking. After a few days, Robert returned and said mockingly, "I couldn't find any mistake—did you really do this alone?" All of Born's students knew that their professor wasn't the greatest at math. But Born recalled that Robert "was the only one frank and rude enough to say it without joking." Rather than being offended by Robert's blunt behavior, Born admired him for having such a "remarkable personality."

"OPPENHEIMER IS TURNING OUT TO BE EVEN MORE BRILLIANT THAN WE THOUGHT WHEN WE HAD HIM AT HARVARD."

During his time at Göttingen, young, brilliant scientists like Robert made new quantum mechanics discoveries so fast it was hard to keep up. In 1926, Werner Heisenberg and Paul Dirac were only twenty-four years old. Wolfgang Pauli was twenty-six, and Pascual Jordan was twenty-three.

They competed fiercely to be first to publish new, exciting breakthroughs. Older physicists like Edward Condon and Albert

Einstein were used to progress unfolding slowly. They watched in utter astonishment as their younger colleagues cranked out new ideas at lightning speed. It seemed that by the time a new paper came off the press, its findings were already outdated, or disproven, or revised, or challenged.

The pressure pushed Robert to perform. He eventually published seven papers from Göttingen, an incredible feat for a twenty-three-year-old graduate student. Born was so impressed that he wrote in a letter to the president of the Massachusetts Institute of Technology (MIT), "We have here a number of Americans . . . One man is quite excellent, Mr. Oppenheimer." Robert's peers ranked him right up there with Dirac and Jordan: "There are three young geniuses in theory here," reported one American student.

Robert made it a point to associate himself with those whom people respected the most. Others began to resent him. "[Robert] and Born became very close friends," Condon said peevishly years later, "and saw a great deal of each other, so much so, that Born did not see much" of his other students.

Robert got into the habit of working all night and sleeping through most of the day. Göttingen's damp weather and poorly heated buildings wreaked havoc on his delicate body. He walked around with a chronic cough caused by his frequent colds or his chain-smoking.

His nocturnal work produced a new theory about "why molecules were molecules." He showed it to Born, who was startled and very pleased. The older man agreed to work with Robert on a paper to present it. Robert wrote his notes into a first draft. But Born was horrified when he received it—it was only four or five pages. "I thought that this was about right," Robert recalled. "It seemed to me all that was necessary."

Born disagreed. He lengthened it to thirty pages. Robert thought the extra writing was unnecessary fluff: "I didn't like it, but it was obviously not possible for me to protest to a senior author." To Robert, the central idea was paramount. Everything else was just word salad.

Robert and Born titled the paper "On the Quantum Theory of Molecules." It was published in 1927. With Born's support, Robert had made a major breakthrough in understanding how molecules behave. Together, they laid the foundation for developments more than nine decades later in high-energy physics.

"I GOT OUT OF THERE JUST IN TIME. HE WAS BEGINNING TO ASK *ME* QUESTIONS."

In spring 1927, after an incredibly rich and productive school year, Robert completed his doctoral thesis. Born, again impressed with Robert's excellent work, recommended that it be accepted "with distinction." The only fault Born could find was that it was "difficult to read." Nevertheless, he remarked that Robert had written "a complicated paper and he did it very well."

On May 11, Robert sat down for his oral examination. He emerged a few hours later with excellent grades. Afterward, one of his examiners, James Franck, remarked, "I got out of there just in time. He was beginning to ask *me* questions."

Harvard professor Edwin Kemble happened to be visiting

around the same time. He wrote to a colleague, "Oppenheimer is turning out to be even more brilliant than we thought when we had him at Harvard. He is turning out new work very rapidly and is able to hold his own with any of the galaxy of young . . . physicists here."

Robert's time in Göttingen had drawn to a close. In that small German town, he had made the transition from depressed and insecure to confident and accomplished. The young man had finally, yet triumphantly, come of age. Becoming a scientist, he later remarked, is "like climbing a mountain in a tunnel: you wouldn't know whether you were coming out above the valley or whether you were ever coming out at all." Robert had shown that he had the raw intellect and motivation to make physics his life's work. In nine short months he had combined academic success with a renewal of his personality and his own sense of worth. Born was sad to see Robert leave. "It's all right for you to leave, but I cannot," he told him. "You have left me too much homework."

Robert sailed for New York in mid-July on a head of steam. It felt good to be going home. He had not only survived but also triumphed, bringing back a hard-earned doctorate. Physicists in Europe now knew that young Robert was a rising star in the field of quantum mechanics. But it would be on American soil that Robert would change the world forever.

CHAPTER SEVEN

"Perro caliente!"

Frank Oppenheimer, Robert's younger brother, had the same icy blue eyes and shock of black bushy hair as Robert. Born with the Oppenheimer lankiness, Frank stood six feet tall and weighed 135 pounds. He was in many ways as gifted intellectually as his brother and at fifteen was far more mature than Robert had been at the same age. But he didn't have the same nervous energy as Robert; Frank was calm and easy to get along with.

Eight years younger than Robert, Frank had only known his brother at a distance growing up. The two only had time to bond on family vacations or when Robert returned home from wherever he happened to be. Still, Frank worshipped his brother and relished the times they spent together.

When Robert returned home from Europe, he spent six weeks catching up with his parents and deepening his relationship with Frank. The Oppenheimers had sold their vacation house the previous winter, but the *Trimethy* was still moored nearby. Robert took Frank out, as he had many times in the past, for a wild sail along the Long Island coast. In August the brothers joined their parents for a short vacation on Nantucket Island. "My brother and I," Frank recalled, "spent most of the days painting with oils on canvas the dunes and grassy hills."

Robert and his younger brother Frank, circa 1918

Frank was a student at the Ethical Culture School. He, too, was gravitating toward a career in physics. Unlike Robert, he was good with his hands and loved tinkering with things, taking apart motors and watches and putting them back together. When Frank was younger, Robert had given him a microscope as a gift. Frank enjoyed using it immensely.

Robert took a keen interest in helping his younger brother navigate the rough-and-tumble waves of adolescence—a difficult voyage he knew only too well. The following spring, Frank confessed to Robert that a girl was distracting him from his schoolwork. Robert told him from his own experience that dating was "only important for people who have time to waste. For you, and for me, it isn't . . . Don't worry about girls, and don't make love to girls, unless you have to: DON'T DO IT AS A DUTY. Try to find out, by watching yourself, what you really want; if you approve of it, try to get it; if you disapprove of it, try to get over it." Robert gave his brother all kinds of advice. Frank eagerly accepted it.

Dreaming of the desert that he had been away from for so long and relishing the time he had recently spent with Frank, Robert suggested that the two of them go out to New Mexico for a couple of weeks sometime—without their parents. The two brothers arrived in Los Pinos in the summer of 1928. This trip would be the first time the two siblings bonded as adults.

They bunked at Katherine Page's ranch. Robert insisted on a series of long trips on horseback into the surrounding hills. They made do with a little peanut butter, some canned artichokes, Vienna sausages, and Kirschwasser and whiskey. As they rode, Frank listened as Robert talked excitedly about physics and literature. In the evenings, Robert pulled out a worn copy of Baudelaire and read to Frank aloud by the light of a campfire.

One day in July, Katherine took Robert and Frank on a ride a mile up into the mountains above Los Pinos. After riding through a pass at ten thousand feet, they came upon a meadow perched on Grass Mountain and covered with thick clover and blue and purple alpine flowers. Ponderosa and white pine trees framed a magnificent view of the Sangre de Cristos and the Pecos River. Nestled in the meadow at an altitude of ninety-five hundred feet was a rustic cabin built from half-trunks and adobe mortar. A hardened clay fireplace dominated one wall of the cabin and a narrow wooden staircase led upstairs to two small bedrooms. The kitchen had a sink and wood stove, but there was no running water. The only bathroom was a windy outhouse built at the end of a covered porch.

"Like it?" Katherine asked.

Robert nodded. Then Katherine told them that the cabin and 154 acres of pasture and brook were for rent.

"Hot dog!" Robert exclaimed.

"No, perro caliente!" quipped Katherine, translating Robert's exclamation into Spanish.

Captivated, Robert and Frank persuaded their father to rent it. They named it Perro Caliente. It became their private haven for years to come.

Oppenheimer spent his summers at Perro Caliente, his 154-acre ranch with a view of the Sangre de Cristo Mountains.

After two weeks in New Mexico, the brothers left to join their parents at the luxurious Broadmoor Hotel in Colorado Springs. Both Robert and Frank took some basic driving lessons. Then they bought a used six-cylinder Chrysler roadster and set off for California. "We had a variety of mishaps," Frank remembered, "but finally got there."

"Mishaps" was an understatement. Outside of Cortez, Colorado, with Frank at the wheel, the car skidded on some loose gravel and landed upside down in a gully. The windshield shattered, and the car's cloth top was ruined. Robert fractured his right arm and two bones in his right wrist.

They managed to get the car towed into town. There, they got the roadster running again—but the very next evening Frank managed to run the car up onto a slab of rock. Unable to move, they spent the night lying on the desert floor, "sipping from a bottle of spirits . . . and sucking on some lemons we had with us."

A year later, the brothers returned to Perro Caliente with two of Frank's friends from the Ethical Culture School. Robert arrived with two gallons of bootleg whiskey, some chocolate, and his standard peanut butter and sausages. For the next three weeks,

Robert and the younger boys spent their days hiking and riding through the mountains.

At night, Robert sat by the light of a Coleman lantern, reading his physics books and preparing his lectures. On one trip, fully eight days long, they rode all the way to Colorado and back, more than two hundred miles. Frank recalled, "We'd all act kind of silly [high up in the mountains]. Everything my brother did would sort of be special. If he went off into the woods to take a leak, he'd come back with a flower. Not to disguise the fact that he'd [taken] a leak, but just to make it an occasion, I guess." If he picked wild strawberries, Robert would serve them with Cointreau.

The Oppenheimer brothers spent hours in the saddle together, talking. "I think we probably rode about a thousand miles a summer," Frank recalled. "We'd start off very early in the morning, and saddle up a horse, sometimes a packhorse, and start riding. Usually we'd have some new place that we wanted to go, often where there was no trail, and we really knew the mountains, the Upper Pecos, the surface of the whole mountain range . . . There were wonderful flowers all the time. The place was very lush."

Robert adored his kid brother. He mentored him on love, music, art, physics—and his own philosophy of life. He also showered him with gifts—a fine watch at the end of that summer, and two years later a used Packard roadster. The time Robert and Frank spent at Perro Caliente cemented a deep bond between them. Frank would look up to Robert, and Robert would look out for Frank as they faced the choppy waters of an uncertain future.

CHAPTER EIGHT

"Well, Robert, that was beautiful, but I didn't understand a damn word."

In 1929, the University of California, Berkeley, hired Robert to teach physics. There, he would introduce quantum mechanics to a new generation of American scientists. In his very first class, he decided to explain Heisenberg's uncertainty principle, the Schrödinger equation, Dirac's synthesis, field theory, and Pauli's latest thinking on quantum electrodynamics.

Of course, his students had no idea what he was talking about.

They told him he was moving too fast. He complained tartly, "I'm [already] going so slowly that I'm not getting anywhere."

In front of the class, he mumbled in a soft, low voice that got even lower when he tried to emphasize a point. He stammered a lot as he laced his lectures with quotes from famous scientists and the occasional poet. He played with words and invented complicated puns, but he always spoke in complete, grammatically correct sentences. Strangely, he would pause every once in a while and stutter an odd hum that sounded like "nim-nim-nim" as he puffed on a cigarette. Every so often, he twirled around to the blackboard to write out an equation.

One of his students recalled, "We were always expecting him to write on the board with [the cigarette] and smoke the chalk." As his students filed out of the classroom one day, Robert spotted his friend Professor Richard Tolman sitting in the back. He asked Tolman what he thought of the lecture. Tolman replied, "Well, Robert, that was beautiful, but I didn't understand a damn word."

While teaching, every so often Robert twirled around to the blackboard to write out an equation.

Over time and with more experience, Robert became a better teacher. He liked his students. Most of them liked him back. He encouraged them to call him "Opje," a nickname that his friends had given him in Europe. Gradually, they began pronouncing "Opje" as "Oppie." He praised their efforts and always tried to clarify ideas when they didn't understand. Sometimes he stayed with students until midnight, helping them grasp very complicated scientific questions. When one of them was stumped and just couldn't finish a paper, sometimes Robert completed it himself.

"He was very keenly aware," recalled one of his students, "of the people in his class." He nurtured them as a father would have treated a baby learning to walk. When students came up with ideas, he allowed them time and space to develop them. While brusque with some students, he supported all of them with love, sympathy, and understanding. He wasn't an easy professor, but that seemed to motivate many students to take his classes more than once. One even went on a hunger strike after finding out Robert wouldn't let her take the same class a fourth time!

THE RADIATION LABORATORY WAS "LIKE MECCA."

Very soon, Robert developed a reputation for being *the* professor to study with if you wanted to enter the field of quantum mechanics in America. Students descended upon Berkeley to learn from him and the experimental physicist Ernest Lawrence. The two very boyish men became fast friends. They talked daily and hung out together in the evenings. On weekends, they went horseback riding.

Lawrence wanted to find a way to penetrate the nucleus—the atom's tiny center containing protons and neutrons. This was easier said than done. Not only was the nucleus tiny, but it was protected by an electrical energy barrier scientists believed to be impenetrable, called the Coulomb barrier. Some physicists thought it would take a stream of charged protons from the nuclei of hydrogen atoms, propelled by perhaps a million electron volts of energy, to break through it. Generating such energy seemed impossible.

But Lawrence thought he had a way around the impossible. Just as a baseball will break through a window at a certain speed, he believed a proton could break through the Coulomb barrier if it was moving fast enough. He wanted to build a machine that could accelerate protons to such a speed, and believed he could do so by using vacuum tubes and an electromagnet. Lawrence wasn't sure how big the machine had to be to penetrate an atom's nucleus.

But he was convinced that with a large enough magnet and a big enough chamber, he could surpass the million-electron-volt mark. That just might do the trick.

In early 1931, Lawrence built the first version of his accelerator. He called it the "cyclotron." In the cyclotron, a magnetic field forced protons to travel in a circle. Each time around, an electric field increased their speed. The machine could generate protons with an energy of eighty thousand electron volts. By the next year, he had an eleven-inch machine that accelerated protons to the speed and energy he aimed for: a million electron volts.

Robert and Ernest Lawrence next to the cyclotron at Berkeley Radiation Laboratory

Lawrence dreamed of building even bigger accelerators, machines weighing many hundreds of tons and costing tens of thousands of dollars. His invention caused a sensation across the scientific world. Theoretical physicists soon realized that the accelerator would allow them to explore the innermost reaches of the atom.

Lawrence named his new laboratory the Berkeley Radiation Laboratory, or "Rad Lab" for short. With Lawrence at the helm, the Rad Lab quickly became the hub for quantum mechanics experimentation in America. "It was like Mecca," according to chemist Martin Kamen. Using the cyclotron, Kamen and another chemist, Samuel Ruben, were able to discover the radioactive isotope carbon-14, the basis of carbon dating—a method that scientists and archaeologists now use to determine the ages of animal and plant fossils. By the end of the decade, Lawrence would win the Nobel Prize in Physics.

While Lawrence worked on the cyclotron, Robert embarked upon the most stunning and original work of his career. On September 1, 1939, Robert and his student Hartland Snyder published one of the most important papers in twentieth-century physics, called "On Continued Gravitational Contraction." They concluded that instead of collapsing into white dwarf stars as scientists previously believed, stars with cores beyond a certain mass would keep getting smaller under the force of their own gravity. Then their gravity would overwhelm them, and the stars would be crushed so completely that not even their light could survive. Seen from afar, the stars would literally disappear. Even light would not escape their gravitational pull. Though scientists didn't use the term then, they would become known as "black holes."

As has been the case with the work of other geniuses, many scientists didn't fully appreciate Oppenheimer and Snyder's black-hole theory until after their deaths. It wasn't until the early 1970s that telescopes became powerful enough for astronomers to confirm that black holes did exist. Once they did, the theory became a centerpiece of astrophysics.

CHAPTER NINE

"Strike! Strike! Strike!"

Robert wasn't very interested in politics until he arrived at Berkeley. Then, all of a sudden, he couldn't ignore them. He found himself surrounded with friends and co-workers who were becoming more and more involved in the political issues of the day, which, in the early 1930s, were becoming more and more worrisome. In January 1933, Adolf Hitler seized power in Germany. The Nazis fired German Jewish professors from their jobs. Many had no choice but to pack their things and flee the country. Greatly disturbed, Robert decided he would set aside 3 percent of his salary to help them safely move to other parts of the world.

The money helped people like James Franck, whom Robert had studied with at Göttingen. Hitler had initially allowed Franck to keep his job there. But when the Nazis demanded he fire other Jews below him, he refused and quit his job in protest. Franck fled to the United States, where he began teaching physics at Johns Hopkins.

The news from Germany was getting worse by the day. But there were also serious problems right in Berkeley's backyard. Five years of economic depression had forced millions of ordinary Americans into poverty. Many of those who still had jobs went on strike for better pay. Some of the strikes turned violent. Three thousand lettuce pickers in California's Imperial Valley walked off the job. Acting on behalf of their bosses, police arrested the pickers by the hundreds, crushing the strike. Their pay was then slashed from twenty cents to fifteen cents an hour.

Then on May 9, 1934, more than twelve thousand dockworkers went on strike up and down the Pacific coast. The dockworkers performed backbreaking work loading and unloading containers of extremely heavy cargo for infuriatingly little pay. By the end of June, they strangled the economies of California, Oregon, and Washington. Police tried to break up the strike in San Francisco by firing tear gas bombs into the picket lines. Picketers threw rocks and canisters right back at them. Riots broke out. After four days of running skirmishes, several police officers fired their guns into the crowd. Three men were wounded. Two of them died. July 5, 1934, became known as "Bloody Thursday." That same day, California's governor ordered the state National Guard to take control of the streets.

That was just the beginning. On July 16, San Francisco labor unions called a general strike. For four days the city was paralyzed as workers in other industries walked off the job in solidarity with the dockworkers. Federal officials had to step in to negotiate a truce between bosses and their employees.

The dockworkers went back to work. They didn't get the pay raises they demanded. But they gained support and sympathy from people all over the country who read about what happened in newspapers and were shocked at how their bosses and the cops had treated them.

Robert, his students, and his Berkeley colleagues couldn't help but pay attention to the dramatic events unfolding just across the bay. Berkeley was split between supporters and critics of the strike. When the dockworkers first walked off the job, a conservative physics professor, Leonard Loeb, recruited football players to go down to the docks and do the jobs that the strikers wouldn't. Robert, along with some of his students, including Melba Phillips and Robert (Bob) Serber, decided they would support the workers by going to San Francisco to attend a large rally. "We were sitting up high in a balcony," recalled Serber, "and by the end we were caught up in the enthusiasm of the strikers, shouting with them, 'Strike! Strike! Strike!'"

FELLOW TRAVELERS

In Berkeley, Robert rented a first-floor apartment in the home of Mary Ellen and John Washburn, who also passionately supported the strikers. The couple cared deeply about the plight of California's workers and believed that their capitalist bosses had too much power. Their house was a hive of activity day and night. It seemed like there was always a party going on with a who's who of Berkeley professors, students, and local intellectuals and activists coming and going, talking and laughing, hypothesizing and philosophizing. Some of them were members of the Communist Party of the United States of America (CPUSA).

CPUSA was inspired by the 1917 Bolshevik Revolution in Russia, which dethroned the Russian emperor (tsar). The revolution proved that a movement led by workers could take down an entire empire. The party invited American workers and those who defended them with open arms, in hopes that they might one day unite with others around the world to continue the revolution the Bolsheviks started. While some members believed a full-fledged revolution could topple the American capitalist system, most weren't as revolutionary—they just saw it as a better alternative for workers than either the Democratic or Republican parties. But many admired what the Bolsheviks were trying to achieve in Russia (known from 1922 as the Soviet Union) and wondered how some of their ideas might work in the United States.[5]

In the Soviet Union, unlike in capitalist countries, private corporations didn't produce and sell the goods that citizens needed to live. Instead, workers contributed what they produced to collective supplies. Then a central "socialist" government set prices for those goods and sold them to citizens.

The idea for a socialist government was based in part upon the nineteenth-century ideas of Karl Marx and Friedrich Engels, who hated how capitalism made a minority of the population (the bourgeoisie) rich while they took advantage of the majority's (the proletariat's) labor. They believed that to make society more equal, the government should make sure people could afford food, clothing, and shelter; tax the richest people the most; get rid of inheritance and private property; end child labor; make education free for everyone; nationalize communication and transportation; establish a national bank to provide credit for all; and expand public ownership of land. Together, those conditions could one day eliminate the gap between rich and poor. If that happened, there would no longer be the need for a central government. Such a utopia would be called "communism."[6]

In the 1930s, some Americans believed that if the United States became more of a socialist country, workers' lives would improve. A tiny minority wanted to replace the American capitalist system with Soviet-style socialism. Others called themselves "communists" even though they weren't really seeking true utopian "communism." Some believed that capitalism could work, but only if the government strongly regulated corporations to make it harder for them to take advantage of workers. Many people also thought the government should provide free or cheap medical care, free housing for those who couldn't afford it, and a national retirement program and ensure that there was enough competition in each industry to keep prices low enough for everyone to afford what they needed.

With so many people out of work and so many others fighting for improved pay and working conditions after a century of cutthroat industrialization, CPUSA became more mainstream in the 1930s. Some Democrats who supported Franklin Delano Roosevelt's "New Deal" also supported those who joined.[7]

CPUSA routinely held parties, picnics, and seminars that created a sense of community and tried to build hope among workers that tomorrow could be better than today. People who never joined the Communist Party hung out with party members, volunteered for party events, and donated to party causes. They became known as "fellow travelers." Robert was one of them.

In autumn 1935, inspired by the boldness of the dockworkers and others in the movement for social justice, Robert and a group of

Berkeley faculty started a union to fight for higher teaching wages. Older, more conservative professors frowned upon the union, but younger, more liberal ones embraced it. Many of them were barely scraping by with their low salaries.

Robert worked as hard as he could to bring more people into the union. He rarely missed a meeting. Sometimes he hosted them in his home. One night, he stayed up with others until 2:00 in the morning addressing envelopes for a mailing to union members. In just a few months, the union had close to one hundred members, including forty professors and teaching assistants.

At one of the meetings, Robert met a fellow professor named Haakon Chevalier. Chevalier taught French literature. His friends called him "Hoke." He always opened his rambling redwood home in Oakland to all sorts of students, artists, activists, and writers. Hoke frequently partied late into the night. He was so often late to his morning classes that his department finally banned him from teaching in the morning.

Hoke was very smart and very political. He was a member of the American Civil Liberties Union, the Teachers' Union, and the Consumer's Union. He was convinced that the United States of America could change from "a society based on the pursuit of profit and exploitation of man . . . to a society based on production . . . and on human cooperation." By the time he and Robert met, Hoke was probably a member of the Communist Party and an advisor to party leaders.

Neither man could remember exactly how they first met, only that they liked each other immediately. From the moment Hoke met Robert, he felt like he had known him forever. Hoke was dazzled by his new friend's intellect and charmed by his "naturalness and simplicity." That very day, they decided to hold regular discussion groups of six to ten people who met every week to talk politics. They held the meetings from 1937 through 1942.

During those years, Hoke regarded Robert "as my most intimate and steadfast friend." Hoke quickly learned to call his new friend by his nickname, Oppie, and Robert found himself dropping by Hoke's house for dinner. They went to movies and concerts together. They shared with each other their most private troubles and secrets.

Haakon Chevalier, called "Hoke" by his friends

CHAPTER TEN

"Jean was Robert's truest love."

In the spring of 1936, at one of the parties the Washburns frequently hosted, Mary Ellen introduced Robert to twenty-two-year-old Jean Tatlock, a first-year medical student at Stanford University. Jean immediately captivated Robert with her striking beauty and her free spirit. The two began dating.

Jean drove around Berkeley in a roadster with the top down, singing in her beautiful voice lyrics from *Twelfth Night*. Her mind was hungry and poetic. She was always the one person in the room who was unforgettable. She hated Hitler and Italy's fascist leader, Benito Mussolini, and viewed socialism as the best system to give workers the power they desperately needed. Like Mary Ellen, Jean paid dues to the Communist Party. She also wrote for *Western Worker*, a party newspaper, and attended two party meetings each week. Whenever she heard stories about social injustice or inequity, she became passionately angry, and channeled that anger into writing.

But, like Robert, communism didn't consume her, and it didn't define her. In fact, nothing seemed to fully define her. She was her own person. Her career aspirations and political activism flew in the face of what most people in the early twentieth century expected of women. Robert loved that.

"Jean was Robert's truest love," a friend would later say. "He loved her the most. He was devoted to her." Jean's activism and fiery social conscience awakened in Robert the sense of social responsibility that the Ethical Culture School encoded in him as a child. She forced him to look outward, to empathize with those less fortunate than him, to speak out against grave injustices.

Jean Tatlock: American psychiatrist and a Communist Party member, although with reservations. Robert's "truest love."

"Beginning in late 1936," Robert recalled, "my interests began to change . . . I had had a continuing, smoldering fury about the treatment of Jews in Germany. I had relatives there [an aunt and several cousins], and [would] later . . . help in extricating them and bringing them to this country. I saw what the Depression was doing to my students. Often they could get no jobs, or jobs which were wholly inadequate. And through them, I began to understand how deeply political and economic events could affect men's lives. I began to feel the need to participate more fully in the life of the community."

Along with his sympathies for dockworkers, Robert felt deeply for migrant farmworkers and their families, whom the Dust Bowl swept from Oklahoma and Arkansas to California. An extreme drought, lasting four years, destroyed their farms, their homes, and their communities. They had no choice but to pack up all their possessions and move west in search of something else. In all, the Dust Bowl rendered five hundred thousand people homeless across the United States.

Jean helped Robert open the door to California's world of political activism. She and her many friends broadened his awareness and fueled his desire to learn more about alternatives to capitalism. While never a communist himself, Robert greatly enjoyed being a part of such a strong progressive political environment. "I liked the new sense of companionship," he later remarked, "and at the time felt that I was coming to be part of the life of my time and country."

Robert and Jean were together for three years. Robert loved her deeply and wanted to marry her. "We were at least twice close enough to marriage to consider ourselves engaged," he later recalled.

But their relationship was very stormy. They would have deep and intense conversations about the state of the world one moment but would go at each other's throats the next. Little things triggered big fights. Robert loved to shower Jean with gifts. She couldn't stand that. She didn't want to be catered to or doted on in any way.

"No more flowers, please, Robert," she told him one day. But he didn't listen—the next time he picked her up at a friend's house, he came bearing another bouquet of bright gardenias. Jean's face flushed red with anger. She grabbed them and threw them to the ground. Then she turned her back on Robert, instructing her friend, "Tell him to go away, tell him I am not here."

Jean's moods were often gloomy and unpredictable. Sometimes she would disappear for weeks or months on end, then return to taunt Robert about whom she had been with and what they had been doing. She seemed determined to hurt Robert, maybe because she knew he loved her so much.

In the end, Jean couldn't handle being together with him. Confused and deeply upset, she rejected his latest offer of marriage. Robert was devastated. But Jean's indefatigable spirit and fiery passion for social justice made a lasting impact on Robert, shaping his actions and decisions for the rest of his life.

KITTY

Newly single and on the rebound, Robert went to a party at a friend's house in August 1939. There, he met a twenty-nine-year-old married woman named Katherine "Kitty" Puening Harrison. Kitty was immediately mesmerized by Robert. "I fell in love with [him] that day," she later wrote, "but hoped to conceal it." Quickly, the two began dating.

Kitty was very different from Jean. For one thing, she loved flowers. Robert didn't have to give her any—she grew flaming orchids herself in her apartment and wore them to make a statement when she went out. Unlike Jean, she was vivacious and outgoing in social settings. She was spunky, cheerful, assertive, and a little wild. Botany was her main interest, and she was about to begin graduate school at UCLA.

Though only twenty-nine, Kitty had been married three times.

Her first husband, Frank Ramseyer, was a Boston-born musician. They had the marriage annulled when she found out he was gay.

Her second husband, Joe Dallet, was the twenty-six-year-old son of a wealthy Long Island businessman. He went on to join CPUSA and fought to organize Ohio steelworkers into a union. After she married him, Kitty also joined the party. She sold copies of party newspaper *The Daily Worker* to workers on the streets of Youngstown. "I used to wear tennis shoes," she recalled, "when I handed out Communist Party leaflets at factory gates so that I could get a fast running start when the police arrived." She paid the party ten cents per week in dues.

She and Joe lived in a dilapidated boardinghouse for five dollars' rent a month and survived on government relief checks of $12.50 every two weeks. They lived with two other party members, one who went on to become party chairman. "The house had a kitchen," Kitty later said, "but the stove leaked and it was impossible to cook. Our food consisted of two meals a day, which we got at a grimy restaurant."

Kitty stuck it out until 1936. "The poverty became more and more depressing to me," she recalled. She and Joe began arguing. Joe's whole life was the party. Kitty wasn't nearly as committed. Joe belittled her as a middle-class girl who couldn't possibly understand the struggles of the working class. Though he may have been right, Kitty resented his condescension. Finally, in June 1936, she stopped paying party dues and fled to live with her parents in London.

Dallet traveled to Spain. There, he volunteered to defend the Spanish Republic against Francisco Franco's army, which was trying to overthrow the country's democratically elected government.

He died in the trenches fighting for the freedoms of industrial laborers and farmworkers as fascism continued its terrible march across Europe.

SUMMER ROMANCE

Kitty returned to America the twenty-seven-year-old widow of a Communist Party war hero. She enrolled at the University of Pennsylvania in 1938, where she received her undergraduate degree in botany. There, she ran into a British-born doctor, Richard Stewart Harrison, whom she had known as a teenager. Older and apolitical, Harrison offered Kitty something she desperately wanted: stability. Impulsively, she decided to marry him. The two moved to California together. But from the very beginning, she knew her heart wasn't in it. He probably knew it too.

Though Kitty was still married to Harrison, she and Robert made no effort to hide their budding relationship. Friends frequently saw them driving together in Robert's Chrysler. "He would ride up [near my office] with this cute young girl," recalled one of Robert's friends. "She was very attractive. She was tiny, skinny as a rail, just like he was. They'd give each other a fond kiss and go their separate ways. Robert always had that porkpie hat on."

Boldly, Robert invited Kitty and Harrison to Perro Caliente the next summer to vacation with him and his friends Bob and Charlotte Serber. Harrison declined but told Kitty to go without him. After just two days, Kitty joined Robert on horseback. Together, they rode to Katherine Page's ranch at Los Pinos. There, they spent the night and rode back the next morning. Their summer romance was off to an intense and passionate start and would remain that way throughout the next two months.

At the end of the summer, Robert called Harrison to tell him that his wife was pregnant. The two men agreed that the thing to do was for Harrison to divorce Kitty so that Robert could marry her.

Kitty obtained a divorce decree on November 1, 1940. She married Robert that very day at a courthouse in Virginia City, Nevada. A court janitor and a local clerk signed the marriage certificate as witnesses.

Most of Robert's relatives didn't think Kitty was right for him. Jackie Oppenheimer, Frank's wife, thought Kitty kept Robert from being able to spend time with his friends. "She could not stand sharing [him] with anyone," Jackie recalled. "Kitty was a schemer. If [she] wanted anything, she would always get it . . . She was a phony. All her political convictions were phony, all her ideas were borrowed."

Kitty certainly had a sharp tongue and rubbed Robert's friends and family the wrong way. But she was very smart and brought stability to his life. After they got married, the couple traded in Robert's old Chrysler for a new Cadillac. Then they bought a house in the hills overlooking Berkeley. A Spanish-style, one-story villa with whitewashed walls and a red-tiled roof, their new home stood on a knoll surrounded on three sides by a steep wooded canyon. They had a stunning view of the sunset over the Golden Gate Bridge. The large living room had redwood floors, twelve-foot-high beamed ceilings, and windows on three sides. An image of a ferocious lion was carved into a massive stone fireplace. Floor-to-ceiling bookcases lined each end of the living room. French doors opened onto a lovely garden framed by live oak trees. The house came with the well-equipped kitchen that Kitty always wanted. She was an excel-

lent cook, and they began inviting friends over frequently for dinner. On May 12, 1941, Kitty gave birth to their first child, Peter.

Kitty Oppenheimer

CHAPTER ELEVEN

"You're too good a physicist to get mixed up in politics and causes."

While Robert made new friends, his political activism began to annoy some of his older ones. Ernest Lawrence, head of the Radiation Laboratory, understood why Robert cared so much about victims of the Nazis, San Francisco dockworkers, and homeless farmers. But he thought those problems weren't a scientist's to solve. He told Robert, "You're too good a physicist to get mixed up in politics and causes."

At first, Robert's politics were a nuisance to Lawrence. But then Robert tried to organize the scientists at the laboratory into a union. There really wasn't a good reason for them to unionize. They made decent money. None of them complained about the working conditions. Everyone in the lab was eager to put in as many hours as they could. Nevertheless, Robert held a meeting at his house and invited his colleagues to attend.

Everyone, it seemed, except Lawrence.

Martin Kamen recalled, "We all sat in a circle in [Robert's] living room. Everybody said, 'Yeah, it's great, it's marvelous.'" They agreed that a union was a good idea. But then Kamen threw cold water on the room. "Wait. Has anybody told Lawrence about this?

We're working in the Radiation Lab and have no independence in this matter. We have to get permission from Lawrence." Robert hadn't thought it necessary to invite Lawrence. But he was shaken by Kamen's words.

When Lawrence found out about the meeting, he blasted Robert for wasting his time and the lab's resources and scolded him about his "leftwandering activities." He strongly opposed his scientists joining a union. But Robert shot back that scientists had a responsibility to help society's "underdogs."

Those "underdogs" had to live and work in an industrial world that scientists helped create. Certainly science had made it much easier to make the steel necessary for skyscrapers, or to send it far and wide on sophisticated oceangoing freighters. But that came at a deep cost for those who toiled to make the steel or off-load the goods from those ships.

Robert believed that in addition to celebrating their achievements, scientists needed to understand the consequences of their work for all human beings.

CHAPTER TWELVE

Fission

"A single bomb of this type, carried by a boat and exploded in a port, might very well destroy the whole port together with some of the surrounding territory." —Leo Szilard (drafted) and Albert Einstein (signed), letter to President Franklin D. Roosevelt, August 2, 1939

On Sunday, January 29, 1939, Luis W. Alvarez—a prominent young physicist who worked closely with Lawrence—sat in a barber's chair reading the *San Francisco Chronicle*. Alvarez stopped the barber mid-snip. The newspaper reported that two German chemists, Otto Hahn and Fritz Strassman, had successfully shown that the nucleus of a uranium atom could be split in two by bombarding it with neutrons. Physicists Lise Meitner and Otto Robert Frisch called the reaction "nuclear fission."

Alvarez ran all the way back to the laboratory to spread the word. Breathlessly, he told Robert the news. "That's impossible." Robert went to the blackboard and tried to prove that it was a mistake.

But it wasn't a mistake. Alvarez showed Robert that it was possible in an experiment he conducted with an oscilloscope. In less than fifteen minutes, Robert agreed that it would be possible to split the uranium atom. Like other physicists around the world, he couldn't contain his excitement. This was a stunning discovery.

But quickly, he realized that the reaction would fire off extra neutrons, causing a chain reaction that would split more uranium atoms. The consequences immediately dawned on him: fission could produce unimaginable amounts of energy. If it wasn't properly contained, it might result in disaster.

What did all this mean? That soon somebody, somewhere, could harness fission to build "atomic" bombs.

Who would build them first? What might they be used for? Immediately, suspicion turned to Germany. The Nazis had already taken over neighboring Austria. Then they threatened war unless Czechoslovakia surrendered the Sudetenland region to them.

In late summer 1939, amid the gathering war clouds, Hungarian physicist Leo Szilard pleaded with Albert Einstein to sign a letter to President Franklin Roosevelt, warning the president "that extremely powerful bombs of a new type might be constructed." He went on, "A single bomb of this type, carried by a boat and exploded in a port, might very well destroy the whole port together with some of the surrounding territory." Ominously, Szilard suggested that the Nazis might already be building the bomb, and that they might be trying to mine uranium in Europe.

One month later, at dawn on September 1, 1939, German forces launched a surprise attack on Poland. World War II had begun.

Roosevelt read Einstein's letter intently and told physicist Lyman Briggs to put together a "Uranium Committee" to investigate the issue. For two years, not much happened. But by June 1941, the war had taken a terrible turn. Germany launched a surprise attack on the Soviet Union, violating a pact of neutrality both countries had signed in 1939. It became clear to the world that the Nazis would continue to roll across Europe and perhaps beyond if they were allowed to. If Hitler did get his hands on an atomic bomb, would anything hold him back from using it?

Roosevelt realized he needed to act. He created the Office of Scientific Research and Development (OSRD) to connect American scientists with the military and put engineer Vannevar Bush in charge. Bush made sure the president knew that, if made, atomic bombs "would be thousands of times more powerful than existing explosives." Roosevelt understood.

Things began to happen fast. The Uranium Committee became the S-1 Committee. It included Bush, chemist and Harvard University president James Conant, Secretary of War Henry Stimson, U.S. Army Chief of Staff George C. Marshall, and Vice President Henry A. Wallace. These men believed that they were in a race against the Nazis to build a nuclear weapon—a race that might very well determine the outcome of World War II. They recruited the best scientists from across the country.

War quickly consumed the world. Germany continued its assault on countries in both eastern and western Europe.

Meanwhile, Japan flexed its imperial muscle in the Pacific. For forty-five years, the island nation in need of natural resources for its growing population had expanded its territory by seizing island after island. By 1931, Japan had built a strong enough fighting force to conquer parts of China, beginning with Manchuria. Then it wrested control of Indochina (present-day Vietnam, Laos, and Cambodia) from the French, who could no longer hold on to their colony. When they invaded China's capital city of Nanking in late 1937, Japanese forces committed one of the worst atrocities in twentieth-century warfare. Over the next two months, in anarchic rage, they killed many thousands of civilians, hunted and killed those they suspected of being Chinese soldiers, and raped tens of thousands of women. Then they ransacked and burned the city. Such behavior inspired Japanese soldiers to engage in more slaughter throughout the countryside.[8]

In 1941, the Japanese allied with the Nazis as they set their sights on the Malay Peninsula, Indonesia, and the Philippines. The U.S., Great Britain, China, and the Netherlands worried that Japan's rapid and ruthless expansion threatened their interests in the Pacific. They stopped trading with Japan and cut off its supply of oil in hopes they could bleed Japan's economy dry.[9]

They underestimated Japan's capabilities—and its will. On Sunday, December 7, 1941, two hundred Japanese planes swooped down on the U.S. Pacific Fleet at Pearl Harbor, Hawaii, in a surprise early-morning attack. Within minutes, the USS *Arizona* was in flames, blown up in a massive explosion. It capsized shortly thereafter. Japanese pilots then picked off seven more American battleships with bombs and torpedoes, setting them on fire too and blasting some of their hulking steel hulls to the bottom of the shallow harbor. When it was all over, twenty-three hundred American servicemen were dead and eleven hundred more wounded.[10]

USS *Arizona* burn after Japanese air crews bombed Pearl Harbor on December 7, 1941.

Americans suddenly found themselves embroiled in what would become the bloodiest war in human history. They were up against an enemy most of them knew very little about. For the next two and a half years, American servicemen battled the Japanese for control of island after island in the Pacific so they could draw close enough to Japan to attack the country's mainland by air.

CHAPTER THIRTEEN

The Luminaries

The S-1 Committee asked Lawrence which scientists he thought would be best suited for the bomb project. Robert was at the top of the list. At the Radiation Laboratory, he was steadily and brilliantly contributing to discussions about splitting the uranium atom. He had become one of the most respected and insightful scientists there. In less than a decade and a half, Robert had transformed himself from an awkward scientific prodigy into a sophisticated and charismatic intellectual leader.

Lawrence knew Robert would be crucial to the project's success. But Robert would need a top-secret security clearance, and Lawrence suspected the government probably wouldn't approve one for someone friendly with so many communists. To people like FBI director J. Edgar Hoover, it didn't matter if you were someone hell-bent on destroying the United States or a fellow traveler who flew the American flag on your front lawn—if you knew someone suspected of being a communist, you earned yourself a secret file. That's why Lawrence had gotten so steamed when Robert tried to organize the union at the Rad Lab. He understood that Robert was trustworthy. But he worried others might see him as a troublemaker.

Lawrence believed Robert was worth the risk and vouched for him. He told James Conant that Robert "would be a tremendous asset [to the project] in every way." So in May 1942, the S-1 Committee formally appointed Robert director of fast-neutron research. His official title was "coordinator of rapid rupture." The title made clear his mission: to rupture the uranium atom as rapidly as possible.

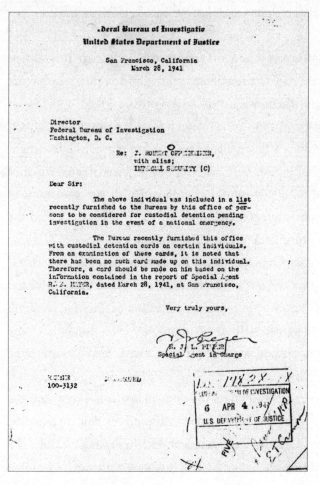

By 1941, Robert was on an FBI list of suspected radicals to be detained in the event of a national emergency.

Robert took on his new role with great urgency. Furious about what the Nazis were doing to Jews in Europe, he now had the power to do something about it. All of his ethical upbringing and scientific education had prepared him for this moment. Now he took a giant step out of the classrooms and parlors of Berkeley into a wider world of consequence, where he could actually change the world for the better, as his teachers at the Ethical Culture School hoped he would. After being uncertain as a young man about what his future would hold, he finally found his purpose.

With high secrecy and extreme urgency, Robert brought in scientists from across the country to begin designing an atomic bomb. Among them were thirty-six-year-old Hans Bethe, who had fled Europe in 1935 and ended up teaching physics at Cornell University; Edward Teller, a Hungarian-born physicist who taught at George Washington University; Swiss physicists Felix Bloch of Stanford and Emil Konopinski of Indiana University; and a few of Robert's former students, including Bob Serber. Robert called the outstanding group of physicists his "luminaries."

Robert's leadership impressed the luminaries. "As Chairman," Teller recalled, "Oppenheimer showed a refined, sure, informal touch. I don't know how he had acquired this facility for handling people." Bethe agreed: "His grasp of problems was immediate—he could often understand an entire problem after he had heard a single sentence."

They started by studying a previous man-made explosion: the 1917 detonation of a fully loaded ammunition ship in Halifax, Nova Scotia. In that horrific accident, five thousand tons of TNT completely destroyed two and a half square miles of downtown Halifax. Four thousand people were killed. Quickly, they realized that an atomic bomb would blow with a force two to three times as powerful as that.

Next, they turned their attention to size. How could they design a bomb that could be small enough for the military to transport and deploy? They figured out that a fission reaction could be achieved with a uranium core placed inside a metal sphere only eight inches in diameter. How much uranium would they need? They didn't know. But they understood that the uranium would have to be processed. It would take a space much larger than a lab to do that.

SUPER BOMB

One morning, Teller burst into the lab. Breathlessly, he shared a stunning revelation. While the other luminaries worked on ways to build a fission bomb, Teller believed that that bomb could be used to ignite an even bigger bomb. If an atomic bomb could somehow blow up a heavy form of hydrogen, it might produce an even more powerful *fusion* explosion—a "super bomb." A super bomb might produce an explosion equal to one million tons of TNT.

One million tons of TNT?! If five thousand tons of TNT destroyed downtown Halifax, what might a million tons destroy? But maybe that wouldn't even matter. Teller went on to tell them that just one atomic bomb exploded in the air might be enough to light the earth's atmosphere on fire. The results could be apocalyptic.

Robert was shaken and alarmed. Were they about to build something that could destroy the earth? He immediately hopped on a train eastward. He had to warn Arthur Holly Compton, his

S-1 boss who was working with a team of other physicists at the University of Chicago on how to produce atomic chain reactions.

Robert tracked Compton down at his summer cottage on a lake in northern Michigan. "I'll never forget that morning," Compton wrote. "I drove Oppenheimer from the railroad station down to the beach looking out over the peaceful lake. There I listened to his story . . . Was there really any chance that an atomic bomb would trigger the explosion of the nitrogen in the atmosphere or the hydrogen in the ocean? . . . Better to accept the slavery of the Nazis than to run a chance of drawing the final curtain on mankind." Eventually Hans Bethe ran calculations and reassured them the chances of lighting the atmosphere on fire were very small. But they weren't zero. They were "near zero."

"I DON'T WANT TO LET ANYTHING INTERFERE WITH MY USEFULNESS TO THE NATION."

Destruction of the earth aside, the luminaries concluded by August 1942 that atomic bombs were possible. But they would be expensive and would require massive technical, scientific, and industrial resources. The project to build them would need a scientific leader who was brilliant enough to quickly solve complicated problems, and charismatic enough to command the respect of many people at once.

And it would have to be kept entirely secret.

Bush and Conant realized that Robert was perfect to lead the project. But as Lawrence predicted, the army worried about Robert's politics. Throughout his time at Berkeley, though Robert didn't know it, the army had been watching him. They knew he was friends with members of the Communist Party like Hoke, Jean, Mary Ellen, John, and others. Was Robert a communist too? If chosen, would he tell others about the bomb project? *Could he be trusted?*

Robert knew his friendships with many communists might be a problem. He told Compton on the phone, "I'm cutting off every communist connection, for if I don't, the government will find it difficult to use me. I don't want to let anything interfere with my usefulness to the nation." Nevertheless, the army told Compton that the War Department didn't trust Robert enough to approve his security clearance.

Bush and Conant pushed the army to reconsider. *They* trusted Robert. They knew he would be crucial to the project's success. Reluctantly, the army relented and cleared him for work.

But they would keep watching him.

CHAPTER FOURTEEN

The Kitchen Conversation

One evening in the winter of 1942–43, Robert had a small conversation with Hoke that, at the time, didn't seem to be of much consequence. But it would forever alter the course of his life, the lives of his family members—and the civic life of the entire country.

As they had done many times before, Robert and Kitty invited Hoke and his wife, Barbara, to the house for a quiet dinner. When the Chevaliers arrived, Robert went into the kitchen to prepare a tray of martinis. Hoke followed. As Robert swished vermouth around conical glasses and stirred gin with the ease of a veteran bartender, Hoke told him about a conversation he had just had with someone they both knew—George C. Eltenton, a British-born physicist who worked at Shell Oil Company.

Exactly what each man said is lost to history. Neither made notes of the conversation. Neither thought it was an important exchange—it was just two friends talking across a kitchen counter. But it haunted Robert in the decades that followed.

Hoke told Robert that Eltenton had asked him to find out if Robert might be willing to share information about the bomb project, which Eltenton could then share with someone he knew in the Soviet Union.

Robert stopped stirring the gin. His mood changed from jovial to angry. Was Hoke out of his mind? Sharing secret information with the Soviets about his new work at the Rad Lab wouldn't just be unethical—it could be treason. And it was precisely the sort of thing the army worried Robert might do. He told Hoke he would have nothing to do with it.

That quickly ended the conversation. Robert finished mixing the martinis. Then the two friends rejoined their wives for the rest of the evening.

Should Robert have called the army intelligence office or the FBI immediately to report that the Soviet Union was trying to get secret information from him? His life would have been very different if he had. But he couldn't do so without betraying his best friend, Hoke.

A few days later, Hoke met up with Eltenton. He told him that he had seen Robert, but "there was no chance whatsoever of obtaining any data and Dr. Oppenheimer did not approve." Eltenton could have been a Soviet spy. But he might just have wanted to help the Soviets get information about the atomic bomb to defeat the Nazis more quickly. After all, the Soviet Union was now allied with the United States against the Nazis.

At the time, the Soviets were fighting Nazi troops fiercely to hold on to the city of Stalingrad. It was the bloodiest battle of the war. All told, 1.1 million Soviets died there alone—thousands each day—to prevent the Nazis from advancing across the Volga River and capturing vital Soviet oil supplies. Eltenton believed that if the United States wasn't going to tell the Soviet Union about a bomb that might end the war faster and save Soviet lives, maybe someone should.

One thing was for certain: that someone wouldn't be Robert. It was becoming clear to him and many others around the world that though the Soviet Union was fighting bravely against the Nazis, it hadn't become the communist utopia the Bolsheviks had fought and died for. Instead, it was becoming a place of terror and hardship for tens of millions of people.

Joseph Stalin, who took control of the country in 1924, believed that waiting for the rest of the world to unite against capitalism would be a fool's errand. Instead, he wanted the Soviet Union to build a strong socialist government on its own—and fast. This put him in direct conflict with his main political rival, Leon Trotsky, who still believed that a global communist revolution could happen.

Stalin was ruthless and intolerant of dissent. First, he threw Trotsky—and many others who agreed with him—out of the Soviet Communist Party. Then he deported him to Turkey. Trotsky became a man without a country. Between 1933 and 1940, he moved to France, then Norway, then Mexico. But it turned out that he wouldn't be safe anywhere. In May 1940, gunmen armed with machine guns stormed his house in Mexico City. Trotsky survived the attack, only to be mortally wounded three months later by a Soviet agent with an ice pick.

After Stalin eliminated his chief political rivals and terrified others who might challenge him, he forced millions of peasants to combine their land and crops into new collective farms controlled by the state. When some tried to fight back, Stalin's political police either rounded them up and shot them on the spot or sent them to concentration camps where they were worked to death. The chaos caused by Stalin's policy caused a horrific famine in Ukraine, called the Holodomor. More than ten million people may have died there between 1928 and 1934.

Emboldened and seemingly invincible, Stalin launched a terror campaign against more of the original Bolsheviks between 1936 and 1938. He held three public "show" trials in Moscow along with a set of other trials that were conducted in secret. After Stalin's political rivals "confessed" to treason under intense torture and intimidation, they were declared guilty and either thrown in prison or killed. Stalin and his secret police declared millions more "enemies of the people" and sent them to prison camps, many never to be seen again. A climate of extreme fear swept the Soviet Union. With the secret police at his back, Stalin had achieved total power.[11]

By 1938, American newspapers regularly reported on Stalin's reign of terror. Robert read them. There was no way he could defend what was happening in the Soviet Union. He remarked that he "could never find a view of [the trials] which was not damning to the Soviet system."

That summer, two physicists who had spent several months in the Soviet Union—George Placzek and Victor Weisskopf—visited Robert in New Mexico. They spent a week telling Robert all about what was really going on there. "Russia is not what you think it is," they told him. They explained that an Austrian engineer named Alex Weissberg had been arrested out of the blue just for having a conversation with them. "It was an absolutely scary experience," Weisskopf told Robert. "We called up our friends, and they said they didn't know us. It's worse than you could imagine." Deeply disturbed, Robert peppered them with more questions. He couldn't believe what he was hearing.

Later, Robert reflected on the conversations: "What they reported seemed to me so solid, so unfanatical, so true, that it made a great impression; and it presented Russia . . . as a land of purge and terror, of ludicrously bad management and of a long-suffering people." Weisskopf could tell Robert was really shaken by what he and Placzek had told him. "I know that these conversations had a very deep influence on Robert. This was a very decisive week in his life, and he told me so . . ." That weekend, Robert began his turn away from the Communist Party.

PART TWO

LOS ALAMOS

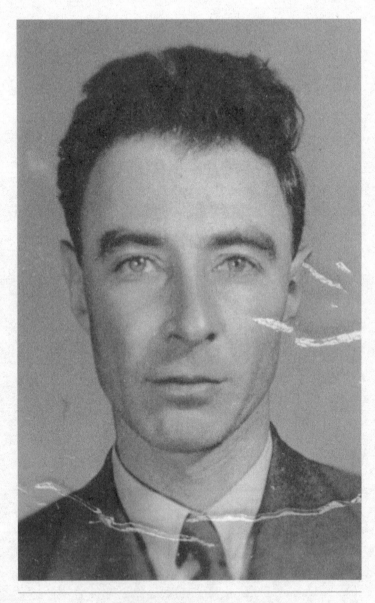

Robert's U.S. government badge photo

CHAPTER FIFTEEN

The Manhattan Project

"He's a genius. A real genius."   —*General Leslie R. Groves*
"He couldn't run a hamburger stand."   —*Berkeley scientist*

The project to build the bomb was formally called the Manhattan Engineer District. Most called it the "Manhattan Project." The army put Colonel Leslie R. Groves in charge. Groves didn't want anything to do with another massive army project. He had just finished work building the Pentagon and wanted to finally get out of Washington. But the army convinced him that if he did this job right, it would win the war. They promised they would make him a general.

The son of a Presbyterian army chaplain, Groves had studied engineering at the University of Washington and MIT. He graduated fourth in his class at West Point. Men serving under him grudgingly admired how smart he was, and how able he was to get things done fast. He was demanding, critical, abrasive, and sarcastic. He didn't take any nonsense. Many people hated his guts. But they understood why he behaved the way he did.

On September 8, 1942, General Groves took control of the

Manhattan Project. That same day, he arranged to buy twelve hundred tons of uranium. The next day, he ordered the purchase of a site in Oak Ridge, Tennessee, where the uranium could be processed.

On October 8, 1942, Groves met Robert Oppenheimer.

Groves was immediately impressed. "He's a genius," Groves said. "A real genius. While Lawrence is very bright, he's not a genius, just a good hard worker. Why, Oppenheimer knows about everything. He can talk to you about anything you bring up. Well, not exactly. I guess there are a few things he doesn't know about. He doesn't know anything about sports."

Robert told Groves that to build the bomb properly, they had to bring together a key group of scientists at one central location—a new lab. The lab needed to be isolated in a rural area rather than in a large city for safety reasons. Groves liked the idea immediately because it would be easier to keep the project secret.

A week after their first meeting, Groves flew Robert to Chicago, where they continued to New York aboard a luxury passenger train. On board, they continued to talk. By then Groves already had Robert in mind to direct the new laboratory. But there were three drawbacks to choosing him. First, Robert lacked a Nobel Prize, and Groves thought that might make it difficult for him to direct other scientists who had won one. Second, he didn't have any experience leading a project like this. And third, "[his political] background included much that was not to our liking by any means."

For those reasons, nobody else imagined that Groves would approve Robert for the job. "It was not obvious that Oppenheimer would be director," Hans Bethe noted. "He had . . . no experience in directing a large group of people." Robert's great friend and admirer I. I. Rabi also thought him a strange choice: "He was a very impractical fellow. He walked about with scuffed shoes and a funny hat . . . and he didn't know anything about equipment." One scientist remarked, "He couldn't run a hamburger stand."

But after a few weeks, Groves knew he wasn't going to be able to find a better candidate and hired Robert to direct the project. Rabi, who didn't like Groves, grudgingly admitted that the appointment "was a real stroke of genius on the part of General Groves, who was not generally considered to be a genius . . . I was astonished."

Groves and Oppenheimer

"THIS IS THE PLACE."

Robert had always wanted to combine his passion for physics with his fierce attraction to the desert high country of New Mexico. Now he had his chance. On November 16, 1942, he and Edwin McMillan, another Radiation Laboratory physicist, set out with army major John H. Dudley to Jemez Springs, a deep canyon forty miles northwest of Santa Fe. Dudley had already inspected many possible sites across the Southwest for the secret laboratory and decided that Jemez Springs would be the best place.

But when they arrived, Robert and McMillan began arguing with Dudley that the snake of land at the bottom of the canyon was too narrow and confined. To house the scientists, their families, army people, and their families, they needed enough open space to build a whole town from scratch.

Robert complained that Jemez Springs had no view of the magnificent mountains. The steep canyons would also make it impossible to fence in. "We were arguing about this when General Groves showed up," recalled McMillan. Groves took one look at the site and said, "This will never do." He turned to Robert and asked if he knew of a better location.

Robert knew the perfect location. "If you go on up the canyon, you come out on top of the mesa and there's a boys' school there which might be a usable site." Exasperated, the men piled back into their cars and drove northwest about thirty miles across a lava mesa called the Pajarito Plateau.

In late afternoon, they pulled up to the Los Alamos Ranch School. Through the haze of drizzly snowfall, Robert, Groves, and McMillan saw a group of schoolboys out on a playing field running around in shorts. The school's eight-hundred-acre grounds included the "Big House," its main building; Fuller Lodge, a beautiful manor house built in 1928 from eight hundred ponderosa logs; a rustic dormitory; and a few other smaller buildings. Behind the lodge there was a pond that the boys used for ice skating in the winter and canoeing during the summer. The school stood at an elevation of seventy-two hundred feet, just about at timberline. To the west, the snowcapped Jemez Mountains rose to eleven thousand feet. From the spacious porch of Fuller Lodge, one could look forty miles east across the Rio Grande Valley to the majestic Sangre de Cristo mountain range, rising to a height of thirteen thousand feet. Groves suddenly announced, "This is the place."

CHAPTER SIXTEEN

"Suddenly we knew the war had arrived here."

An armada of bulldozers and construction crews soon invaded the campus. Student Sterling Colgate recalled seeing Robert and Lawrence roaming the grounds: "Suddenly we knew the war had arrived here. These two characters showed up . . . one wearing a porkpie hat and the other a normal hat, and these two guys went around as if they owned the place."

The War Department wrote a letter to the school's headmaster, A. J. Connell, telling him that the army was taking over the property for military purposes. Connell and others had worked and lived at the school for over twenty years. They had poured their time and talents into shaping their students' minds and lives. Now the school would have to close suddenly—and permanently.

View from Los Alamos Ranch School

Schoolhouse at Los
Alamos Ranch School

Ranch school students reading
together in their living
quarters

The army had no
time to spare in its
race to build a bomb.
It ordered all students
and faculty off the
property by February 8, 1943. Shocked and heartbroken, Connell obeyed. He canceled holiday break and quickened students'
coursework. Students worked straight through to January 21. Then
they packed up and moved out fast. There would be no ceremony
for the four boys graduating that year—no traditional entry on
horseback by the student body, no San Ildefonso Pueblo dancers,
no parents applauding in the audience.[12]

Though Robert and army officials considered the land surrounding the school to be virtually uninhabited, the Pajarito Plateau

had been home to many people for over ten thousand years. Long before New Mexico became a state, Paleo-Indians populated the region, expertly hunting bison with sophisticated weapons. Later, between 6000 BCE and 1150 CE, Archaic hunters migrated to the plateau. To survive, they hunted rabbits and deer, and harvested wild seeds and nuts from piñon trees.

Around 1150, Ancestral Pueblo people arrived from other places across the western continent. Using rock formed by volcanic ash, they erected canyon-side dwellings and whole villages on top of the mesa. There, they harvested beans, corn, and squash, foraged native plants, and hunted deer and small game to round out their diet. Ancestral Pueblo society thrived on the plateau until 1550, when a severe drought forced them to nearby areas along the Rio Grande. But the plateau remained a special place for their descendants. They routinely visited the breathtakingly beautiful landscape to practice and honor their traditions, which were deeply connected to the unique physical surroundings. When the army took over the plateau for the Manhattan Project, it cut them off from their ancestral and spiritual homeland.

In addition to the Pueblos, about thirty-six homesteaders made the plateau their home beginning in 1887, after the Homestead Act of 1862 allowed adult citizens to claim 160 acres of government land and cultivate it. Those who moved there were mostly Hispanic farmers and ranchers who initially lived basic lives off many of the same resources the Native people did before them but built their own farms and dwellings over time.

When the army arrived in 1942, it took over their land and their homes. The army paid them a small amount in return, but it was less than one-eighth of what they paid the white landowners of the Ranch School and other larger properties. Shirley Roybal, a descendant of one of the homesteaders, explained that her ancestors willingly gave up the land to the government: "They were patriotic . . . and like other homesteaders, they hoped to get their land back after the war." When two strangers, one in uniform and one in a formal suit, showed up at their door, Shirley's grandparents, who spoke only Spanish, were taken by surprise. They didn't understand why the strangers were there or what they wanted. "My mother was sixteen or seventeen years old, and she remembers two men coming to the door and asking them to sign over the land."

Ezequiel Garcia began farming his 42.5 acres in 1915. In April 1919, after a herculean effort to clear the land of ponderosa stumps, he was finally able to build a log cabin and settle there with his family. Over time, he built another small log house, a corral, a chicken coop, a bread oven, and a water tank for livestock. Even though the land was extremely difficult to farm, he was able to plant corn and beans, then expand his crops to potatoes, wheat, and oats. Since there was no fresh water on his land, Ezequiel and his family had to haul all their water from a spring a half mile away. In 1941, Ezequiel died and left the property to his wife and their eight children. He had no way of knowing that the very next year, the army would come and take it all away.[13]

Years later, Robert confessed, "I am responsible for ruining a beautiful place."

Over the next three months, construction crews moved in. They built cheap army-green-colored barracks with shingled or tin roofs. Similar buildings popped up to serve as crude chemistry or physics labs.

A makeshift city came to life. Furnished and electrified homes sprung up in neat rows for scientists, soldiers, and their families. Kitchens had fireplaces and refrigerators. They were equipped with wood-fired stoves and hot-water heaters. The homes had no telephones for security reasons. The army erected a school and a hospital, arranged for regular garbage collection, and built a small grocery store and mail-order depot where residents could receive packages. They recruited some of the very same Pueblos and Hispanos (people of Mexican and Spanish descent) they had forced off their land to work as janitors, gardeners, furnace stokers, waiters, housekeepers, babysitters, bodyguards, and maids for the scientists' wives.

A makeshift city came to life at Los Alamos.

Adrienne Lowry, the wife of chemist Joseph Kennedy, remembered: "I had a bodyguard, who was a Spanish-American, and spoke very little English. He wore a gun around his waist on a belt and followed me to where I had to go, to the post office and so on. He was protecting me from who knows what. It was amusing, walking with—I think his name was Juan Lujan—walking with Juan in downtown Santa Fe because he had friends that were around in the streets. I remember him making comments to his friends and I could not understand what they were saying."

The children of the workers went to school with the scientists' and soldiers' children. Esther Vigil, one of the workers' children, remembered her experience fondly: "The opportunities we had were far beyond anything that I had seen . . . We had activities that went beyond reading, writing, and arithmetic. There was a pond, and during the wintertime they would take us ice skating there. [Being in Los Alamos] was an education in itself. It was a tremendous opportunity." Dolores Heaton remembered, "All of my area where we lived, the majority of people were Hispanics. Secundino Sandoval helped me get through geometry. I was terrible in math, horrible. So, you know, 'Would you help me with this?' They were wonderful."

While some Pueblos and Hispanos remembered Los Alamos fondly, others remember being discriminated against. "There were elements of blatant discrimination," reflected Dimas Chavez. "I can recall going to birthday parties, not that many but a few, where my cake and ice cream was served to me outside. In later years, there were families whose daughters were not allowed to date Mexican Americans. Thankfully there was not that much, but it was there." Haskell Sheinberg, who worked in the engineering division, recalled seeing derogatory signs aimed at Hispanos: One said "How do you say, 'Don't spit on the floor'?" in Spanish only, "so that you knew that the signs referred to the Hispanic people. It's like expecting them not to have the same manners or do the things the same way as the non-Hispanics."[14]

CHAPTER SEVENTEEN

Life on the Mesa

To entertain residents who weren't allowed to leave the complex, a recreation officer planned movie showings and hiking trips in the nearby mountains. A cantina served beer, Cokes, and light lunches. Many residents ate their meals in a regular mess hall, while married couples sometimes enjoyed evenings out at a separate "fancy" café.

When Los Alamos opened in March 1943, a hundred scientists, engineers, and support staff converged in the new town. Within six months there were a thousand. A year later, thirty-five hundred people lived out on the mesa. The "Technical Area" alone was made up of thirty-seven separate buildings, including a plutonium purification plant, a foundry, a library, an auditorium, and dozens of labs, warehouses, and offices.

Fuller Lodge mess hall

Los Alamos living quarters

Groves wanted all scientists at Los Alamos to become officers in the army. To do so, they would have to undergo physical exams. Robert failed his. He weighed in at 128 pounds, eleven pounds under the minimum weight and twenty-seven pounds under the ideal weight for a man his age and height. He also had a chronic cough dating back to 1927, when X-rays of his chest confirmed a case of tuberculosis. Every ten days or so, moderate pains shot down his left leg. Army doctors declared him "permanently incapacitated for active service." But Groves ordered the doctors to clear him for duty regardless. He was far too important to the project to be disqualified for medical reasons.

Some of the scientists Robert recruited to Los Alamos flatly refused to work under the army's control. Rabi thought Robert was a fool for letting the army control a scientific project. "[Robert] thought it would be fine to go in uniform because we were at war; it would bring us closer to the American people . . . I know he wanted seriously to win the war, but we couldn't make a bomb that way."

Groves agreed to compromise. When they conducted experiments at the lab, scientists could remain civilians. But when it came time to test the bomb, everyone would put on uniforms. That wasn't good enough for Rabi. He refused to relocate to Los Alamos. He couldn't understand why they had to build such a weapon in the first place. "I was strongly opposed to bombing ever since 1931, when I saw those pictures of the Japanese bombing that suburb of Shanghai. You drop a bomb, and it falls on the just and the unjust. There is no escape from it."

Though Robert was deeply disappointed that Rabi wouldn't join him in New Mexico, he appreciated his friend's passionate misgivings. But as the Nazis murdered Jews in the streets and sent millions more to their deaths in concentration camps, what mattered to Robert most was building the bomb before Germany did.

Robert's uniform at Los Alamos was quite different from those of the military men.

Radioactivity group at Los Alamos

Isidor Isaac (I. I.) Rabi

Los Alamos personnel entering and leaving the main Technical Area

"WE WERE VERY FAR FROM ANYTHING, VERY FAR FROM ANYBODY."

In March 1943, Robert, Kitty, and their son, Peter, moved into their new home on the mesa. It was a rustic one-story log-and-stone house that had been originally built for the sister of the Ranch School's director. It sat at the end of "Bathtub Row"—named that because it and five other log homes on the street were the only houses that had bathtubs. The

Physicists Ernest Lawrence, Enrico Fermi, and I. I. Rabi

small two-bedroom house was partially shielded by shrubbery. Originally it lacked a kitchen, but Kitty insisted that one be built. The living room was pleasant, with high ceilings, a stone fireplace, and a huge plate glass window overlooking a small garden. There, twenty-one months later, Kitty would give birth to their daughter, Toni.

The first spring on the mesa turned out to be a nightmare. As snow melted off the nearby mountains, mud covered the entire town. Everyone's shoes were caked in it. On some days the mud engulfed car tires in a quicksand-like grip. Newly arrived residents had to live temporarily in tin-roofed plywood barracks that weren't a match for the elements.

Hans Bethe was disheartened by what he saw. "I was rather shocked," he said. "I was shocked by the isolation, and I was shocked by the shoddy buildings . . . Everybody was always afraid that a fire would break out and the whole project might burn down." Still, Bethe admitted that the setting was "absolutely beautiful . . . Mountains behind us, desert in front of us, mountains again on the other side. It was late winter, and in April there's still snow on the mountains, so it was lovely to look at. But clearly, we were very far from anything, very far from anybody. We learned to live with it."

Everyone had to get used to new habits and routines. At Berkeley, Robert had refused to schedule classes before 11:00 a.m. so he could socialize late into the evening. At Los Alamos, he was awake, showered, dressed, and on the way to the Technical Area by 7:30 a.m. The Technical Area—known simply as the "T"—was surrounded by a nine-and-a-half-foot woven wire fence, topped with two strands of barbed wire.

Military police guarded the gates. They inspected everyone's color-coded badges. A white badge designated a physicist or other scientist who had the right to roam freely. One day, Robert drove up to the gate and, without even slowing down, whizzed through. The astonished military police shouted a warning and then fired a shot at the car's tires. Robert stopped, backed up the car, murmured an apology, then drove off. After hearing about what happened, Groves wrote Robert a letter asking him not to drive for more than a few miles—and, for good measure, "refrain from flying in airplanes."

Pickup trucks entering Los Alamos

Everyone worked long hours. But even on workdays, Robert wore his New Mexico wardrobe of jeans or khakis with a blue tieless work shirt. His colleagues followed suit. "I don't recall seeing a shined pair of shoes during working hours," recalled one of them. As Robert walked to the "T," scientists fell in behind him and listened quietly as he softly murmured his thoughts of the morning. "There goes the mother hen and all the little chickens," observed one Los Alamos resident. "His porkpie hat, his pipe, and something about his eyes gave him a certain aura," recalled another. "He never needed to show off or shout."

The lab was open day and night. Robert told people to set their own schedules. He refused to allow time clocks to be installed. "The work was terribly demanding," Bethe recalled. The deadlines were incredibly stressful. "I had the feeling, and this came in my dreams," he said, "that I was behind a terribly heavy cart which I had to push up a hill." Scientists who were used to having no deadlines now had to adjust to a world of exacting ones.

"HE BROUGHT OUT THE BEST IN ALL OF US."

The atmosphere at Los Alamos changed Robert. Before the war, he had been more hesitant and modest. Now he was in charge. He assumed his new role with the energy and confidence of a decisive leader.

He didn't give orders. Instead, as one scientist recalled, Robert communicated his desires "very easily and naturally, with just his eyes, his two hands, and a half-lighted pipe." Bethe remembered that Robert "never dictated what should be done. He brought out the best in all of us, like a good host with his guests." Robert Wilson, chief of the experimental physics division, felt similarly: "In his presence, I became more intelligent, more vocal, more intense, more prescient, more poetic myself."

Robert's authority at Los Alamos was nearly absolute. He reported directly to Groves and invested much into their relationship. Each man arrogantly figured he could dominate the other. Groves knew Robert was crucial to the project's success. He thought he could use Robert's political baggage to control him. Robert understood that he could keep his job only if Groves kept thinking of him as the best possible director by far. He knew his political baggage gave Groves power over him, but by showing how important he was, he believed he could convince Groves to run the lab however he wanted. Groves needed Robert's skill as much as Robert needed Groves's approval. They were the perfect team to lead the effort to beat the Germans in the race to build the bomb.

That first winter, in 1943–44, the snows came early and stayed late. Some mornings, the temperature fell to well below zero,

Harold M. Agnew

Luis Alvarez

Robert Bacher

Kenneth T. Bainbridge

Robert F. Christy

Priscilla Duffield

Enrico Fermi

Richard P. Feynman

Louis H. Hemplem

Joseph W. Kennedy

George B. Kistiakowsky

John Manley

William G. Penney

Norman F. Ramsey

Frederick Reines

Emilio Segrè

Staislaw M. Ulam

John R. Von Neumann

Arthur C. Wahl

Victor F. Weisskopf

Hans A. Bethe

Norris E. Bradbury

Hugh Bradner

en Chamberlain

Otto R. Frisch

K. E. J. Fuchs

Gen. Leslie R. Groves

Theordore A. Hall

Edwin M. McMillan

J. R. Oppenheimer

Katherine Oppenheimer

William E. Parsons

Charlotte Serber

Robert Serber

Cyril S. Smith

Edward Teller

Robert R. Wilson

OFFICIAL U.S. GOVERNMENT
BADGE PHOTOS OF
LOS ALAMOS PERSONNEL

draping the valley below in a thick fog. But the harshness of the winter served only to enhance the natural beauty of the mesa, and to connect the transplanted urbanites to this new and unfamiliar mystical landscape.

When the snows finally melted, the drenched highlands blossomed with lavender mariposas and other wildflowers. Almost every day in the spring and summer, dramatic thunderstorms rolled in over the mountains for an hour or two in the late afternoon, cooling the terrain. Flocks of bluebirds, juncos, and towhees perched in the spring-green cottonwoods around Los Alamos. "We learned to watch the snow on the Sangres, and to look for deer in Water Canyon," physicist Philip Morrison later wrote. "We found that on the mesas and in the valley there was an old and strange culture; there were our neighbors, the people of the pueblos, and there were the caves in Otowi canyon to remind us that other men had sought water in the dry land."

Gradually, those who lived and worked at Los Alamos forged a sense of community—and Robert was coming into his own as their leader. Exhibiting his commitment to democracy, he appointed a town council, which met regularly and helped him understand the community's needs. In front of the council, Los Alamos residents vented their frustrations. Why was the food so bad? Why couldn't the houses be built better? Couldn't the army police give fewer parking tickets?

Robert understood and appreciated the sacrifices everyone was making to uproot their lives and move to such a challenging place. Despite the lack of privacy, the spartan conditions, and the recurring shortages in water, milk, and even electricity, he infected people with his playful enthusiasm. When the local theater group put on a production of *Arsenic and Old Lace*, the audience was stunned and delighted to see Robert, powdered white with flour and looking stiff as a corpse, carried onstage and laid out on the floor. He also displayed deep empathy toward residents who were going through tough times. When, in the autumn of 1943, a young woman suddenly died of a mysterious paralysis, Robert was the first to visit her grieving husband.

At home, Robert became the cook. He enjoyed spicy dishes like the Southeast Asian dish nasi goreng, but one of his regular dinners included steak, fresh asparagus, and potatoes, prefaced by a gin sour or one of his signature martinis. On April 22, 1943, he hosted the first big party at Los Alamos—to celebrate his thirty-ninth birthday. Food and drinks flowed. Everyone was dancing and carrying on. Robert danced the foxtrot in his usual old-world style, holding his arm stiffly in front of him. Rabi amused everyone when he took out his comb and played it like a harmonica.

On Saturday evenings, the lodge became packed with square dancers—the men dressed in jeans, cowboy boots, and colorful shirts; the women wore long dresses bulging with petticoats. Afterward, some of the younger scientists threw the rowdiest parties. Sometimes one of them played an accordion while everyone danced.

Occasionally, some of the physicists gave piano and violin recitals. Robert dressed up for these Saturday-evening affairs, wearing one of his tweedy suits. He was always the center of attention. "If you were in a large hall," a resident recalled, "the largest group of people would be hovering around what, if you could get your way through, would be Oppenheimer. He was great at a party and women simply loved him."

Scientists and their families put on a skit inside Fuller Lodge.

On Sundays, many residents went for hikes or picnics in the nearby mountains, or rented the horses boarded at the Los Alamos Ranch School's former stables. Robert rode his own horse, Chico, a beautiful fourteen-year-old chestnut, on a regular route from the east side of town west toward the mountain trails. Robert could make Chico "single foot"—trot by placing each of his hooves down at a different time—over the roughest trails. Along the way, he greeted everyone he encountered with a wave of his mud-colored porkpie hat and a passing remark. He would often go with Kitty, who was a "very good horsewoman, really European trained." An armed guard always went with them.

A group of physicists
out for a Sunday hike

Robert's physical stamina atop a horse or hiking in the mountains surprised his companions. "He always looked so frail," recalled Dr. Louis Hempelmann, director of the Los Alamos health group. "He was always so painfully thin, of course, but he was amazingly strong." During the summer of 1944, Robert and Hempelmann rode together over the Sangre de Cristos to Perro Caliente. "It nearly killed me," said Hempelmann. "He was on his horse with the 'single-foot' gait, perfectly comfortable, and my horse had to go into a hard trot to keep up with him. I think the first day we must have ridden thirty to thirty-five miles, and I was nearly dead."

Though rarely sick, Robert suffered from smoker's cough, the result of a four- or five-pack-a-day habit. "I think he only picked up a pipe," said one of his secretaries, "as an interlude from the chain smoking."

Sometimes he would break down in uncontrolled spasms of coughing, and his face would flush purple as he kept trying to talk through his cough. Just as he made a ceremony of mixing his martinis, Robert smoked his cigarettes with a singular style. Where most

people used their index finger to tap ashes off the end of their cigarettes, he had the peculiar mannerism of brushing the ash from the tip by using the end of his little finger. The habit had so callused the tip of his finger that it appeared almost charred.

Robert with his standard cigarette

CHAPTER EIGHTEEN

Near-Total Surveillance

On the mesa, security was paramount. What happened at Los Alamos had to stay at Los Alamos. One day, Robert learned that rumors were flying around Santa Fe about a secret facility way out on the mesa. He suggested to Groves that they plant their own rumor as a diversion. He asked two Los Alamos couples to go out to some of the bars in Santa Fe at night. "Talk. Talk too much," Robert told them. "Talk as if you had too many drinks . . . I don't care how you manage it, say we are building an electric rocket." The couples drove down to Santa Fe and tried to spread the rumor.

Security rules greatly annoyed everyone. Edward Teller told Robert that some people were complaining about the army opening their mail. Robert replied bitterly, "What are they griping about? I am not allowed to talk to my own brother." Robert himself complained all the time that his phone calls were being listened to. He told his friend Robert Wilson, who thought he was being paranoid.

But Robert wasn't being paranoid. He *had* been under near-total surveillance. Even before Los Alamos opened, J. Edgar Hoover's FBI had been spying on Robert's friends and family. They tried mightily to connect dots between him and the Communist Party.

Army Counter Intelligence Corps (CIC) officers were already in place when Robert arrived on the mesa. One agent doubled as Robert's personal driver and bodyguard. CIC officers monitored Robert's mail and tapped his home phone. They wiretapped his office too.

No matter what Robert said or did to ease their suspicions, the FBI and CIC wouldn't let up. In June 1943, Colonel Boris Pash, West Coast chief of CIC, a virulent anti-communist who fought for the White Army in the Russian Civil War, became convinced that Robert was still connected to his old communist friends. Pash told Groves's security aide, Lieutenant Colonel John Lansdale, that Robert should be fired.

Lansdale liked Robert and trusted him. He thought firing him was too extreme and knew Robert was essential to the project. But he also thought Groves should know what Pash suspected. What if Robert *was* a spy and Lansdale failed to say anything? Lansdale wrote Groves a memo that laid out Pash's so-called evidence: Robert had been a member of both the American Civil Liberties Union and the American Committee for Democracy and Intellectual Freedom. He was friends with people the FBI said were known or suspected communists, including his old flame Jean Tatlock, whom he had visited in June—an event that prompted Pash's conviction.

Lansdale and Pash decided to bait Robert. They told him they suspected there were already traitors out on the mesa sharing secrets with the Soviet Union. If Robert was indeed one of them, as Pash believed, maybe he would be scared enough to rat them out.

Robert was worried. He could tell something was going on but didn't know what. Hounded by all the investigations into his past, he thought maybe he should just quit the project. The strain of the job was getting to be too much.

No, he decided. He had come too far and invested way too much to quit now. He racked his brain. Was there anything the FBI or CIC had that might really hurt him?

Suddenly, the kitchen conversation he had with Hoke six months earlier popped into his mind. He didn't report it at the time because he wanted to protect his friend, but what if Eltenton really was trying to get him to share information about the bomb with the Soviets? How would it look if the FBI or CIC found out about it and believed he was covering it up? Or maybe the Soviets knew about it already? *He had to tell somebody.*

Robert told Groves first. But he didn't stop there. On a trip to Berkeley for other project business, he sought out Lieutenant Lyall Johnson, the army security officer at Radiation Laboratory. He told Johnson that there was a man in town named Eltenton who might be trying to get information about the lab's work, and that he should be watched.

Alarmed, Johnson immediately told Pash. Already deeply suspicious of Robert, Pash told Johnson to tell Robert to come back the next day for an interview. That night, while Robert slept, they placed a tiny microphone into the phone on Johnson's desk and ran a wire to a recording device in the next room.

Robert had no way of knowing that Pash had already recommended he be fired *and prosecuted* under the Espionage Act. Instead, he naively assumed Pash had the best intentions. After all, Robert was about to give him important information about someone who could be an *actual* threat to the project. He figured Pash would respect him for that.

The next morning, with the hidden microphone on, Pash got right to the point. Who, he asked Robert, was interested in what was going on at the Rad Lab? Robert said he didn't know. But he told Pash there was a man whose name he had never heard, who may have been trying to get Rad Lab scientists to send information to the Soviet Union.

Robert *had* heard the man's name, though. Hoke had told him in the kitchen it was Eltenton. And not only that, he'd already told both Groves and Johnson that Eltenton should be watched. But at that moment, intimidated by Pash's icy interrogation, Robert chose not to mention Eltenton's name.

Pash pressed Robert further, "Could you give me a little more specific information as to exactly what information you have?"

Robert clarified, "Well, I might say that the *approaches* were always to other people, who were troubled by them, and sometimes came and discussed *them* with me."

Approaches. Plural. Robert was digging himself a hole—continuing to sabotage himself as he often did under such strain. Now he had made Pash believe that more than one person was trying to get information for the Soviets.

Pash stared at Robert. By then Robert had figured out that this wasn't someone to mess with. What information might Pash already have about Eltenton? If Robert knew more than he was letting on and he didn't come clean, Pash might decide he was being deliberately evasive.

Colonel Boris Pash, West Coast chief of the Army Counter Intelligence Corps (CIC)

Robert therefore decided to tell Pash what he had already told Groves and Johnson: that George Eltenton should be watched. Eltenton, he said, had talked to one of his friends who knew someone on the project. Of course, Eltenton's "friend" was Hoke, and the "someone on the project" was Robert, but Robert knew better than to admit that.

Pash was relentless. He pressed Robert to name those who had been approached. Politely, Robert refused. He certainly wasn't going to rat out his friend Hoke, whom he believed to be innocent. Instead, he responded, "I'll tell you one thing. I have known of two or three cases, and I think two of the men were with me at Los Alamos—they are men who are very closely associated with me."

Naively thinking that Pash would understand, Robert tried to convince him that the people who were trying to get information for the Soviets were innocent and well-meaning. He explained to Pash that if the United States government wasn't going to share important scientific knowledge that might help its ally win the war against the Nazis sooner, they saw it as their duty to share it themselves.

Robert admitted, "The actual fact is that since it is not a communication which ought to be taking place, it is treasonable." But Robert didn't believe the *spirit* of their actions was treasonable. They were trying to end the war sooner.

Robert didn't realize whom he was talking to. Pash was a lifelong hater of the Soviet Union who would do anything in his power to go after those who defended it. He saw things in black and white: no one trying to get information to the Soviet Union was innocent or well-meaning. And this wasn't just any information—it was information about the most sensitive project in American history. By trying to share it with a foreign power, they were committing espionage! Pure and simple. How could Robert admit in one breath that he knew people who may have committed treason, but then refuse to name their names in the next?

If he hadn't been convinced enough before, Pash now believed wholeheartedly that Robert was up to no good. And now he had Robert's voice on tape sympathizing with those who would try to share information about the bomb with the Soviets. Robert agreed to speak with Pash because he wanted to do what he thought best for his country. But he had now given one of his most powerful enemies more ammunition to destroy him.

CHAPTER NINETEEN

Misgivings

By spring 1944, many scientists realized that the Germans hadn't made much progress on building atomic bombs. Because he was cleared to read top-secret information, Robert had known that for quite some time. But still, the Manhattan Project continued at full speed.

Restless and determined, Robert and most of the other scientists pressed forward without stopping to rest or reflect. But one of them, Joseph Rotblat, paused. At dinner one night with Groves, the general shocked the Polish physicist with an ominous comment: "You realize of course that the main purpose of this project is to subdue the Russians."

Rotblat did a double take. Groves had just said the quiet part out loud. *Subdue the Russians?* The scientists had been told they were building the bomb to keep the *Nazis* in check. Now the director of the project himself was saying they were building it for another purpose entirely. Rotblat felt betrayed.

Though the United States and the Soviets had teamed up against the Nazis, the two countries were far from true friends. After the Bolshevik Revolution in 1917, the United States and other Western countries had tried to strangle the infant communist government in its cradle by backing the "white" army in its fight against the Bolshevik "reds." After that, though American companies did some business with Russia in the 1920s, the two countries didn't have an official relationship until 1933. But just as the relationship seemed like it might thaw, Americans found out more about Stalin's horrific behavior toward those who dared challenge him.

Making matters worse, as war clouds gathered in the late 1930s, Stalin signed a pact with Hitler that the Soviet Union and Germany wouldn't attack each other. Then both countries invaded Poland. By August 1940, Stalin's army became so powerful that it attacked Finland and swallowed Lithuania, Estonia, Latvia, and parts of Romania into a rapidly expanding "Soviet Union."[15] President Roosevelt publicly called Stalin out for running "a dictatorship as absolute as any other dictatorship in the world."[16]

It wasn't until Germany betrayed the pact and invaded the Soviet Union on June 22, 1941, that the United States and the Soviets became allies. But even as allies, their relationship was anything but smooth. As Stalin's troops went head-to-head with the Nazis in the east, they pleaded desperately with the U.S., Britain, and France to send troops to help squeeze them from the west. Roosevelt promised Stalin that they would open a "second front" in fall 1942. But 1943 rolled around, and there was still no second front. Meanwhile, hundreds of thousands of Russian soldiers died to keep the Nazis at bay. In 1944, after the United States still hadn't delivered on its promise, Stalin finally recalled his ambassadors from Washington and London in protest. [17]

It wasn't until June 6, 1944, that U.S., British, and Canadian troops stormed ashore at Normandy, France, and began their march toward Germany to confront the Nazis and relieve the Soviets from the carnage.[18]

Rotblat understood that the United States and the Soviet Union were only held together by their common goal of defeating the Nazis. He also understood that many Americans, after reading about Stalin's atrocities and his army's takeover of neighboring countries, worried more and more that the Soviet Union might one day become powerful enough to challenge or threaten the United States. But still . . . the scientists had been told that their goal was to build the bomb to stop the Nazis, not as a tool to threaten the Soviets. Rotblat reflected, "Until then I had thought that our work was to prevent a Nazi victory . . . and now I was told that the weapon we were preparing was intended for use against the people who were making extreme sacrifices for that aim."

By the end of 1944, it was clear that the war in Europe would soon be over. After six months of fierce fighting, American, British, and Canadian troops had liberated France, occupied Belgium, and part of the Netherlands, and now closed in on the German border. The Nazis would be defeated. Rotblat thought it was pointless to continue work on a weapon that was no longer necessary to defeat them. He said goodbye to Robert and left Los Alamos on December 8, 1944.

Other Los Alamos scientists began to question why they needed to keep building such a powerful and destructive bomb. Small groups of them began meeting wherever they could find space— first in their apartments and in the Los Alamos chapel. Then, as the meetings became more formal, they tried to organize space in laboratory lecture rooms.

Robert Wilson wanted to know how the bomb might be used if it wasn't going to be used against the Nazis. He asked Robert to hold a formal meeting to talk about it. Robert worried that Wilson could get in trouble with CIC for questioning the mission. He tried to talk him down. Wilson didn't care about getting in trouble. Bravely, he put notices up all over the lab, announcing a public meeting to discuss "The Impact of the Gadget on Civilization."

Robert Wilson, Robert's friend and chief of the Los Alamos experimental physics division

Robert tried his best to discourage scientists from attending. Senior physicist Victor Weisskopf recalled, "He said . . . this is politics, and we should not do this." Some of them wondered what had happened to the Robert they knew—the Robert who would have organized those types of meetings himself not so long ago. Had their esteemed colleague become so fixed on building the bomb—and so beholden to his military and government bosses—that he had turned away from his conscience?

Despite Robert's admonishments, twenty people showed up. Why, they wondered, did they need to keep building a bomb now that the Allies were on the cusp of winning the war in Europe? Together, they contemplated what the future of the world might look like after a war with atomic weapons.

Robert knew it would reflect poorly on him as the project's leader if he didn't attend. Shocking some of the scientists, he walked through the door. Wilson understood why he felt he needed to be there: "You know, you're the director, a little bit like a general. Sometimes you have got to be in front of your troops, sometimes you've got to be in back of them."

With Robert in the room, the scientists voiced their chief worry—one that kept some of them awake at night: If the bomb wasn't going to be used on the Nazis, who *might* it be used on? Would it be possible to stop the project, to put the genie back in the bottle?

At another meeting, Robert took the floor. As usual, he immediately dominated the discussion and commanded the room. Everyone fell into absolute silence. In his soft voice, he argued that the war shouldn't end without the world knowing about this primordial new weapon. The worst outcome would be if the bomb remained one nation's military secret. If that happened, the next war would almost certainly be fought with atomic weapons.

No, Robert told them—they had to forge ahead. The bomb had to be tested. Regardless of the Nazis' impending defeat, the world needed to know that humankind had invented these weapons of mass destruction, so the weapons could be better understood and controlled.

It was a defining moment for everyone. Robert's charismatic energy and his ever-present logic cut through the scientists' uncertainty. He was able to convince them to press ahead with the mission. Wilson recalled, "My feeling about [Robert] was, at that time, that this was a man who is angelic, true, and honest and he could do no wrong . . . I believed in him."

CHAPTER TWENTY

The War in the Pacific Raged On

April 12, 1945: "Sunday morning found the mesa deep in snow. A night's fall had covered the rude textures of the town, silenced its business, and unified the view in a soft whiteness, over which the bright sun shone, casting deep blue shadows behind every wall. It was no costume for mourning, but it seemed recognition of something we needed, a gesture of consolation. Everybody came to the theater, where [Robert] spoke very quietly for two or three minutes out of his heart and ours." —Phil Morrison, physicist

Franklin Delano Roosevelt, the president who had inspired millions around the globe to have faith that the terrible sacrifices of World War II would yield "a world more fit for human habitation," was dead. Looking out over the solemn crowd of scientists, Robert declared, "We have been living through years of great evil, and great terror." And during this time, Roosevelt had been, "in an old and unperverted sense, our leader." Characteristically, he quoted the two-thousand-year-old Hindu scripture the Bhagavad Gita, which he had studied in-depth with a fellow professor at Berkeley: "Man is a creature whose substance is faith. What his faith is, he is." He concluded, "We should dedicate ourselves to the hope that his good works will not have ended with his death."

Robert, along with many of the scientists, held out hope that FDR's men in Washington would commit themselves to telling other world leaders about the bomb before the United States used it. He desperately hoped that the new president, Harry Truman, would agree.

When Truman took office, he didn't know anything about the Manhattan Project. He had been FDR's vice president for only eighty-two days before the president's death. At no time during that period did FDR think it necessary to tell him that the United States was building a secret bomb that could destroy an entire city.

The war in Europe was nearly over. On April 30, Hitler died by suicide. Eight days later, Germany surrendered. Tens of thousands of Americans took to the streets in celebration. Spontaneous parties erupted across Paris. Russians of all ages wept with both glee and sorrow on May 9, which they declared "Victory Day." To many, it seemed unfathomable that the Allies had finally brought Nazi Germany to its knees. Allied soldiers liberated concentration camps, arrested disgraced Nazi officers, and shared stories about the death camps with international newspapers.

But the war in the Pacific raged on. After years of island-hopping and ferocious fighting, American forces finally drew close enough to Japan to bomb its cities mercilessly from the air. On the evening of March 9–10, 1945, 334 American B-29 aircraft dropped tons of jellied gasoline—napalm—and high explosives on Tokyo. The horrific firestorm killed an estimated one hundred thousand people and completely burned 15.8 square miles of the Japanese capital. By July 1945, all but five of Japan's major cities had been destroyed. Hundreds of thousands of Japanese civilians were dead. Japan fought on.

The firebombings were no secret. Ordinary Americans read about them in their newspapers. Thoughtful people understood that such bombing of civilians raised deep ethical questions. "I remember Mr. Stimson [the secretary of war] saying to me," Robert later remarked, "that he thought it appalling that there should be no protest over the air raids which we were conducting against Japan, which in the case of Tokyo led to such extraordinarily heavy loss of life. He didn't say that the air strikes shouldn't be carried on, but he did think there was something wrong with a country where no one questioned that . . ."

More Los Alamos scientists began to wonder if the entire project should be scuttled. If the original purpose for building the bomb was to keep the Nazis in check, why continue building such a powerful weapon now that they were defeated?

At the University of Chicago, Leo Szilard was frantic. Atomic bombs would soon be ready. He had a terrible feeling that now that the Nazis had been defeated, the U.S. would drop them on Japan.

Before the war, Szilard had been petrified the Nazis would develop the bomb first. He was the first to urge President Roosevelt to build them. Now he was hell-bent on convincing Truman *not* to use them. Szilard understood that if the United States used the bombs against the Japanese, other countries, especially the Soviet Union, would move heaven and earth to build their own bombs.

Szilard made an appointment with Truman. He arrived at the

White House on May 25 with two other scientists, determined to convince the new president not to drop the horrific new weapon on Japan. But their hopes were dashed when they got to the gates of the executive mansion. There, they learned that Truman wouldn't meet with them after all. Instead, the president sent them to meet with James F. Byrnes, soon to be appointed secretary of state. Dejected but determined, they traveled to meet Byrnes in Spartanburg, South Carolina.

Byrnes invited them into his house. Anxiously, Szilard told Byrnes that if the United States dropped the atomic bomb on Japan, the Soviet Union would likely build its own bombs. Once the Soviets saw that the U.S. would drop such a weapon on Japanese cities, wouldn't they fear the U.S. might drop it on their cities if push ever came to shove?

Byrnes shook his head. He shot back that dropping the bomb on Japan would show the Soviets how powerful the United States had become. Maybe that would force them to withdraw their troops from eastern Europe after the war.

Byrnes's reply shocked Szilard. Was he actually saying that the United States should drop the bomb, possibly on civilians, just to intimidate the Soviets into changing their behavior?

And what if they didn't listen?

Szilard thought that dropping the bomb on a military target was terrible enough. But if countries started using atomic bombs as tools to scare or control other countries, it would set an incredibly dangerous precedent. The United States would only be the first country to use nuclear weapons. Others would shortly follow. Szilard left in a somber mood. "I was rarely," he wrote, "as depressed as when we left Byrnes's house and walked toward the station."

Undeterred, Szilard decided to share his concerns with Robert. Surely Robert would understand what he was saying. Perhaps *he* could convince Truman and Byrnes to listen to reason.

Robert met with Szilard on May 30. It's difficult to know exactly how Robert felt at that point about dropping the bomb on Japan. It was clear that he was fixated on finishing what he had started regardless of the Nazi defeat. But curiously, he didn't believe the bomb would be useful in combat. The atomic bomb "is a weapon which has no military significance," he told Szilard. "It will make a big bang—a very big bang—but it is not a weapon which is useful in war." Robert told Szilard that if it *were* to be used, it would be important to tell the Soviets about it beforehand. Szilard shot back that merely telling Stalin about the bomb wouldn't prevent a race between the countries to build more bombs after the war.

"Well," Robert insisted, "don't you think that if we tell the Russians what we intend to do and then use the bomb on Japan, the Russians will understand it?"

"They'll understand it all too well," Szilard replied.

Robert seemed to believe, naively, that if the United States dropped the bomb on Japan, the Russians would see how terrible a weapon it was, compelling them to work together with the U.S. and the rest of the world to control the bombs' future construction and use. Paradoxically, he also believed that once the world realized how destructive those new bombs could be, all future wars might be eliminated. The price of waging them would just be too great.

Szilard thought Robert was giving the Soviets, and humankind, way too much credit. As he had already expressed to Byrnes, Szilard believed that the Soviets would learn the opposite lesson—that they needed to build their own bombs quickly and in secrecy to counter what they perceived as a growing American threat.

In a meeting on May 31, Robert advised Secretary of War Henry Stimson and other American government officials to tell other countries, particularly the Soviet Union, about the bomb before using it. Maybe, instead of building more bombs, the world could work together after the war to harness atomic energy for the betterment of humankind. Perhaps it could be used for peaceful purposes instead, like generating energy to heat homes, power vehicles, and move goods more efficiently. Telling the world would send a powerful message that the United States, having been the first to build such a horrible weapon, was committed to a peaceful and productive future at the very moment the world needed to hear it.

At first, Stimson seemed to listen. He thought it might be possible to form an international organization, which would guarantee "complete scientific freedom" and prevent countries from building bombs in secret.

Five-star general and eventual Nobel Peace Prize winner George C. Marshall didn't go that far. But he reassured nervous American officials that he believed the Soviets would remain loyal allies and not say a word to the Japanese. He even suggested that the Americans might invite Soviet scientists to witness the first bomb test.

Such words from the country's top military officer put Robert at ease. It seemed he was beginning to convince them that openness and cooperation would prevent disaster. But Byrnes shot Marshall's idea straight down. Byrnes, fearful that the Soviets might ask to take part in the bomb project, didn't want them anywhere near the bomb test. He believed the United States must "push ahead as fast as possible . . . to make certain that we stay ahead" of the Soviet Union.

Byrnes's view won out. The Manhattan Project would stay secret from the Soviets, and the bomb would be dropped on a Japanese city without warning. Though Robert didn't believe the bomb would be "useful in war," and though he was anxious about how many Japanese people might die, he trusted the word of military commanders that dropping it on Japan would prevent an American invasion and end the war quickly, thereby saving American lives.

But there was much that Robert did not know as the bomb project barreled toward completion. He later recalled, "We didn't know beans about the military situation in Japan. We didn't know whether they could be caused to surrender by other means or whether the invasion was really inevitable. But in the backs of our minds was the notion that the invasion was inevitable because we had been told that." Robert didn't know that the United States had decoded messages from Japan indicating that the Japanese government understood that the war was lost and was seeking acceptable surrender terms.

No one can be certain how Robert may have reacted if he had learned on the eve of the bombing in Hiroshima that Truman *knew* the Japanese were "asking for peace," and that the military use of atomic bombs on cities was an option rather than a necessity for ending the war. But we do know that after the war he came to believe that he had been misled, and that this knowledge constantly reminded him that he should be wary of what government officials told him.

CHAPTER TWENTY-ONE

Jornada del Muerto

The summer of 1945 was hot and dry out on the mesa. Robert pushed his men to work longer hours. Tensions rose. Activity accelerated. Explosions increased. Everyone seemed on edge. The bomb was nearing completion. It was almost time to test it.

More than a year earlier, Robert had spent three days and nights bouncing around the barren, dry valleys of southern New Mexico in a three-quarter-ton army truck, looking for an isolated patch of wilderness where the bomb could be safely tested. With him went Kenneth Bainbridge, a scientist from Harvard, and several army officers. At night, the men slept in the truck's flatbed to avoid rattlesnakes.

There, under the stars, Robert reminisced about his days as a student in Göttingen. How exciting it had been to be a young physicist surrounded by so many great minds, competing with one another so fiercely to produce breakthrough after breakthrough. The work of Heisenberg, Dirac, Pauli, Jordan, Born, and so many others made it possible to split the atom—to harness energy so limitless that it could power the future, which at the time had seemed so bright.

But as Robert and his fellow officers lay there almost twenty years later, on land sacred to many prior generations of fellow humans, the weight of the world was on all of them. Hundreds of thousands of years of human knowledge and almost a half century of advances in quantum mechanics were about to yield the most powerful bomb in history. What might the future be like after it was used?

The men selected a test site sixty miles northwest of Alamogordo, in an area the Spanish had called the Jornada del Muerto—the "Journey of Death." There, they staked out an area eighteen by twenty-four miles in size and built hardened bunkers from which to observe the first explosion of an atomic bomb. Robert called the test site "Trinity." He wasn't sure later why he chose that name. He remembered vaguely a John Donne poem that opens with the line "Batter my heart, three-person'd God . . ." Perhaps he was drawing from the Bhagavad Gita and the trinity of Hindu gods: Brahma the creator, Vishnu the preserver, and Shiva the destroyer.

Robert and army personnel on a trip to select a site for the Trinity test

To Robert's delight, his brother Frank came to join him at Los Alamos in late May 1945. Conditions were spartan, to say the least. Frank, Bainbridge, and the army officers slept in tents and toiled in hundred-degree temperatures to prepare the site. As the target date approached, Frank thought they should prepare for disaster just in case. "We spent several days finding escape routes through the desert," he recalled, "and making little maps so everybody could be evacuated."

Everyone was exhausted. The pressure was relentless. Groves pushed for speed. He knew that Truman was scheduled to meet with Joseph Stalin and Winston Churchill, the prime minister of the United Kingdom, in mid-July in Potsdam, Germany. Groves wanted a tested and usable bomb in the president's hands before that conference ended. Robert first thought that the bomb would be ready by July 4—but that proved to be unrealistic. By the end of June, he told his team that they were now aiming for Monday, July 16.

On the evening of July 11, Robert walked home and said goodbye to Kitty. For good luck, she gave him a four-leaf clover from their garden. Then he drove to Albuquerque and checked into the Hilton Hotel. Joining him were top government officials who had flown in from Washington to observe the test. "He was very nervous," observed Joseph O. Hirschfelder, a chemist. As if people were not already anxious enough, a last-minute test had just indicated that the bomb was likely to be a dud. Explosives division head George Kistiakowsky recalled, "[Robert] became so emotional that I offered him a month's salary against ten dollars that [it] would work." That evening Robert, jittery with nerves, recited a stanza from the Gita that he had translated from Sanskrit:

In battle, in forest, at the precipice in the mountains,
On the dark great sea, in the midst of javelins and arrows,
In sleep, in confusion, in the depths of shame,
The good deeds a man has done before defend him.

Robert only slept four hours that night. General Thomas Farrell, who was trying to sleep in the next room, heard him coughing miserably half the night. Robert awoke exhausted and depressed on July 15, the day before the test. But as he ate breakfast, he received a phone call from Hans Bethe telling him that the last-minute test had failed only because of a minor wiring problem. There was no reason why the bomb test wouldn't work.

Relieved, Robert then turned his attention to the weather. That morning the skies over Trinity were clear. But winds around the site were picking up. He called Groves and warned him, "The weather is whimsical."

In the late afternoon, thunderclouds moved in. Robert drove to the Trinity tower for one last look at the unexploded bomb. Alone, he climbed up to the top and inspected his creation. It was an ugly

metal globe studded with detonator plugs.

Everything seemed in order. After surveying the landscape, he climbed down, got into his vehicle, and drove back to base camp. Violent storms

Partially assembled Trinity bomb atop the test tower

darkened the horizon by the time he arrived. Against the threatening skies, Robert encountered Cyril Smith, one of the project's chief metallurgists. The two began chatting aimlessly about family and life on the mesa. The conversation then turned philosophical. Robert gazed out at the thunderclouds billowing up over the mesa toward the ridgeline of the Sangre de Cristos and reflected, "Funny how the mountains always inspire our work." To many of the scientists and government officials who hailed from other parts of the country and across the globe, the otherworldly landscape was simply beautiful. To Robert, it had become so much more.

CHAPTER TWENTY-TWO

"We knew the world would not be the same."

At the test site the night of July 15, 1945, a sleepless Robert hung out in the base camp mess hall, gulping down black coffee and rolling cigarette after cigarette, smoking them nervously down to the butt. As rain pelted the tin roof, he pulled out a book of poetry by Baudelaire and began to read. Lightning illuminated the darkness outside.

Enrico Fermi feared that the storm's winds might drench them with radioactive rain. He wanted to postpone the test. "There could be a catastrophe," he warned Robert. The scientists were tense.

After years of hypothesizing, theorizing, and modeling, the moment of truth was rapidly approaching. Would the bomb work? What would it look like? Sound like? Feel like?

How big would the explosion be?

To pass the time and relieve their anxiety, some of the scientists organized a betting pool. They each bet a dollar to predict the size of the explosion. Edward Teller bet high, putting his dollar on forty-five thousand tons of TNT. Robert bet low, a modest three thousand tons. I. I. Rabi staked his dollar on twenty thousand tons. Fermi took side bets on whether the bomb would actually light the atmosphere on fire.

The few scientists who managed to sleep were awakened by an extraordinary noise. Frank recalled, "All the frogs in [the] area had gathered in a little pond by the camp and copulated and squawked all night long."

Robert's chief meteorologist, Jack Hubbard, assured him the storm would pass. To be on the safe side, Hubbard suggested moving the hour of detonation from 4:00 to 5:00 a.m. At that moment, an agitated Groves paced back and forth across the mess hall. He disliked Hubbard and didn't trust him. Groves thought that any postponement at all might mean delaying the test for at least two or three more days. Worried that some of the more cautious scientists might convince Robert to postpone if they stayed at base camp, Groves whisked him away to the South Shelter control center, which was less than six miles from the Trinity site.

At 2:30 a.m., thirty-mile-an-hour winds and severe thundershowers pounded the test site. Still, Hubbard predicted the storm would clear. Oppenheimer and Groves stalked the ground nervously, glancing to the skies every few minutes to see if they could detect a change in the weather. Around 3:00 a.m., they went inside the control center bunker and talked. Neither man could stomach a delay. Groves was even more adamant that the test should proceed.

Finally, they announced their decision: They would schedule the test for 5:30 a.m. and hope for the best. One hour later, true to Hubbard's prediction, the skies began to clear and the wind died down.

At 5:10 a.m., a loud voice boomed across a loudspeaker for all to hear, "It is now zero minus twenty minutes."

Robert was lying facedown as 5:30 approached. The countdown reached two minutes. He muttered to himself, "Lord, these affairs are hard on the heart." As he lay there in anticipation, an army general watched him closely: "Dr. Oppenheimer . . . grew tenser as the last seconds ticked off. He scarcely breathed . . . For the last few seconds he stared directly ahead and then . . . the announcer shouted 'Now!'"

THE DAWN OF THE NUCLEAR AGE

Physicist Richard Feynman stood twenty miles from ground zero when he was handed dark glasses. They were so dark he determined that he wouldn't see anything through them. Instead, he climbed into the cab of a truck. He figured the windshield would protect his eyes from harmful ultraviolet rays, and he'd be able to actually see the explosion.

All of a sudden the horizon lit up with a tremendous flash. Feynman ducked reflexively. He looked up again. A white light changed into yellow and then orange: "A big ball of orange, the center that was so bright, becomes a ball of orange that starts to rise and billow a little bit and get a little black around the edges, and then you see it's a big ball of smoke with flashes on the inside of the fire going out, the heat." A full minute and a half after the explosion, he finally heard an enormous bang, followed by a rumble of man-made thunder.

James Conant had expected a relatively quick flash of light. But the white light flooded the sky so much that for a moment he thought "something had gone wrong" and the "whole world [had] gone up in flames."

Bob Serber was also twenty miles away, lying facedown and holding a piece of welder's glass to his eyes. "Of course," he wrote later, "just at [that] moment my arm got tired and I lowered the glass for a second, the bomb went off. I was completely blinded by the flash." When his vision returned thirty seconds later, he saw a bright violet column rising twenty or thirty thousand feet into the air. "I could feel the heat on my face a full twenty miles away."

Chemist Joe Hirschfelder also described the moment: "All of a sudden, the night turned into day, and it was tremendously bright, the chill turned into warmth; the fireball gradually turned from white to yellow to red as it grew in size and climbed into the sky; after about five seconds the darkness returned but with the sky and the air filled with a purple glow, just as though we were surrounded by an aurora borealis . . . We stood there in awe as the blast wave picked up chunks of dirt from the desert soil and soon passed us by."

Frank lay right next to his big brother when the bomb exploded. Though he was lying on the ground, "the light of the first flash penetrated and came up from the ground through one's [eye]lids. When one first looked up, one saw the fireball, and then almost immediately afterwards, this unearthly hovering cloud. It was very bright and very purple." Frank thought, "Maybe it's going to drift over the area and engulf us." In a few moments, the thunder of the blast was bouncing back and forth on the distant mountains. "But I think the most terrifying thing," Frank recalled, "was this really brilliant purple cloud, black with radioactive dust, that hung there, and you had no feeling of whether it would go up or would drift towards you."

After the explosion, Rabi caught sight of Robert from a distance. Tremendously relieved, Robert walked easily with the stride of a man fully in command of his destiny. Rabi's skin tingled: "I'll never forget his walk; I'll never forget the way he stepped out of the car . . . his walk was like *High Noon* . . . this kind of strut. He had done it."

Robert later said that when he saw the unearthly mushroom cloud soaring into the heavens, "we knew the world would not be the same. A few people laughed, a few people cried. Most people were silent. I remembered the line from . . . the Bhagavad Gita; Vishnu is trying to persuade the prince that he should do his duty, and to impress him, takes on his multi-armed form and says, 'Now I am become death, the destroyer of worlds.' I suppose we all thought that, one way or another."

Whatever horror flashed through Robert's mind, those around him were intensely excited after realizing their stunning achievement. The journalist William Laurence described their mood: "The big boom came about 100 seconds after the Great Flash—the first cry of a new-born world. It brought the silent, motionless silhouettes to life, gave them a voice. A loud cry filled the air. The little groups that hitherto had stood rooted to the earth like desert plants broke into dance." They danced for only a few seconds. Then the men started shaking hands, "slapping each other on the back, laughing like happy children." Robert and Frank shared a celebratory drink.

Robert left the control center and walked back to base camp. On the way he encountered physicist Ken Bainbridge and turned to shake his hand. Bainbridge looked Robert in the eye and muttered, "Now we're all sons of bitches."

BOMB COUNT
July 1945

United States: 1

CHAPTER TWENTY-THREE

The Day After

Just before 5:30 in the morning on July 16, 1945, twelve-year-old Barbara Kent was sound asleep in the top bunk of her cabin at camp in Ruidoso, New Mexico. She, along with eleven other girls, had been enjoying a summer vacation from real life—sleeping together, eating together, and learning new ballet and tap dance routines from their teacher, Karma Deane, who had organized it all.

Suddenly, something lurched the girls awake. Barbara crashed down on the floor. "It was the biggest jolt you could imagine," she recalled. She looked around. "We were all sitting there on the floor wondering what [was] happening . . . [Ms. Deane] thought the water heater had exploded so we rushed outside. We were all just shocked . . . and then, all of a sudden, there was this big cloud overhead, and lights in the sky. It even hurt our eyes when we looked up. The whole sky turned strange. It was as if the sun came out tremendous."

As the day went on, the girls noticed a fine white powder falling from the sky. "It was snowing in July," Barbara recalled. Excited and confused by the strange weather, they threw open the door of the cabin and ran outside. "We were catching it on our tongues like snowflakes. Scooping the ash and putting it all over our faces."

Other campers emerged from their cabins to watch the strange "snow" cover roads, grass, and even the surface of the river that flowed nearby. The girls decided to jump in. "We were all having such a good time in that river, trying to catch what we thought was snow. There was a lot, let me tell you." But strangely the snow was hot, not cold.

Barbara Kent and her bunkmates play in a river amid cancerous fallout from the Trinity test.

In Oscuro, New Mexico, the snow fell for days, covering everything around: fruit orchards, vegetable gardens, farm animals, ponds, rivers, and the wells that supplied townspeople with their only fresh drinking water. One family hung bedsheets in the windows to keep it from entering their house.

Then their pets began to die.

Ruidoso and Oscuro were fifty miles away from Trinity. Some people lived as close as twelve miles from the site. But nobody warned any of the five hundred thousand living within 150 miles that the world's first atomic bomb would explode so close to them. They had no idea that their lives and the lives of their descendants were in great danger.

At precisely 5:30, Trinity's massive mushroom cloud billowed up into the sky. The strong winds that had blown the storm out hours before divided the cloud into three sections. One drifted eastward, another to the west and northwest, and the third to the northeast.

The cloud contained cancer-causing radioactive dust, which "fell out" over an area one hundred miles long and thirty miles wide. The "fallout" then spread farther, over thousands of miles, eventually as far away as western New York state. The United States had bombed itself, and New Mexico was ground zero.

Nineteen New Mexico counties were downwind of Trinity, including seventy-eight towns and cities, and many villages and ranches. Five days after the test, the Manhattan Project's chief medical officer, Stafford Warren, told Groves, "There is still a tremendous quantity of radioactive dust floating in the air," and explained that "a very serious hazard" existed across twenty-seven hundred square miles.

Groves wanted to keep the test secret at all costs. But he soon realized that an explosion that flashed across hundreds of miles, turning night into day in some places, couldn't be kept entirely under wraps. He had one of his army commanders tell journalists that "a remotely located ammunition magazine containing a considerable amount of high explosives and pyrotechnics exploded." He made sure to emphasize that there had been "no loss of life or injury." New Mexico newspapers reported the lie without thinking twice.

In Tularosa, New Mexico, eleven-year-old Henry Herrera woke up early in the morning on July 16 to help his father work on their car. "I remember I was helping my dad pour water in the radiator, holding the funnel. Just as we got done with it there was a hell of a blast and the cloud went up." Henry ran inside to tell his mom. "I very well remember because [she] was so angry. She had just hung up our clothes on the line—you can imagine what they looked like." Henry's dad figured that the explosion came from the nearby missile range but couldn't believe how incredible the mushroom cloud was. "I watched it outside for hours. It rose up and to the east. The bottom half kept on going, but the top half pushed back and landed right here."

The day after Trinity, Karma Deane took Barbara and the rest of her campers into the town of Ruidoso. There, government officials were going to give a speech addressing people's concerns about the explosion. "It was so crowded downtown—everyone was shoulder to shoulder. What they told us—there was an explosion at a dump. They said, 'No one worry about anything, everything's fine, just go along with your own business.' Everyone was confused. Some people believed it, but some people thought they couldn't imagine that a dump explosion would do this. They lied to us. I didn't learn the truth until years later."

A hundred miles away in Roswell, a health care worker observed in August that thirty-five infants died in the month after Trinity alone. She wrote an urgent letter to Warren to tell him. His assistant dismissed her concerns and reassured her that "the safety and health of the people at large is not in any way endangered."

As the years passed, Barbara started hearing disturbing news from her bunkmates. They were all getting terrible cancers. Barbara too contracted skin and endometrial cancer, and eventually had to have her thyroid removed. She was one of the lucky ones. Only she and one other would live past the age of forty.

Henry Herrera also lost many of his friends and family members to cancer. "People around here were dying right and left. Nobody knew what was going on, they just died."[19]

CHAPTER TWENTY-FOUR

"Those poor little people, those poor little people."

Back at Los Alamos, everyone seemed to be partying. Feynman sat on the hood of a jeep, beating his bongo drums. "But one man," Feynman remembered, "[Robert] Wilson, was just sitting there moping."

"What are you moping about?" asked Feynman.

"It's a terrible thing that we made," replied Wilson.

To Feynman, Wilson seemed to be the only man with misgivings. This staggering scientific achievement, to accomplish what seemed nearly impossible, infused everyone else with overwhelming excitement. But Feynman was wrong. Oppenheimer was also thinking about the consequences of the successful test.

In the days after Trinity, Robert's mood began to shift from relief to deep concern and inner conflict. Now that it had been tested, his "gadget," as Robert called it, had become a weapon. And weapons were controlled not by scientists but by governments. If the bomb was to be used, it wouldn't be up to the scientists who built it—it would be up to the president of the United States.

Robert now knew the names of the Japanese cities the army had chosen to bomb. The knowledge was painfully sobering; he understood the devastation about to be unloaded. He shuddered to think about the people who would be killed. But American military commanders had convinced him that the bomb he and others had built would save American lives and end the horrific war sooner. Perhaps that would be the greater purpose he had so passionately sought his whole life.

In the Bhagavad Gita, which Robert had studied so intently, Krishna, a manifestation of God, tells Arjuna, a conflicted warrior whose body trembled at the thought of going to war with his kin, that he has to understand his duty and become disciplined. To Krishna, Arjuna could never find a greater purpose than to fight in a righteous war. Krishna reassures Arjuna, "If you are killed, you shall reach heaven; or if you triumph, you shall enjoy the earth; so stand up . . . firm in your resolve, To fight!"[20]

There's no way to know for sure exactly what was going through Robert's mind. But perhaps his inner Krishna and Arjuna were duking it out, and Krishna's focus on discipline was winning. Years earlier, Robert wrote to his brother Frank, "I believe that through discipline . . . we can achieve serenity . . . through discipline we learn to preserve what is essential to our happiness in more and more adverse circumstances . . . Therefore, I think that all things which evoke discipline: study, and our duties to men and to the commonwealth, and war . . . ought to be greeted by us with profound gratitude." Would he have remained so disciplined if he had known that at that moment, the Japanese were looking for a way to surrender?

As he walked from his house to the Technical Area, Robert's secretary bumped into him. As he puffed on his pipe, obviously in deep thought, she heard him repeating, "Those poor little people, those poor little people."

But that very week, Robert was working hard to make sure that the bomb exploded efficiently over those "poor little people." On the evening of July 23, 1945, he met with two senior officers who would supervise the bombing run over Hiroshima. It was a clear, cool, starry night. Pacing nervously in his office, chain-smoking, Robert wanted to make sure they understood his precise instructions for delivering the weapon on target.

According to one of the officers, "'Don't let them bomb through clouds or through an overcast,' [Robert said.] He was emphatic, tense, his nerves talking. 'Got to see the target. No radar bombing; it must be dropped visually.' Long strides, feet turned out, another cigarette. 'Of course, it doesn't matter if they check the drop with radar, but it must be a visual drop.' More strides. 'If they drop it at night there should be a moon; that would be best. Of course, they must not drop it in rain or fog . . . Don't let them detonate it too high. The figure fixed on is just right. Don't let it go up [higher], or the target won't get as much damage.'"

August 6, 1945
8:14 a.m.
Hiroshima, Japan

The American B-29 aircraft Enola Gay, *named after pilot Paul Tibbets's mother, dropped one uranium bomb over Hiroshima, Japan, incinerating the city and the people who lived there.*

Hiroshima after the atomic bomb   A city in ruins

At 2:00 p.m., General Groves, who was in Washington, picked up the phone. He called Robert at Los Alamos. Groves was in a congratulatory mood. "I'm proud of you and all of your people," he said.

"It went all right?" Robert asked.

"Apparently it went with a tremendous bang . . ."

"Everybody is feeling reasonably good about it," Robert said, "and I extend my heartiest congratulations. It's been a long road."

"Yes," Groves replied, "it has been a long road, and I think one of the wisest things I ever did was when I selected [you to be] the director of Los Alamos."

"Well," replied Robert hesitantly, "I have my doubts, General Groves."

Later that day, the news   Nagasaki after the atomic bomb

blared over the Los Alamos public address system: "Attention, please. Attention, please. One of our units has just been successfully dropped on Japan." Frank was standing right outside his brother's office when he heard the news. His first reaction was "Thank God, it wasn't a dud." But within seconds, a terrible thought entered his mind, "One suddenly got this horror of all the people that had been killed."

Despite such thoughts, the atmosphere was jubilant. One soldier, Ed Doty, recalled the excitement: "Everyone has been keyed up to a pitch higher than anything I have ever seen on such a mass scale before . . . People came out into the hallways . . . and milled around like a Times Square New Year's crowd. Everyone was looking for a radio."

That evening, a large crowd gathered in the Los Alamos auditorium. Scientists and soldiers cheered and stamped their feet. They fixed their eyes on the stage and waited for the man of the hour to appear. But rather than entering from the wings directly onto the stage, Robert entered dramatically from the rear of the auditorium and made his way up the center aisle. Once onstage, he surveyed his audience. Then, suddenly, he clasped his hands together and pumped them over his head like a prize fighter. The crowd hollered. Robert, playing to the room, declared, "[It's] too early to determine what the results of the bombing might have been, but [I'm] sure that the Japanese didn't like it!"

As the night went on, Doty remembered that "there were parties galore. [I was] invited to three of them, I managed to get to only one . . . It lasted until three . . . [People were] happy, very happy. We listened to the radio and danced and listened to the radio again . . . and laughed and laughed at all that was said."

Three days later, news that the United States had dropped a second bomb, on Nagasaki, echoed across the plateau like a thunderclap. When Wilson heard, he became "just ill . . . sick . . . to the point that I thought I would be—you know, vomit." Wilson wasn't alone. A powerful sense of doom descended over Los Alamos. "The revulsion grew," recalled historian Alice Kimball Smith, "bringing with it—even for those who believed the end of the war justified the bombing—an intensely personal experience of the reality of evil."

Robert, despite playing to the crowd earlier, was a wreck. He was tired, depressed, and consumed with doubt about what happened. It had all happened so quickly, without the warning to world leaders he had so strongly recommended. At that moment, the United States had a monopoly over atomic bombs. But soon other countries would develop their own. What could possibly protect American cities from suffering the same fate as Hiroshima and Nagasaki?

Or much worse once the bombs got bigger?

Robert could no longer keep those thoughts to himself. He wrote a letter to Secretary of War Stimson on behalf of Los Alamos scientists, which he personally carried by hand to Washington, D.C. In the letter, he explained that the priority of the U.S. government shouldn't be to "inflict damage on an enemy power." Rather, it should be to make "future wars impossible." He suggested that future bombs be made illegal, "just like poison gases after the last war."

But folks in Washington refused to listen. Truman made clear that he wanted the Manhattan Project to continue, full steam ahead.

Robert returned to New Mexico bereft of hope.

Three centuries of incredible progress in physics and decades of dizzying advances in quantum mechanics had led to the creation of a weapon of mass destruction so horrible it could lead to the end of life on the planet. Though Robert rationalized with himself that the bomb should be dropped to end a brutal war, nevertheless he had been the instrument of that monstrous creation. Was that the legacy he was now destined to leave behind as a scientist and a human being? What would become of him, and the world, now that the genie had been released from the bottle?

BOMB COUNT
August 1945

United States: 2

Estimated Total Destructive Capability:
2 "Hiroshimas"[21]

CHAPTER TWENTY-FIVE

"The peoples of this world must unite, or they will perish."

After the United States dropped the atomic bombs on Hiroshima and Nagasaki, Robert became a celebrity. Millions of Americans, who also believed that the bombs ended the war in Japan, deemed him a hero. Photos of his chiseled face beamed out from magazine covers and newsprint across the nation. He had become a symbol of all that science could achieve.

"Hats off to the men of research," gushed the *Milwaukee Journal*. Never again, chimed in the *St. Louis Post-Dispatch*, should America's "science-explorers . . . be denied anything needful for their adventures." We must admire their "glorious achievement," declared *Scientific Monthly*. *Life* magazine observed that physicists now wore the cape "of Superman."

Robert quickly became comfortable with the praise. It was as if he had spent the previous two and a half years atop the mesa training for this new role of statesman and icon. Even his behaviors and wardrobe, including the pipe-smoking and his ever-present porkpie hat, became recognizable around the world.

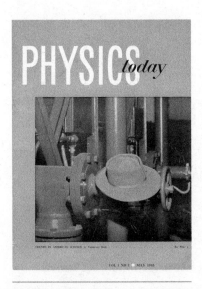

Everyone knew Robert by his porkpie hat.
Physics Today put it on its cover, May 1948.

Taking advantage of his new-found fame, he made his private feelings public: "We have made a thing, a most terrible weapon," he told one audience, "that has altered abruptly and profoundly the nature of the world . . . a thing that by all the standards of the world we grew up in is an evil thing. And by so doing . . . we have raised again the question of whether science is good for man . . ."

The "father" of the atomic bomb admitted to the country that the weapon he helped create was one of terror. And that one day it might prove deadly to whole civilizations. The bombs at Hiroshima and Nagasaki were used "against an essentially defeated enemy . . . [They are weapons] for aggressors, and the elements of surprise and of terror are as intrinsic to [them] as are the fissionable nuclei."

Thousands packed auditoriums to hear Robert speak. One of his friends, Harold Cherniss, was in the audience when Robert addressed a big crowd of students at Berkeley. There, at his old stomping ground, Robert got up and spoke without notes for almost an hour. Cherniss was stunned by the hold he had on the audience: "From the moment he began to speak until the end, not a whisper in the whole place. This was the kind of magic that he exercised."

Robert flew back and forth between Los Alamos and Washington. He hoped that his fame would allow him to influence people in government who were making decisions about how atomic bombs might now be controlled. On one trip, he brought with him a statement signed by over three hundred Los Alamos scientists to the War Department about how dangerous it would be if nations started racing each other to build bombs.

The scientists explained that if other countries obtained their own bombs, there would be no way to defend the United States against them in future wars. They believed nations should share information about the bombs in order to tame their threat to humanity. They recommended launching an international project to control them.

The scientists hoped that the War Department would release their statement to the press. After all, the American people should know about the danger nuclear weapons posed to life on Earth. But rather than release it, the government kept it secret.

Curiously, Robert agreed with the government's decision, stunning many of his closest colleagues. Some of them were now more convinced than ever that he had become just another tool of the

Secretary of War Robert Patterson awards Oppenheimer the Medal of Merit, March 5, 1946

Robert and other dignitaries at Harvard Commencement, June 1947

Washington establishment. But Robert still believed that change was possible within the government, and that before scientists shared such weighty concerns with the public, they should give President Truman the courtesy to share his own thoughts with Congress.

Robert also wanted to stay on Truman's good side. He believed he could convince the president to listen to reason. He worried that if Truman saw him as a troublemaker, he would lose his influence.

Members of the General Advisory Committee of the Atomic Energy Commission, April 1947

Others didn't give Truman as much credit as Robert did. They thought the president was a small-minded man in way over his head. Truman "was not a man of imagination," said Rabi. Even the seasoned Wall Street lawyer John J. McCloy wrote that Truman was "a simple man, prone to make up his mind quickly and decisively, perhaps too quickly." This was not a great president, according to McCloy, "not distinguished at all . . . not Lincolnesque, but an instinctive, common, hearty-natured man."

Behind closed doors, Robert felt he was doing his best to share the deep concerns his fellow scientists held for the future. He told Under Secretary of State Dean Acheson that most Manhattan Project scientists didn't want to work on any more weapons. After Hiroshima and all the horrors of World War II, building more bombs was "against the dictates of their hearts and spirits." Robert agreed with them. He told a reporter that he was a scientist, not a weapons manufacturer.

On October 16, 1945, Robert resigned as director of Los Alamos.

Thousands of people, virtually the entire population of the mesa, turned out to say goodbye. Under a blazing New Mexico sun, Robert came forward to accept a certificate of appreciation from General Groves. Speaking in a low, quiet voice, Robert told his friends and colleagues that in the years ahead, he hoped that they would all be able to look back on their achievements with pride.

But then, on a sober note, he warned those who would keep building bombs to temper their pride with a profound concern: "If atomic bombs are to be added as new weapons to the arsenals of a warring world . . . then the time will come when mankind will curse the names of Los Alamos and Hiroshima . . . The peoples of this world must unite, or they will perish."

General Leslie Groves presents Robert with a Certificate of Appreciation for his work on the Manhattan Project, October 16, 1945.

"MR. PRESIDENT, I FEEL I HAVE BLOOD ON MY HANDS."

Two days later, Robert stood in front of a half dozen senators and once again warned about the dangers of future bomb-building. Henry A. Wallace, vice president during Roosevelt's third term (1941–45), now serving as Truman's commerce secretary, sat in the audience, listening. Robert asked Wallace if they could meet privately. Wallace invited him to take a walk the following morning.

The two men walked through downtown Washington toward the Commerce Department. Robert told the former vice president how anxious he was about the future of the world. Wallace recalled afterward, "I never saw a man in such an extremely nervous state as Oppenheimer. He seemed to feel that the destruction of the entire human race was imminent."

Robert complained bitterly that Secretary of State Byrnes "felt that we could use the bomb as a pistol to get what we wanted." He thought it was extremely dangerous for Byrnes to talk that way. For if one person has a pistol, others would get their own to protect themselves. He told Wallace that that the Soviets would simply build their own bomb—that they had good scientists and plenty of resources and would put everything they had into making plenty of atomic bombs as soon as they could.

Robert asked Wallace if he thought it would do any good to share his feelings with Truman. Maybe if the president could see the whites of his eyes and feel the spirit of his determination, it might convince him to end the American bomb program before it was too late. Wallace encouraged him to try to get an appointment.

Six days later, at 10:30 a.m. on October 25, 1945, Robert walked into the Oval Office. Truman ushered him in and asked him to have a seat on one of the couches in the center of the room. The president spoke first. He asked Robert to support his effort to give the army permanent control over atomic energy.

Robert sighed. How could he support giving power over future bomb-building to an army commission who would make their decisions in secret, probably without any civilian or scientific input at all?

Robert sat, uncomfortable and silent. He hesitated to challenge the president directly. Rather than answer Truman's question, he decided to change the subject. "Perhaps it would be best first to define the international problem," he told the president. Robert meant that the United States should work with other countries to control atomic weapons, to stop their spread.

Impatient, Truman brushed the suggestion aside. Then, abruptly, he asked Robert to guess when the Soviets would build their own atomic bomb. Knocked off guard, Robert replied that he didn't know. Truman confidently said he knew: "Never."

Robert was stunned. It was beginning to dawn on him that his fellow scientists might be right: Truman was a fool. Of course the Soviets would get their own bombs! It was only a matter of time.

Sensing that Truman didn't understand the deadly urgency of his message, Robert wrung his hands and uttered the sort of regrettable remark that he often made under pressure. "Mr. President," he said quietly, "I feel I have blood on my hands." Truman's face flushed with anger. He snapped back, "The blood [is] on my hands . . . let me worry about that." Then the president stood up. The meeting was over.

After Robert left, Truman muttered, "Blood on his hands, damn it, he hasn't half as much blood on his hands as I have. You just don't go around bellyaching about it." Later, still fuming, Truman told Dean Acheson, "I don't want to see that son of a bitch in this office ever again."

CHAPTER TWENTY-SIX

The Acheson-Lilienthal Report

On a late afternoon during the bitterly cold Christmas week of 1945, Robert visited Rabi in his New York City apartment on Riverside Drive. Watching the sun set from Rabi's living room window, the two friends could see ice floes bathed in yellow and pink floating down the Hudson River.

Afterward, they sat alone in the spreading darkness, smoking their pipes and talking about the danger of countries racing to build bigger and bigger bombs. Both men believed that the only way to prevent that from happening was to create an international organization that fully understood the risks atomic bombs posed to humanity, and that had the power to control them. Of course, to do that, the U.S. government would have to agree to share the very information Truman and others were determined to keep secret at all costs.

Robert and Rabi didn't realize it then, but the United States, the Soviet Union, and other countries *had* already been trying to do just that. At that moment, the countries were talking about establishing a United Nations Atomic Energy Commission (UNAEC). Secretary of State James Byrnes had appointed a special committee, chaired by Under Secretary of State Dean Acheson, to explore the idea of an international system that would control nuclear weapons.

When Robert found out about the committee, his hopes swelled. Were Truman and Byrnes finally listening to what he and his fellow scientists were telling them? And furthermore, to Robert's great delight, he learned that he had been chosen to be the only physicist on the committee's board of consultants. Here, at last, was the opportunity he was waiting for.

Robert quickly dominated the discussions and impressed fellow consultants and committee members with his clear vision for international control. David Lilienthal, the chairman of the committee's board of consultants, remembered Robert from their very first meeting in Robert's Washington hotel room. "He walked back and forth," Lilienthal noted, "making funny 'hugh' sounds between sentences or phrases as he paced the room, looking at the floor—a mannerism quite strange." Later, after spending more time with him, Lilienthal gushed, "[Robert] is worth living a lifetime just to know that mankind has been able to produce such a being . . ."

Robert stimulated the committee with his creative ideas. He was constructive and attentive. He picked fights when necessary. Acheson admired his quick wit, his clear vision—and his sharp tongue.

One night, Acheson invited Robert to his house in Georgetown. After dinner, he stood by a small blackboard, chalk in hand, lecturing his host and former assistant secretary of war Jack McCloy on the atom. As a visual aid, Robert drew little stick figures to represent electrons, neutrons, and protons chasing one another about and carrying on in unpredictable ways. When the two men appeared bewildered, "he put down the chalk in gentle despair," saying, "It's hopeless! I really think you two believe neutrons and electrons *are* little men!"

Though Robert wrote the board's thirty-four-thousand-word report himself, it became known as the Acheson-Lilienthal report. In it, Robert proposed that an international agency control all aspects of atomic energy. The agency would control the technology and develop it for civilian purposes only, like electricity production.

Robert believed that in the long run, "without world government there could be no permanent peace . . . without peace there would be atomic warfare." The agency would own all uranium mines, nuclear power plants, and laboratories. No nation would be permitted to build bombs—but scientists everywhere would still be allowed to harness the atom for peaceful purposes. Most importantly, nations would share information about nuclear weapons with each other so that the rest of the world would at least have warning if a rogue government decided to build bombs.

Robert and the committee sent the report straight to the White House. Even after his disastrous meeting with the president, he still believed Truman would understand the urgent need to control the atom. But again, Robert was naive. He should have known by then that Truman wasn't going to listen to reason.

If Truman really cared about cooperating with other countries to control nuclear weapons, he might have shared Robert's report with the UNAEC himself. Instead, Truman asked Wall Street financier Bernard Baruch to do it. A staunch capitalist and passionate defender of American power, Baruch was never going to agree to share American atomic secrets with other countries. Certainly not with the Soviet Union. Baruch believed that keeping the atomic bomb secret was essential to making sure the United States of America remained the most powerful nation on Earth. He also owned stock in a company that owned uranium mines and didn't want an international agency to control them.

Rather than share the Acheson-Lilienthal plan with the UNAEC, Baruch presented his own plan. He wanted the United States to build a stockpile of atomic bombs to deter other countries from attacking. That idea became known as "deterrence." He wanted privately owned American companies to control uranium mines. And he didn't want an agency to have the power to limit any country's development of atomic energy.

When Robert found out what was in Baruch's plan, he knew the Soviets on the UNAEC Committee would reject it immediately. On June 14, 1946, they did. Instead, they proposed a simple treaty to ban the building and use of atomic weapons.

That would have been the best opportunity to prevent an uncontrolled nuclear arms race between the two major powers. But Truman immediately said no.

The decision deeply anguished and saddened Robert. He had been so hopeful that the Acheson-Lilienthal plan might prevent a nuclear arms race. Now he understood more than ever that Truman was doing more to provoke the Soviet Union than calm the waters.

Every day, newspaper headlines warned that the world might once again be on the road to war. Robert wrote in despair on June 1, 1946, "Every American knows that if there is another major war, atomic weapons will be used." He told Lilienthal, "I am ready to go anywhere and do anything, but I am bankrupt of further ideas.

And I find that physics and the teaching of physics, which is my life, now seems irrelevant."

Robert was becoming frustrated with the government that employed him. By the end of 1945, he knew that contrary to what he had been told before Hiroshima and Nagasaki—and what the American people had been led to believe afterward—the Japanese had been essentially defeated before the United States dropped atomic bombs on them. He couldn't bear to think that in future wars, other innocent people might suffer the same fate.

And what crucial information might the government keep secret from future scientists who, like Robert, trusted that their government was making decisions in humanity's best interest?

"FOLLOW OPPENHEIMER'S ACTIVITIES AND CONTACTS CLOSELY."

Robert's increasingly vocal criticism of American policy drew the ire of FBI director J. Edgar Hoover. Hoover, paranoid and ruthless, was incensed that Robert would dare challenge the idea that the bomb should be kept secret. He believed Robert was being disloyal to the United States.

Hoover had gotten his start spying on suspected anarchists twenty-five years earlier. Ever since, he had collected massive amounts of information about others he suspected of being disloyal. The information in those files would later be used to justify questioning them and, in some cases, arresting them.

J. Edgar Hoover

On November 15, 1945, Hoover sent Robert's file to the White House. He told Truman and Byrnes that the FBI overheard Communist Party members saying that Robert was a "regularly registered" member of the party. A few months later, Hoover ordered his agents to step up surveillance on Robert. Then he told Truman, without a shred of evidence, that he suspected Robert was a Soviet sympathizer and intended to leave the U.S. for the Soviet Union, where he would share everything he knew about how to build bombs. Hoover ordered his agents to "follow Oppenheimer's activities and contacts closely."

Hoover's investigation of Robert foreshadowed a new FBI playbook—the use of the charge of "communist," "communist sympathizer," or "fellow traveler" to silence or destroy political opponents. Now, as the rift grew bigger between the United States and the Soviet Union, the FBI suspected anyone who questioned the need for the government to keep secret information about the atomic bomb or U.S. nuclear research.

The problem was that there was a big difference between people *saying* that Robert was a registered member of the party and the FBI being able to prove it. Beyond what they heard, Hoover had no evidence that Robert was a communist. In fact, Hoover would never be able to prove it—because it wasn't true. But that didn't stop him and his agents. Over the next eight years, the FBI generated about a thousand pages each year of memos, surveillance reports, and wiretap logs on Robert. They were out to smear him.

On May 8, 1946, the FBI tapped Robert's home phone. He and Kitty knew about it. On one call, they heard the clicking sound of an operator cutting in and out. Robert asked Kitty, "Are you still there? I wonder who is listening to us?" Kitty replied, "The FBI, dear." Robert said, "They are—the FBI?" He then quipped, "The FBI must just have hung up." Kitty giggled, and then they resumed their conversation.

The constant surveillance angered Robert. It also made him paranoid. One day at Berkeley, he was talking to a former student when he suddenly pointed to a brass plate on the wall and said, "What the hell is that?" His student explained that the university had ripped out an old intercom system and covered the hole in the wall with this brass spacer. But Robert interrupted him and said, "That was and always has been a concealed microphone." He then stomped out of the room, slamming the door behind him.

On September 5, 1946, FBI agents descended upon Robert's office. They wanted to know more about his kitchen conversation with Hoke in 1943. Gracious as always, Robert told them that in the kitchen, Hoke had told him about Eltenton's scheme and that he had immediately rejected it. He remembered telling Hoke that "to do such a thing was treason or close to treason."

The agents weren't satisfied. Could he be more specific? What *exact* words had he used? But the conversation had taken place almost four years before. Robert couldn't remember exactly—but he was sure he either used the word "treason" or "treasonous."

Then they hounded him about the other Soviet *approaches* to scientists he had told Boris Pash about when they met in 1943. Robert now admitted to them that he had made up that part of the story. There hadn't been more than one approach—at least that he was aware of. He had only known of one—Eltenton's attempted approach through his dear friend Hoke.

Why had Robert made up a different story? Had he simply panicked when Pash confronted him, and made up the story about fictional approaches to other fictional scientists to divert attention from himself and Hoke? That was the most logical explanation. Or maybe in the kitchen, Hoke had made it *sound like* Eltenton had approached other scientists, but he actually hadn't. Or maybe, Robert had actually told Pash the truth in 1943—that there were other approaches—but now felt like he had to change his story to protect Hoke and the other unnamed scientists. It was now all so confusing. Regardless of what had actually happened, one thing was crystal clear—the more Robert spoke out, the more the FBI was determined to stop him.

CHAPTER TWENTY-SEVEN

"We will go believing that everything is in the hands of God."

At thirty-four seconds after 9:00 a.m. on July 1, 1946, the United States tested its fourth atomic bomb by dropping it over the lagoon of Bikini Atoll, a part of the Marshall Islands in the Pacific Ocean.

A fleet of abandoned navy vessels of all shapes and sizes were either sunk or exposed to lethal amounts of radiation. A large crowd of congressmen, journalists, and diplomats from numerous countries witnessed the demonstration. Some of the ships were stocked with pigs, rats, and other animals to study the effects of nuclear fallout on live creatures. Robert refused to attend.

Two months earlier, he had sent Truman a letter objecting to the test. The government said that its purpose was to show how atomic bombs might be used in sea warfare. Robert thought that was ridiculous. It was pretty obvious: "If an atomic bomb comes close enough to a ship . . . it will sink it." So why waste $100 million on it? And, if the United States really cared about international control of nuclear weapons, how could it justify setting one off for no good reason? Yet again, Robert thought the letter might convince the president to listen to reason.

But predictably, the letter just insulted Truman. He forwarded it to acting secretary of state Dean Acheson with a short note calling Robert the "crybaby scientist" who had claimed to have blood on his hands during their Oval Office meeting eight months earlier. As it turned out, it was Truman who once again had blood on *his*.

"Baker" test, part of "Operation Crossroads," detonated underwater, July 25, 1946

Though remote, Bikini Atoll had been populated for thousands of years. Until the nineteenth century, Bikinians had very little interaction with the rest of the world. They survived primarily on fish and fruits and vegetables that grew on the island, including coconut, breadfruit, and taro.

Between 1914 and 1944, Japan occupied the islands. They were an important base in the nation's crusade to control the wider Pacific. But in early 1944, the United States invaded and wrested control from Japan. By the end of the year, the U.S. took charge of the islands and installed a military governor, Ben H. Wyatt.

One Sunday afternoon in early 1946, Wyatt called the 167 Bikinians together. He asked them if they would leave their ancestral homeland for another island to allow the United States to test atomic bombs. Wyatt told them the tests would be "for the good of mankind and to end all world wars."

Though cautious and wary of their new American occupiers, they eventually agreed after their leader, King Juda, told them it would be okay. Juda rallied his people: "We will go believing that everything is in the hands of God."

The Bikinians packed up all their belongings. A United States Navy tank ship landed on shore and loaded them on board for the journey to Rongerik. A Bikinian girl recalled:

"[I had] never seen anything like this before, I had fun on the ship. We finally arrived at Rongerik Atoll, and after we unloaded all of our belongings on the beach, the council began to decide on which families would live in the various houses that had been prepared for us. We started dividing up the food that the Navy men had given us, and we tried to fall back into the daily routines of our lives. Routine was difficult now, though, because there were many newsmen on Rongerik taking pictures of us. I guess it was all exciting in a way, but it was also a little scary. Those people who were looking at us were strange. The island itself looked so different from Bikini. It was smaller. And, from the beginning, we had reason to lack confidence in our abilities to provide for our future on that tiny place. We could only remain hopeful and keep thinking that one day soon we would be returned to Bikini."

But they would never return. Between 1946 and 1958, the United States tested sixty-eight nuclear bombs at Bikini. The islands became "hopelessly contaminated." On Rongerik, the Bikinians suffered terribly. Radiation from the bombs killed or poisoned many of them. Some took their own lives to end their pain. People were born with physical deformities, including "jellyfish babies" who looked more like blobs of jelly than human beings. The radiation continues to kill people there today.[22]

The United States military removes 167 native Bikinians from their ancestral homeland in 1946 to begin testing atomic bombs.

Native Bikinians weaving thatch before removal from their ancestral homeland by the United States military

BOMB COUNT
1946

United States: 9

Total Estimated Destructive Capability:
12 "Hiroshimas"

CHAPTER TWENTY-EIGHT

A Man "Ablaze with Power"

In late 1946, Lewis Strauss, a board member of the Institute for Advanced Study in Princeton, New Jersey, flew out to Berkeley. He wanted to meet with Robert. Robert agreed and met him at the airport. As the two men paced back and forth on the tarmac, Strauss told him that the institute was looking for a new director, and Robert's name was at the top of the list. Would he like the job?

Born in 1896 in Charleston, West Virginia, Strauss was the son of a struggling shoe merchant. As a child, he had always been fascinated by physics. He read book after book about radiation and wave mechanics and dreamed of studying physics in college. But, unlike Robert's, his family was poor and his father's business wasn't doing well. So instead of college, Strauss hauled crates of shoe samples across the country as a traveling salesman.[23]

By the time he turned twenty years old in 1916, Strauss had saved up $20,000. Boldly, he went to Washington, where he tracked down Herbert Hoover, who was then in charge of sending American food supplies to feed the Allied army in World War I. Strauss found out which hotel Hoover was staying in and waited there for him to arrive. When he did, he walked up to the future president, introduced himself, and told him that he wanted to work for him for free. Hoover looked at the young man with an amused smile and asked, "When do you want to start?" "Right now," Strauss replied.

Strauss became Hoover's assistant, close friend, and confidant. Hoover introduced him to many people in the halls of American power, including Mortimer Schiff, a partner in the investment bank of Kuhn, Loeb & Co. For the next twenty-five years, Strauss worked at the bank, eventually making a million dollars a year. While there, he remained interested in physics. His mother's death of cancer motivated him to finance a radiation research center for cancer treatment at the California Institute of Technology. He made an effort to seek out and become friends with physicists who were fleeing the Nazis. In 1939, they told him that Otto Hahn and Fritz Strassman had split the atom.

In 1941, Strauss joined the navy, where he worked to inspect weapons and ammunition. After four years, he went back to Washington. There, Truman finally gave him the power he craved, appointing him to a brand-new federal agency—the United States Atomic Energy Commission (AEC).[24] After Hiroshima and Naga-saki, Congress established the AEC to take charge of future bomb-building and figure out how fission might be used for peacetime purposes. Agency members gathered a group of expert advisors to help guide their decision-making, called the General Advisory Committee (GAC). They appointed Robert chair of that com-mittee.

Lewis L. Strauss

Robert was interested in Strauss's job offer. But he needed time to think about it. If he took the job, he certainly wouldn't have to travel as much. That year alone he had made fifteen transcontinental flights between California and Washington. Plus, after all that had happened over the past five years, it might be nice to have a change of scenery.

After thinking it through, he told Kitty that he thought he could do a good job—that "it was a thing he could do rather naturally." He enjoyed being a leader—he was a very good one. It would also be much easier to just jump on a train when he needed to head to Washington for meetings. He promised her that if they moved to Princeton, they could keep their house in Berkeley to visit in the summers.

Robert took his time to mull it over. One evening, he and Kitty were out for a drive when they heard a news broadcast on the radio announcing that Robert Oppenheimer had been appointed director of the Institute for Advanced Study. "Well," Robert said to Kitty, "I guess that settles it."

Kitty was excited to move east. She told a salesman in Berkeley that they "would not be gone long—only fifteen or twenty years." Robert told her that their new home in Princeton, called Olden Manor, had ten bedrooms, five bathrooms, and a "pleasant garden."

Of course, Robert's Berkeley colleagues were disappointed. The chairman of the physics department described his departure as "the greatest blow ever suffered by the department." Ernest Lawrence was miffed to learn of Robert's departure from a radio news report.

But Robert's East Coast friends were delighted. Rabi wrote him, "I am terribly pleased that you are coming . . . It's a sharp break with the past for you and the perfect time of life in which to make it." Mary Ellen Washburn threw Robert a farewell party. Then Kitty, Robert, Peter, and Toni packed their bags and headed east.

The Oppenheimers arrived in Princeton in mid-July 1947 during an unusually hot and humid summer. The institute paid Robert a generous salary of $20,000 a year, plus rent-free use of Olden Manor. Kitty quickly fell in love with the place. It was a rambling, three-story white colonial home, surrounded by 265 acres of lush green woodlands and meadows. A barn and a corral stood behind the house. Robert and Kitty bought two horses, which they named Topper and Step-up.

Soon after their arrival, Robert had an ample greenhouse built at the back of the house, near the kitchen wing. It was his birthday gift to Kitty, who filled it with dozens of varieties of orchids. Robert mounted one of his father's prized paintings, Vincent Van Gogh's *Enclosed Field with Rising Sun*, in the living room, above the formal fireplace. While the house was comfortably furnished, it never had a cluttered, lived-in look. Kitty kept everything neat. Robert's austere study, with its white walls unadorned by pictures, reminded one old friend of their Bathtub Row home at Los Alamos.

Robert, Kitty, Peter, Toni, and dog Buddy at Olden Manor, 1947 (left) and 1949 (right)

From Olden Manor's back terrace, Robert could gaze south across an open field to the grounds of the institute. Not more than a quarter mile away lay Fuld Hall, a four-story redbrick building with two wings and an imposing church-like spire. It housed modest offices for scores of scholars, a wood-paneled library, and a formal common room lined with overstuffed brown leather couches. A cafeteria and boardroom occupied the top floor. Room 225 was the office of the institute's most famous resident—Albert Einstein.

Robert relished his new leadership role and tried hard to play the part well. While most of those at the institute walked around in sports jackets—Einstein favored a rumpled sweater—Robert often wore expensive English wool suits hand-tailored for him at Langrock, the local tailor for Princeton's upper crust. While many scholars traveled around Princeton on bicycles, Robert drove a stunning blue

Albert Einstein

Cadillac convertible. Where once he'd worn his hair long and bushy, now he had it "cut like a monk's, skintight." At forty-three, he seemed delicate, even frail. But he was in fact quite strong and energetic. Physicist Freeman Dyson recalled, "He constantly moved around; he couldn't sit still for five seconds; you had the impression of somebody who was tremendously ill at ease. He smoked all the time."

Visitors to Fuld Hall saw a man "ablaze with power."

Princeton was a world away from the free-spirited, liberal, bohemian atmosphere of Berkeley, not to mention the lifestyle and natural beauty of Los Alamos. In 1947 Princeton, a suburban town of twenty-five thousand residents, had one stoplight and no public transportation—with the exception of the "Dinky" tram that ferried hundreds of daily commuters to the train station at Princeton Junction. From there, bankers, lawyers, and stockbrokers in pinstripe suits boarded trains for the fifty-minute ride into Manhattan. Unlike most American small towns, Princeton possessed a distinguished history and an elite sense of itself. But, as a longtime resident once observed, it was "a town with character but without soul."

Robert in conversation with students and colleagues at the Institute for Advanced Study, Princeton, NJ, 1958

Robert wanted the institute to become a world-class center for theoretical physics to rival Berkeley. Very soon he assembled a concentration of scientific talent unlike anywhere else in the world. His first appointment was Abraham Pais, a bright young physicist who would remain at the institute for sixteen years. Some of the biggest quantum mechanics legends, including Niels Bohr, Paul Dirac, Wolfgang Pauli, Hideki Yukawa, George Uhlenbeck, George Placzek, Sin-Itiro Tomonaga, and others came to study and share their ideas. In 1949, Robert recruited Chen Ning Yang, a brilliant twenty-seven-year-old who would win the 1957 Nobel Prize in Physics with Tsung-Dao (T. D.) Lee, another Chinese-born physicist.

"This is an unreal place," Pais wrote in his diary. "Bohr comes into my office to talk, I look out of the window and see Einstein walking home with his assistant. Two offices away sits Dirac. Downstairs sits Oppenheimer."

Robert's experience at Los Alamos convinced him that scientists couldn't just research and experiment in a vacuum. They needed to think about how their inventions might impact people, both positively and negatively. Science and the humanities had to be studied together. If scientists read philosophy, they might think harder about the "whys" and "what ifs" of what they were doing. If they read psychology, they might better understand how others could use their inventions to control or manipulate others. If they read history, they might understand how their discoveries could change the nature of war and peace. With quantum mechanics exploding so rapidly, scientists had to keep asking the hard questions about what their work might create—and what it might destroy.

So, in addition to scientists, Robert wanted the institute to become a place where a much wider array of scholars could come together to better understand the human condition. He began recruiting experts in other fields, like his old friend from Berkeley, Harold Cherniss, the country's leading scholar on Plato and Aristotle. He brought in his dear friend Francis Fergusson, a theater expert and mythology critic. Next came archaeologist Homer Thompson, poet T. S. Eliot, historian Arnold Toynbee, philosopher Isaiah Berlin, and diplomat George F. Kennan.

As Robert built the institute the way he thought best, it became clear that the man who brought him there, Lewis Strauss, wanted to limit Robert's power. Robert often annoyed Strauss by making decisions himself without running them by the board. In 1948, Strauss told Robert that he was thinking about buying a house on the grounds of the institute. Quickly, Robert got the institute to buy the house and rented it to another scholar. That shut Strauss out for the time being. But it also created tension and distrust between the two men that would only explode over time.

Robert didn't think much of Strauss. In early June 1949, both men traveled to Washington to testify on Capitol Hill. Congress wanted to know why the Atomic Energy Commission voted 4–1 to export radioisotopes to foreign labs for scientific and medical research. Strauss was the only member to vote against it. He and some in Congress didn't think the United States should be sharing any nuclear information, no matter how beneficial it could be for humankind.

Robert thought Strauss was being foolish and said so out loud. "No one can force me to say that you cannot use these isotopes for atomic energy. You can use a shovel for atomic energy. In fact, you do." The audience murmured with laughter. A young reporter, Philip Stern, happened to be sitting in the hearing room. He had no idea whom Robert was making fun of, but "it was clear [he] was making a fool of someone."

Strauss's face turned an angry beet red. More laughter greeted Robert's next statement: "My own rating of the importance of isotopes in this broad sense is that they are far less important than electronic devices, but far more important than, let us say, vitamins, somewhere in between." One of the commissioners remembered "the terrible look on Lewis's face." David Lilienthal vividly recalled, "There was a look of hatred there that you don't see very often."

Robert didn't seem to have a problem with making fun of people he thought less of. It came easily to him and was part of his classroom style as a professor. Just as he had made fun of Max Born in front of his seminar so many years ago in Göttingen, Robert went at Strauss in front of a committee of Congress. "Robert could make grown men feel like schoolchildren," said one of his friends. "He could make giants feel like cockroaches." But Strauss wasn't one of his students; he was a powerful, thin-skinned, vengeful man who was now supremely well-connected in Washington. Robert didn't realize it then, but he had made for himself a dangerous enemy. Strauss didn't forgive, and he didn't forget.

PART THREE

FALLOUT

CHAPTER TWENTY-NINE

"Our atomic monopoly is like a cake of ice melting in the sun."

On September 3, 1949, an American B-29 reconnaissance plane flying over the northern Pacific detected radiation in the atmosphere. The U.S. military broke the news to the White House: the Soviets had successfully tested an atomic bomb. No one wanted to believe it. But less than two weeks later, it was confirmed.

BOMB COUNT
1949

United States: 170

Soviet Union: 1

Total Estimated Destructive Capability:
281 "Hiroshimas"

As Robert and many other scientists predicted, the United States no longer held a monopoly on nuclear weapons. David Lilienthal broke the news to Truman and pleaded with him to tell the public immediately. He tried every argument he could to convince

Truman to tell the Soviets that the Americans knew about their test. He wanted to break the cycle of suspicion between the two countries so that they could work together to control the production of future bombs.

Truman resisted. It had been less than four years since he told Robert in the Oval Office that the Soviets would "never" have their own bomb. Now, stubbornly, he refused to believe that the Soviets had tested one.

He sat on the news for three days. Then, still doubtful, the president reluctantly announced to the nation that an atomic explosion had occurred in the Soviet Union. But he refused to say it was a bomb.

There had never been any doubt in Robert's mind that the Soviets would get the bomb. It was only a matter of time. A year earlier, he had warned *Time* magazine, "Our atomic monopoly is like a cake of ice melting in the sun." Robert couldn't fathom why Truman couldn't understand that.

Maybe now that the Soviets had a bomb, Robert could finally persuade Truman to work with other nations to control them. But he wasn't optimistic. By then he understood that convincing Truman of anything would be next to impossible. While Robert and other scientists saw the Soviet test as proof that the world must share knowledge about nuclear weapons and cooperate to stop their multiplication, the president became more resolute in keeping the American bomb program secret.

The Soviet bomb test convinced Truman that the United States needed *more* bombs to keep the Soviet Union in check. The U.S. stockpile of atomic weapons—which in June 1948 stood at about fifty bombs—skyrocketed to some three hundred weapons by June 1950. And that was just the beginning.

Some in Washington now pushed for what had seemed unthinkable just a few years earlier—the construction of Edward Teller's "Super Bomb"—a thermonuclear "fusion" weapon that would be *thousands* of times more powerful than the ones that obliterated Hiroshima and Nagasaki. It became known as the hydrogen bomb. As it turned out, one of its biggest cheerleaders was Lewis Strauss.

Panicked that the Soviets now had the same city-destroying bombs as the United States, Strauss sent a memo around Washington telling all who would listen that the United States desperately needed something bigger. He believed that any advantage the U.S. had over the Soviets would dissolve without a "quantum jump" in technology. The United States had to build the hydrogen bomb—now.

The idea of a hydrogen bomb had deeply disturbed Robert from the second Teller burst into the Radiation Laboratory to tell him about it back in 1943. From the beginning, it was all Teller cared about; he was obsessed with the idea of building one.

Unlike Teller and Strauss, Robert desperately hoped the hydrogen bomb would prove impossible to build. Atomic weapons were bad enough. But the thought of any country—let alone multiple countries—having bombs thousands of times more powerful was too much for him to bear.

The physics of fusion mimicked the reactions that occur in the interior of the sun, meaning that fusion explosions had no physical limits. Even larger explosions would be possible simply by adding heavier hydrogen. Armed with a hydrogen bomb, a single airplane could kill millions of people in minutes. It would be a weapon of mass, indiscriminate murder—and a grave threat to the future of life on the planet.

The possibility of such an apocalyptic weapon horrified other scientists like Arthur Holly Compton, who as early as 1945 wrote the vice president on their behalf: "We feel that [the H-bomb] should not be undertaken, primarily *because we should prefer defeat in war to victory obtained at the expense of the enormous human disaster that would be caused by its determined use*" (emphasis added).

James Conant was infuriated when he learned about Strauss's memo. He told Robert that the hydrogen bomb should be built "over [his] dead body." He thought a bomb of that magnitude was nothing less than a machine of genocide. Victor Weisskopf argued that a war fought with thermonuclear weapons would be suicidal. Hans Bethe said that he and Weisskopf agreed "that after such a war, even if we were to win it, the world would not be . . . like the world we want to preserve. We would lose the things we were fighting for."

But the hydrogen bomb excited the imaginations of some air force generals and their supporters in Congress. Military commanders pressed Truman hard to approve a crash program to build one before the Soviets could.

Scientists opposed to building the H-bomb were desperate to tell Truman why its creation would be a terrible idea for the country, the world, and the human race. Lilienthal asked to speak with Truman to plead their case. Truman agreed. But in the meeting, the president seemed only to care about one thing. He asked Lilienthal,

"Can the Russians do it?" Lilienthal nodded. "In that case, we have no choice."

Lilienthal knew then that the die had been cast. The president was never going to listen to the scientists who spent their careers building, testing, and understanding the horrors of nuclear weapons. Instead, just as he had given in to the pressure of those around him to drop atomic bombs on Japan, he now gave in to the pressure of military commanders who believed a peaceful society could only be protected with weapons of mass destruction. All they cared about was having a weapon that could "win."

Truman demanded that Lilienthal and his fellow scientists not say a word about the crash H-bomb program. He knew how persuasive Robert could be—how adored he was by so many Americans. He also knew that generations of Americans had been conditioned to trust the words of scientists over politicians, clergy, and other powerful influencers. He didn't need Robert or other "crybaby scientists" challenging his decision in the press. It might make him look weak.

Pale and defeated, Lilienthal left the Oval Office and relayed the bad news to his colleagues. "It was like a funeral party," he recalled, "especially when I [told them the president had gagged us all]."

The news knocked the wind out of Robert. Should he resign his position on the GAC in protest and defy the president of the United States by going public? Might other scientists like Conant break ranks and spill the beans? Dean Acheson warned Conant that if they did so, they would be acting "contrary to the national interest."

Though Robert was determined not to keep his views on the H-bomb to himself, he stayed loyal to his country and respected the chain of command. The president had made a decision. The matter had been settled. Reluctantly, he and Conant decided they would be good soldiers and fall in line.

Years later, both of them realized they should have resigned then and there.

CHAPTER THIRTY

"You would swear the whole world was on fire."

On November 1, 1952, as Americans flocked to theaters to see *Peter Pan*, cheered Mickey Mantle as he bashed home runs out of Yankee Stadium, and argued in court against school segregation, their government blew the island of Elugelab apart with a detonation eight hundred times the explosive force of the Hiroshima bomb—two times more powerful than *all the bombs* dropped during World War II combined. The world's first hydrogen bomb blasted an underwater chasm 164 feet deep and more than a mile wide. Historian Richard Rhodes described what it was like:

> It expanded in seconds to a blinding white fireball more than three miles across . . . and rose over the horizon like a dark sun; the crews of the task force, thirty miles away, felt a swell of heat as if someone had opened a hot oven, heat that persisted long enough to seem menacing. "You would swear the whole world was on fire," one sailor wrote home . . . Swirling and boiling, glowing purplish with gamma-ionized light, the expanding fireball began to rise, becoming a burning mushroom cloud balanced on a wide, dirty stem with a curtain of water around its base that slowly fell back into the sea. The wings of [a plane] orbiting fifteen miles from

ground zero at forty thousand feet heated ninety-three degrees almost instantly. In a minute and a half, the enlarging fireball cloud reached fifty-seven thousand feet; in two and a half minutes, when the shock wave arrived . . . the cloud passed one hundred thousand feet. The shock wave announced itself with a sharp report followed by a long thunder of broken rumbling.[25]

Ivy Mike (yield 10.4 megatons)—an atmospheric nuclear test conducted by the U.S. at Elugelab on November 1, 1952. It was the world's first successful hydrogen bomb.

BOMB COUNT
1952

United States: 841

Soviet Union: 50

Total Estimated Destructive Capability:
3,533 "Hiroshimas"

CANDOR (NOUN): UNRESERVED, HONEST, OR SINCERE EXPRESSION: FORTHRIGHTNESS —MERRIAM-WEBSTER DICTIONARY

Robert had long harbored a vague premonition that something dark and momentous lay in his future. Since Hiroshima, he had lived with the sense that he was a hunted man. The more he spoke out in favor of international arms control, the more his political opponents circled like vultures. But he continued to speak out, even though he was beginning to believe he might pay a hefty price.

On February 17, 1953, Robert strode to the podium at a meeting of the Council of Foreign Relations. Many of Washington's power elite were there, including the young banker David Rockefeller, *Washington Post* publisher Eugene Meyer, *New York Times* military reporter Hanson Baldwin, and the Kuhn, Loeb investment banker Benjamin Buttenwieser. Their attendance ensured that Robert's words would echo loudly throughout Washington. Lewis Strauss was there that night, too.

Bluntly, Robert declared that no country could expect to win a war with atomic and hydrogen bombs. In the very near future, he said, the United States and the Soviet Union "will each be in a position to put an end to civilization and life of the other, though not without risking its own." He added, "We may be likened to two scorpions in a bottle, each capable of killing the other, but only at the risk of his own life."

The only solution, Robert concluded, was "candor." Though news of the 1952 H-bomb test at Elugelab leaked shortly after it happened, the government didn't confirm it took place until April 1, 1954. To that point, though Americans knew their government was working on super bombs, many had trouble grasping just how powerful and dangerous they were. Robert believed the government had to start being more honest with Americans, and the United States had to start being more honest with the world, about the dangers the H-bomb presented. That way, everyone would understand the true stakes as countries built more of them, and perhaps press their leaders to think twice before doing so.

Robert's speech was incredibly daring. Here was the celebrated father of the atomic bomb publicly declaring that United States policy to keep the nuclear threat secret was ignorant and foolish. The country's most famous nuclear scientist was telling the government to release its most closely guarded secrets, and to discuss candidly what a nuclear war would look like. Here was a private citizen, armed with the highest security clearance, openly challenging the nation's war plans. Lewis Strauss was appalled. So were many others in Washington.

But others took the words of America's darling physicist to heart. Initially, newly elected president Dwight D. Eisenhower (nicknamed "Ike") seemed to be one of them. Unlike Truman before him, Ike was moved by Robert's idea of "candor." As a five-star general, he had witnessed firsthand the death and destruction that had so quickly rolled across Europe during World War II, and immediately understood Robert's vivid comparison of the two major powers as "scorpions in a bottle."

Highly skeptical of nuclear weapons and committed to only deploying America's military might when it was absolutely necessary, Ike told one of his aides that "atomic weapons strongly favor the side that attacks aggressively and *by surprise.* This the United States will never do." Later in his presidency, Eisenhower stood up to a group of war-happy advisors who wanted to build more nuclear weapons. In his no-nonsense way, Ike told them, "You can't have this kind of war. There just aren't enough bulldozers to scrape the bodies off the streets."

Robert hadn't been able to convince Truman. But he started to believe he might convince Eisenhower to keep nuclear weapons under control. His hopes were quickly dashed when he found out Eisenhower had made the fateful decision to appoint Strauss director of the Atomic Energy Commission.

Strauss had donated a lot of money to Eisenhower's campaign, so he had the new president's ear. He violently disagreed with Robert that the public should be told about how many nuclear weapons the United States was building, the threat they posed to human existence, or the speed at which the Soviet Union was building their own. Just as he had resented Robert's belittling of him in front of Congress four years earlier, he now resented how openly and brazenly Robert was criticizing the government.

Strauss thought that the candor Robert advocated for would just give the Soviets crucial knowledge about the bombs, which would only make it easier for them to build more. As Strauss had with Truman, he now took every opportunity to plant suspicion in Eisenhower's mind about Robert. He told Ike that "Dr. Oppenheimer was not to be trusted."

On the morning of May 25, 1953, Strauss went to FBI headquarters to meet with D. M. Ladd, an aide to J. Edgar Hoover. Strauss told Ladd he knew Robert had an appointment with Eisenhower in two days, and that he was "very much concerned about [Robert's] activities." He told Ladd that Robert had hired suspected communists to work at Los Alamos in 1943, that he might have been in contact with the Soviets in 1942, and that he might be trying to delay work on the hydrogen bomb. Given all of these "facts," Strauss asked Ladd if the FBI would be okay with him telling Ike about all of that before the president's meeting with Robert. Ladd assured Strauss that would be fine. Strauss didn't know that the FBI had already sent the attorney general's office all the information *it* had collected about Robert.

That afternoon, Strauss walked into the Oval Office. He was hell-bent on sullying Robert's reputation with the president. There, he repeated to Ike what he had just told Ladd at the FBI and explained that he couldn't do his job at the Atomic Energy Commission if Robert still chaired its General Advisory Committee.

Robert met with Eisenhower two days later. After a short meeting, the president asked him if he would share his thoughts with the National Security Council. Robert spent five hours lecturing to some of Ike's most trusted advisors. Again, he explained how important it was that the United States and other countries share information about nuclear energy. Then he urged Ike to create a five-person panel whose job it would be to get rid of nuclear weapons that had already been built.

As usual, Robert had everyone spellbound. But strangely, it seemed that Ike had changed his tune. At the end of the meeting, he cordially thanked Robert but let him leave the room without tipping his hand as to what he was thinking.

Eisenhower was mulling over what Strauss had told him just forty-eight hours earlier—that he couldn't run the AEC if Robert continued to chair its GAC. Ike may also have felt uncomfortable as he watched Robert exert "almost hypnotic power" over the National Security Council. Later, he told one of his advisors that he "did not completely trust" Robert.

Strauss's first blow had found its mark.

Having now smeared Robert in front of the president, Strauss began to disparage him in public. Over the next few months, *Time*, *Life*, and *Fortune* magazines—all controlled by media mogul Henry Luce—published articles attacking Robert and the influence of scientists in Washington. The May 1953 issue of *Fortune* featured an anonymous article titled "The Hidden Struggle for the H-Bomb: The Story of Dr. Oppenheimer's Persistent Campaign to Reverse U.S. Military Strategy." The article scorned Robert for daring to question the government's plan to retaliate with atomic weapons in the event it was attacked. After reading it, Lilienthal wrote in his diary that it was "another nasty and obviously inspired article attacking Robert Oppenheimer . . ." Lilienthal didn't know it, but Strauss had helped the editors of *Fortune* write the article himself.

Regardless of Strauss's smears, Robert was still a sensation and commanded the respect of many Americans who credited him with helping end World War II. On June 19, *Foreign Affairs* magazine published the "candor" speech Robert had given to the Council of Foreign Relations four months earlier. The article quoted him as saying that without "candor" the American people wouldn't understand how terrible nuclear weapons were. And if they didn't understand how terrible they were, they might be more inclined to accept their government's decision to make bigger ones. Only the president, Robert said, "has the authority to transcend the racket and noise, mostly consisting of lies, that have been built up about this subject."

Lies! After reading the article, a smoldering Strauss told Eisenhower that he thought Robert's essay was "dangerous and . . . fatal." But to Strauss's astonishment, Ike told him that Robert had cleared the article with the White House before it went to print. The president had read the essay and agreed with Robert that more candor about nuclear weapons was a good idea. Strauss was dumbstruck.

Strauss responded with great guts. Knowing Ike didn't want to appear soft on communism, he warned the president that journalists were reporting that he fully supported Robert's strategy of "candor," and that the president was okay with disclosing information about the power of the American nuclear arsenal with the public. "That's complete nonsense," Eisenhower replied, unshaken. "You ought not to read what those fellows write. I am at least the one person more security-minded than you are."

Inside the White House, Robert's article sparked strong debate about what the government should tell the public about nuclear weapons. That was exactly what Robert wanted. He had hoped that his blunt description of the dangers the country faced from a nuclear arms race would convince Eisenhower and all Americans that the military shouldn't rely so heavily on nuclear weapons.

Eisenhower wrestled with the issue. "We don't want to scare the country to death," he told one of his aides. But he told Strauss that he also wanted to be honest about the risks of nuclear war while offering the public some "hopeful alternative."

Strauss sensed that the president was really starting to listen to Robert. Strauss was determined to put a stop to that. He contacted *Fortune* magazine again. Together with an editor, he wrote another article bitterly critical of Robert's call for candor on atomic secrets.

BOMB COUNT
1953

United States: 1,169

Soviet Union: 120

United Kingdom: 1

Total Estimated Destructive Capability:
5,354 "Hiroshimas"

CHAPTER THIRTY-ONE

"You'd better tell your friend Oppie to batten down the hatches and prepare for some stormy weather."

Late that August, newspaper headlines across the country blared the news "Reds Test H-Bomb." Only nine months after the first American test of a hydrogen bomb, it appeared that the Soviets had been able to match that feat.

At least, that's what the American people were told.

But the Soviet test was not the achievement it seemed to be: it was neither truly a hydrogen bomb nor a weapon that could be dropped from a plane. Regardless, after reading about it in newspapers under alarming headlines, many Americans believed that the Soviet Union didn't just have the most powerful weapon on Earth—they might even have more than one.

Fear descended upon the nation. The frightening news gave Strauss further ammunition to attack Robert's calls for candor. The voices of "Cold Warriors" like Strauss became louder and louder, pushing for nuclear secrecy at all costs, and pressuring Eisenhower to build even more H-bombs to confront the Soviet threat.

Publicly, Eisenhower walked a fine line between Strauss and Robert. In an address to the United Nations on December 8, 1953, he declared that the United States and the Soviet Union should work together to develop peaceful nuclear power plants that could produce more than enough energy to power homes, buildings, and transportation. But absent from the speech was any information about the size and power of America's nuclear arsenal. Instead of candor, Eisenhower doubled down on secrecy.

In fact, the White House had quietly decided to cut spending on non-nuclear weapons while *building up* the American nuclear arsenal. Against Robert's advice, Eisenhower decided to rely almost exclusively on nuclear weapons to defend the United States. He determined that in future wars, "massive retaliation" would be cheaper and deadlier than boots on the ground.

It might also be suicidal. For in a nuclear war, there very well might be no winners or losers. Only millions of dead on all sides. Dean Acheson called Ike's massive retaliation strategy a "fraud upon the words and upon the facts." Former Illinois governor Adlai Stevenson, a Democrat who had challenged Ike for president in the 1952 election, asked pointedly, "Are we leaving ourselves the grim choice of inaction or thermonuclear holocaust?"

Robert was devastated when he found out. He had spent so much time and energy trying to convince Ike to douse the Promethean fire of what he had created. Now the president had just tossed gasoline on it.

Lewis Strauss had won the battle for Eisenhower's mind. Nuclear secrecy would remain America's policy, and the United States would continue to build new nuclear weapons in dizzying numbers.

Robert had once considered Strauss annoying, but now Strauss was dangerous. He was the head of the Atomic Energy Commission under a new president who'd decided that the only way to respond to a nuclear attack was to retaliate massively with more nukes. And he was obsessed with silencing Robert's powerful voice.

Now Strauss was firmly in the driver's seat with his right foot pressing the accelerator to the floor. Robert and many of his friends knew Strauss was gunning for him. One day, Herbert Marks, Robert's close friend and lawyer, received an anonymous call from someone who worked under Strauss at the AEC. The caller told Marks, "You'd better tell your friend Oppie to batten down the hatches and prepare for some stormy weather."

"MORE PROBABLY THAN NOT, J. ROBERT OPPENHEIMER IS AN AGENT OF THE SOVIET UNION."

Strauss took charge of the Atomic Energy Commission like a captain on the deck of a battleship. His first order of business was to call J. Edgar Hoover and ask him to send him everything the FBI had on Robert. His second order of business was to summon William Liscum Borden to his office.

Borden was a bright, young, and energetic Yale graduate obsessed with keeping the Soviet Union at bay. In 1950, he had attracted the attention of Senator Brien McMahon, who hired the twenty-eight-year-old as his aide to help him advise Congress on nuclear power. Someone who knew Borden well recalled, "Borden was like a new dog on the block who barked louder and bit harder than the old dogs." Borden couldn't stand anyone who believed the United States should slow down its march to build bigger bombs.

He wondered if Robert's opposition to the super bomb was motivated by loyalty to the Soviet Union.

Borden, a Democrat, had lost his job when Republicans took control of the Senate in 1952. Since then, he'd fixated on the idea that Robert was a Soviet spy. He spent a great deal of his time writing a sixty-five-page report tracing Robert's influence in Washington.

Strauss called Borden into his office and shut the door. Borden brought with him a mysterious document that was probably a list of his suspicions about Robert. During the meeting, the two men conspired to shut Robert out of political decision-making once and for all. Strauss would get Borden all the information he needed. Borden would do the dirty work.

Borden began sifting through Robert's files deep in the Atomic Energy Commission's vault. He brought files to Strauss. Strauss reviewed them, then sent them back to the vault. Borden brought up more files. Strauss reviewed them again. Borden spent his evenings studying thousands of pages that contained FBI transcripts of Robert's phone calls, descriptions of people Robert visited, parties he attended, company he kept, and places he went. During the seven months between April and December 1953, Strauss and Borden began to make the case that Robert was untrustworthy.

On November 7, 1953, Borden mailed a letter to J. Edgar Hoover mixed with truths, half-truths, and outright lies. It painted a dire picture:

Robert had sent money to the Communist Party.

His wife and younger brother were communists.

He had an affair with a communist mistress.

He belonged to communist organizations.

The people he recruited to Berkeley were all communists.

He was a recruiter for the Communist Party.

He was in frequent contact with Soviet spies.

He gave jobs to communists at Los Alamos.

His decision to speak out against the building of the hydrogen bomb was done at the direction of the Soviet Union.

And then the bombshell: "More probably than not, J. Robert Oppenheimer is an agent of the Soviet Union."

J. Robert Oppenheimer, 1954

CHAPTER THIRTY-TWO

Witch Hunt

Robert now found himself in the crosshairs of a terrible witch hunt ravaging Washington and the nation. Political leaders told Americans that communism was a threat to the existence of the country. Communists determined to destroy the United States could be hiding *anywhere*. They could be practicing medicine, writing scripts in Hollywood, mowing their lawn next door, or running for public office. Their goal, according to people like Republican senator Joseph McCarthy, was for communism to take over the world, ruin American companies and the bigger economy, and possibly threaten the country's very existence.

Senator McCarthy rabidly launched a series of high-profile investigations into people he suspected had infiltrated the State Department, the Treasury Department, and even the White House.[26] A blanket of fear and distrust wrapped the nation. Parents wondered, "Could my child's teacher be a communist?" Bosses wondered, "Could my employees be spies for the Soviet Union?" Librarians purged books from their shelves that might encourage communist thought. Many banned Karl Marx and other communist philosophers. McCarthy and his followers pressured Americans to report fellow citizens whom they suspected of being communists to the police.

McCarthy gave blistering speeches over radio and television, charging that Eisenhower and his administration were making it easy for communists to sabotage American laws and customs. He accused the president himself of comforting them. One government official told a *New York Times* reporter that "McCarthy had declared war on the President."

The atmosphere was insidious and toxic. McCarthy pressured Eisenhower to prove he was doing something about the suspected communists in his ranks. Secretary of Defense Charles Wilson asked the president if he had seen Robert's FBI report. Ike said no. Wilson said it was "the worst one so far." He warned Ike that Strauss had said, "McCarthy knows about it & might [use] it on us."

Sympathetic to Robert, Ike gave the celebrated scientist the benefit of the doubt. He told Wilson that he wasn't worried about McCarthy. He wasn't going to assassinate Robert's character without further evidence to prove that he was a communist. Wilson shot back, "[Robert's] brother & wife *are* Communists; this fact, plus his past relations, make him a bad risk."

Senator Joseph McCarthy standing at microphone with two other men, probably discussing the Senate Select Committee to Study Censure Charges, June 1954

Guilt by association.

McCarthy and his followers used this tactic to sully the reputations of people whom they suspected of being communists but didn't have enough proof. After a while, people didn't have to be proven communists to have their reputations ruined, lose their careers, or be run out of the public square. They merely had to be seen with someone else who was *suspected* of being a communist, be friends with someone with very liberal views . . . or, in Robert's case, have a brother and wife who once were members of the Communist Party.

"I CLIPPED IT OUT AND SENT IT IN."

Frank Oppenheimer had learned to debate moral and ethical issues just like Robert. When he was sixteen years old, he worked on the presidential campaign of Al Smith, the progressive four-term Democratic governor of New York who stood up for workers, spoke out against the terrorism of the Ku Klux Klan, and fought to prevent women and children from being forced to work more than fifty-four hours per week.

On a trip to Germany in the 1930s, Frank's father's relatives told him about "some of the terrible things" Hitler and the Nazis were doing to Jews and other groups. After hearing their stories, Frank decided to support any group that would "do something about it."

When he returned to the U.S., he was deeply moved by the difficulties that migrant farmworkers and many Black Americans experienced just to survive. The Depression was taking a terrible toll on millions of people.

Frank began reading about workers and conflicts they had with their bosses throughout history. Like Robert, Frank became active in the East Bay Teachers' Union and the Consumer's Union, and supported migrant farmworkers as they struggled.

Frank's wife, Jackie, had always been fired up by politics. "She could drive you crazy with her political rants," recalled a relative. In college, she was a member of the Young Communist League. She was very proud of her working-class roots and aspired to be a social worker.

Jackie wasn't the kind of woman Robert would have chosen for his brother. When Frank told Robert that he intended to marry Jackie, Robert had tried to talk him out of it. He probably thought that Jackie was too radical, and that Frank was being too headstrong. But Frank ignored his brother's advice and married her in September 1936. "It was an act of emancipation and rebellion on his part," wrote Robert, "against his dependence on me."

One day in early 1937, Frank and Jackie saw a membership coupon in *People's World*. "I clipped it out and sent it in," recalled Frank. The party responded by asking Frank to join using an alias. Frank chose the name Frank Folsom. They sent him a green party membership card, which he kept in his shirt pocket.

The party assigned Frank and Jackie to a street unit in Pasadena, California. There, they worked with people in the community, many of them poor, unemployed Black Americans, to integrate the city's swimming pool. Frank recalled, "They just allowed blacks in Wednesday afternoon and evening, and then they drained the pool Thursday morning." But despite their efforts, the pool remained segregated.

In the mid-1930s, it wasn't unusual for progressive Americans who cared about social justice to ally with the communist movement. Many workers, as well as writers, journalists, and teachers, believed that only strong government social welfare and safety programs would release the necks of millions of Americans from the boot of big business. If progressives didn't actually join the Communist Party like Frank, their hearts deeply sympathized with a movement that promised a just and equal world for all.

Though Frank was a card-carrying member of the party, communism didn't define him. He had a lot of noncommunist friends. He played the flute and was incredibly fond of music. He flew airplanes. He loved spending time at Perro Caliente. Given all of those pursuits in addition to his passion for physics, Robert reflected, "He couldn't have been a very hard working Communist."

Still, when Frank told Robert that he had joined the party, Robert was very upset. Frank had taken his brother's advice and pursued his own career in physics. In 1937, he was working on his PhD at the California Institute of Technology in Pasadena. At the time, being associated with the Communist Party was normal for many California liberals. But the University of California administrators who made decisions about whom to hire and fire for faculty positions were hostile to party members. Robert worried that Frank's decision to join would negatively impact his career.

Robert deeply shared his brother's passion for social justice, but there is no hard evidence that he ever desired to join the party. Frank loved and respected Robert, but joining the party allowed Frank to stake out his own personality and destiny—and step out of his brother's shadow.

In 1947, Frank was teaching physics at the University of Minnesota. Late one evening, a newspaper reporter called him on the phone. The reporter told him that he was going to run a story the following morning explaining that Frank had been a member of the party. He asked Frank to comment. "The story was full of all other kinds of allegations that were false," Frank said. "The pre-war party membership was the only true thing in it. They asked me for a statement and I simply said the whole thing was false—which was stupid of me to do. I should have just said nothing."

The story went to press. It shocked and worried Frank's bosses. They worried what people would think once they heard that a University of Minnesota professor had been a Communist Party member. They pressured Frank to give them the same denial in writing. Under great pressure and fearing for his job, Frank wrote a statement swearing that he had never been a member.

His lie came back to haunt him. On June 14, 1949, the House of Representatives called Frank to testify in front of the House Committee on Un-American Activities (HUAC). The committee's purpose was to investigate people suspected of having ties to the Communist Party. They had come for Frank.

Frank had a heart-to-heart with Jackie. He would not lie under oath. He testified that he and Jackie had been members of the party for three and a half years. During those years, he testified, his party alias had been "Frank Folsom." Again and again, various congressmen pressed Frank to give them names of other people with communist ties. Again and again, Frank refused to betray his friends.

"The people whom I have known throughout my life have been decent-thinking and well-meaning people. I know of no instance where they have thought, discussed or said anything which was inimical to the purposes of the Constitution or the laws of the United States."

As Frank testified, anger welled up inside Jackie. As she waited to testify herself, she gazed out the window of the House Committee anteroom. She was startled by the contrast between Capitol Hill's marble buildings, surrounded by manicured grounds, and the rows of dilapidated houses occupied by the city's poor Black population. The children were barefoot and dressed in rags. "They all looked rachitic, and most seemed undernourished. All they had to play with was junk they found in the street. As I sat there reading and listening and looking out the window, I found myself alternately worrying what the committee was going to try to do to me and getting madder and madder at the fact that I had been called down here so that some fellow could question *me* about being un-American."

Reporters gathered around Frank and Jackie as they exited the hearing room. Frank told them that he had joined the party because he wanted to solve the "problems of unemployment and want in the wealthiest and most productive country in the world." He had left the party in 1940, never knew any spies, and never shared any information about his work at Los Alamos.

Barely an hour later, Frank learned from reporters that the University of Minnesota had accepted his resignation. To the university, the only thing that mattered was that he had lied two years earlier. That was reason enough for his banishment from academic life. He had only been three months away from achieving tenure; however, the university president made clear to Frank in a final meeting that he was finished. Frank left the office in tears.

Blacklisted as a communist, Frank couldn't get another job. Devastated, he and Jackie packed their things and moved to the eight-hundred-acre cattle ranch they had purchased a year earlier, high in the Colorado mountains. The ranch was perched at an altitude of eight thousand feet. The winters were unbearably cold. "Jackie would sit in the cabin," recalled a friend, "with binoculars and watch cows ready to give birth in the snow. They'd have to run out to keep the newborn calves from freezing."

For the next decade, Robert Oppenheimer's likable and brilliant younger brother eked out a living as a working rancher, twenty miles from the nearest town. FBI agents showed up from time to time to question his neighbors. They kept trying to get him to rat out his friends. He kept refusing. One agent asked him threateningly, "Don't you want to get a job in a university? If you do, you have to cooperate with us." Frank reflected, "Finally, after all these years, I have gotten wise to the fact that the FBI isn't trying to investigate me, it is trying to poison the atmosphere in which I live. It is trying to punish me for being left wing by turning my friends, my neighbors, my colleagues against me and making them suspicious of me."

Frank received job offers to teach physics abroad in Brazil, Mexico, India, and England. But the U.S. government refused to issue him a passport. To make ends meet, he resorted to selling one of his prized possessions—a Van Gogh painting his father had left him.

CHAPTER THIRTY-THREE

A Blank Wall

The fires of McCarthyism raged all around the White House. Ike was under more pressure than ever before to root out suspected communists from the ranks of government.

Eisenhower still had great respect for Robert. Initially, he had supported Robert's pleas to share America's nuclear knowledge with the world. But the contents of Borden's letter seemed damning. Was Borden correct? Was Robert a Soviet spy? If so, was Robert trying to dupe Ike into going along with a scheme to give America's atomic secrets to the Soviet Union?

On the other hand, if Borden's charges were false, the letter was scandalous. After reading it, Ike wrote in his diary that it "present[ed] little new evidence." Others Ike trusted, who had studied Robert's file over many years, agreed—none of them could find evidence that he had been disloyal to the United States.

Ike sat down at his desk. He had a decision to make and knew he couldn't get it wrong. He wrote in his diary that the reports on Robert's past activities "bring forward very grave charges." Then, he paused to think. Were Borden's charges enough to formally accuse Robert of a crime? No. But the letter weighed heavily on him.

He continued writing, "I very much doubt they will have this kind of evidence, [but] the sad fact is that if this charge is true, we have a man who has been right in the middle of our whole atomic development from the very earliest days."

The next morning, Ike called Strauss into the Oval Office and asked him if he had read Borden's letter. Not only had Strauss read it, he was also the one who pressed Borden to write it in the first place. Ike wrestled with his conscience. Though he wanted to give Robert the benefit of the doubt, the five-star general who had so bravely led Allied troops to victory over the Nazis less than a decade earlier finally caved in to the pressures of McCarthyism.

Not wanting McCarthy or anyone else to think he was protecting someone who might be a security risk, Eisenhower concluded that Robert could no longer be trusted with government secrets. Ike ordered his attorney general to "place a blank wall" between Robert "and any information of a sensitive or classified character."

Admiral William "Deke" Parsons, an old friend of Robert's who worked with him at Los Alamos, was anguished when he heard about what Eisenhower had done to Robert. How ridiculous! Parsons knew Robert would never be a security risk to the United States. He knew that Robert had fought passionately for social justice so many years ago, and that he had been associated with many progressives throughout his life. But Robert was an honest, ethical man intent on protecting both the security of the United States and human life around the world. When Parsons heard that Ike was cutting Robert out of the loop after all he had done for the country, he couldn't contain himself. He told his wife, Martha, "I have to put a stop to it. Ike has to know what's *really* going on. This is the biggest mistake the United States could make!" He told Martha he was going to raise his objections with his boss, the secretary of the navy. Martha responded, "Deke, you're an admiral, why can't you go to the president?"

"No," he told his wife, "the secretary of the navy is my boss. I can't go around him."

That night, Parsons felt a deep pain in his chest. By morning, he was so pale that Martha rushed him to Bethesda Naval Hospital. He died that day of a heart attack before he was able to defend Robert to the secretary. Martha was convinced that the terrible news about Robert caused Deke's death.

With Ike's "blank wall" order, Lewis Strauss had all the ammunition he needed to destroy Robert's reputation for good. Immediately he went back to the White House, where he met with Vice President Richard Nixon, CIA chief Allen Dulles, and other aides to the president. Together, they agreed that Strauss should assemble a panel of people within the Atomic Energy Commission to decide whether Robert should be able to keep his top-secret security clearance.

It wouldn't be a trial. It wouldn't be public. But for Robert, and for the entire species, the weight of it would be enormous. His security clearance was crucial if he was to keep influencing American decisions about how many bombs would be built and what information should be shared with the rest of the world. He was a voice of reason within an ever more war-happy and fearful government that believed it needed more massive hydrogen bombs to protect itself from the rest of the world.

On December 21, 1953, at 3:00 in the afternoon, Strauss confronted Robert in person and broke the news that the commission would immediately revoke his security clearance. He told Robert that Eisenhower had read Borden's letter and, though he admitted himself that it didn't contain any new evidence, ordered an immediate investigation. He also told Robert that the commission was preparing a list of charges against him.

Strauss pushed a copy of the letter across the table to Robert. This was the first time Robert had seen it. Outwardly he appeared calm, but as he read it, his mind raced. Yes, he had donated money to causes that the Communist Party supported. But not to the Communist Party itself! Yes, Kitty had been a member of the Communist Party . . . at a time when membership hadn't been such a big deal. So had Jean Tatlock. Yes, Frank had too, but he would never betray his country! No, he wasn't in frequent contact with Soviet spies! No, he never knowingly gave jobs to communists at Los Alamos! And it was outrageous to suggest that the Soviet Union told him to speak out against the hydrogen bomb. He spoke out about it because he worried about what the world might look like after it was used.

Strauss peered across his desk at Robert. Robert knew what he was thinking without him saying a word. Unless Robert resigned from the commission, the commission would charge him officially and call him in for hearings. That could destroy his career, his life, and his reputation as one of America's most respected scientists. Robert didn't have much time to process what was happening. Strauss told him that he had one day to decide. Robert asked Strauss if he could have a copy of the charges against him. Strauss refused. He could only have them after deciding what he was going to do. Robert asked if Congress knew anything about this. Strauss said no but suggested they would find out soon enough.

Robert left Strauss's office distraught. He couldn't believe what

was happening to him. He had spent much of his career building a
bomb for the U.S. government.

He trusted the government to use the technology for humanity's
protection—to guard the world against the Nazis. Instead, after the
Nazis were defeated, the government dropped not one but two bombs
on civilians in Japan—a country that, contrary to what he had been
told, had been looking to surrender before the attacks. And then, when
he challenged the government's effort to build super bombs that could
wipe out life on the planet, that same government was now trying to
take away his job and rob him of his ethical duty to shape the future of
the weapons he had created.

"IF HE REFUSED, THEY COULD ACCUSE HIM OF BEING PART OF A COVER-UP."

At the exact moment Robert's life irrevocably changed, an FBI
agent knocked on General Groves's door in Connecticut.

For years, the FBI pushed Groves to report what he knew about
Robert's kitchen conversation with Hoke. For years, Groves refused
to tell them. The FBI first questioned him about it in 1944. Groves
didn't bother to respond. In 1946, FBI agents asked him again what
he knew. Groves told them that he wouldn't talk about it because
Robert had told him about it in "strict confidence." Agents pressured him. They told him that they already knew the man who approached Hoke was Eltenton, and that they were about to interview

him. In an extraordinary demonstration of his loyalty to Robert, Groves told them yet again that he wouldn't say anything more. He simply wouldn't betray the man who he had worked with for years—who had guided the bomb project so expertly and so professionally.

Hoover was astonished to learn that an American army general was refusing to cooperate with an FBI investigation. On June 13, 1946, Hoover wrote Groves personally asking him to reveal what Robert had told him about his conversation with Hoke. Again, Groves stood his ground. He politely but firmly replied to America's "top cop" that he would still tell him nothing. He would not put his relationship with Robert in jeopardy. Not many men in Washington would have had the courage to do that.

But now, in 1953, with a federal agent on the doorstep of his home, amid a national witch hunt and a country captivated by exposing communists, even the indefatigable General Groves began to buckle. In this poisonous environment, Groves understood that if he didn't tell the FBI everything he knew, it would look like he had been trying to cover up a Soviet attempt to spy on the American military. That could spell the end of his career. He might even be branded a spy himself.

The problem was that Groves couldn't remember exactly what Robert had told him so many years earlier. The one thing he did remember was that he promised he would never say anything to the FBI—a promise he was now breaking. Reluctantly, Groves told the agent that Robert had come to him in 1943, told him that Hoke had first approached his brother Frank to try to get information for the Soviets, and that Frank had asked Robert for advice about what he should do. But when the FBI asked Frank about this, he denied that Hoke had ever approached him, or that he had ever talked with Robert about it. And Robert had always been very clear that Hoke had approached him directly in the kitchen. FBI interviews with other people, including Kitty, who was there that night, confirmed that.

So why would Groves have said that Frank was involved? Maybe he didn't remember it clearly. Maybe he was basing it on memories of what he thought had happened. Or maybe Robert actually had told him that Frank was involved for another reason. Anything more specific is lost to history.

Groves did make certain to tell the agent that he didn't believe that Hoke or Frank were Soviet spies themselves. But now Groves found himself in hot water. He had just told a federal agent that he knew about the Soviet approach in 1943 and didn't report it. Strauss and Hoover had him where they wanted him—they could now pressure him to testify against Robert. If he refused, they could accuse him of being part of a cover-up.

CHAPTER THIRTY-FOUR

A Terrible Crash

Strauss expected Robert's decision that evening. But the next morning came, and still no word. At noon, he ordered the commission's general manager, Kenneth Nichols, to call Robert. Robert answered the phone. He told Nichols that he needed more time to make up his mind. Nichols replied brusquely that he "could not have any more time."

One hour later, Robert called Nichols back. He told him that he would come to Washington and give his answer in person. He would take an afternoon train and be at Strauss's office at 9:00 the next morning.

Robert and Kitty boarded a train at Trenton and arrived in Washington in the late afternoon. They jumped in a car and took off for Georgetown, where they would spend the night at the home of their friend and lawyer Herbert Marks and his wife, Anne. Staring out the window as they sped through the streets of Washington, Robert exclaimed, "I can't believe what is happening to me." When they arrived, Joseph Volpe, another lawyer, joined them. The five of them sat up late into the evening, debating whether Robert should fight the charges, or resign and avoid Strauss's inquisition.

Finally, with the help of his friends, Robert made up his mind. He wouldn't go down without a fight. The next morning, he would go into Strauss's office and tell him that he wouldn't resign.

Robert was exhausted. The agonizing conversation had taken a great toll on him. With a heavy sigh, he got up from the couch and announced that he was retiring upstairs to the guest bedroom.

A few minutes later, Anne, Herb, and Kitty heard a terrible crash. Anne bounded to the top of the stairs. Robert was nowhere to be seen. She knocked on the bathroom door. "Robert! Robert!" she yelled. No response. She tried to open the door. "I couldn't get [it] open," she said, "and I couldn't get a response."

Inside the bathroom, Robert had collapsed on the floor. His unconscious body blocked the door. Together, Anne, Herb, and Kitty forced it open, pushing Robert's limp form to one side. They carried him to a couch and revived him.

Robert explained what had happened. He had taken a sleeping pill Kitty had given him. Anne called a doctor—who told her, "Don't let him go to sleep." So for an hour they walked him back and forth, coaxing coffee down his throat until the doctor arrived.

Somehow Robert managed to get to Strauss's office by 9:00 the next morning.

He clutched a letter that Marks and Volpe helped him write. In it, Robert explained that by quitting, it would mean that he agreed with "the view that I am not fit to serve this government, that I have now served for some twelve years. This I cannot do. If I were thus unworthy I could hardly have served our country as I have tried . . . or have spoken . . . in the name of our science and our country."

BOMB COUNT
1954

United States: 1,703

Soviet Union: 150

United Kingdom: 5

**Estimated Total Destructive Capability:
24,729 "Hiroshimas"**

PART FOUR

AMERICAN INQUISITION

CHAPTER THIRTY-FIVE

Kangaroo Court: A mock court in which the principles of law and justice are disregarded or perverted. —Merriam-Webster Dictionary

As soon as Robert told Strauss that he wouldn't resign, the commission turned on him for good. Strauss gave them the green light to take Robert down. Nichols told one of his colleagues that Robert was "a slippery sonuvabitch, but we're going to get him this time."

Two FBI agents arrived at Robert's house on Christmas Eve 1953. They demanded Robert give them all the classified papers he had in his files. The same day, he received the commission's letter of charges against him. Like the Borden letter, this one charged that Robert was friends with communists and that he donated money to the Communist Party. It also blasted him for opposing the hydrogen bomb and persuading other scientists not to work on building it.

> Of course Robert had protested the development of the hydrogen bomb—both privately within the government and publicly in the press. He was astonished that any government would build such a profoundly terrible weapon. He couldn't understand why countries needed to build tools that could destroy the world.

But in McCarthy's America, speaking out and criticizing the government was equal to disloyalty. It didn't matter who you were. If you didn't agree with decisions the government made, you became a target.

Robert worked feverishly to prepare his defense. He had thirty days to respond to the charges. Marks and Volpe told him that he needed a good trial lawyer. Robert went immediately to New York. He strode into the law office of Lloyd K. Garrison, whom he had grown to trust over the previous year. Garrison was the great-grandson of the abolitionist William Lloyd Garrison. He was a strong liberal and a board member of the American Civil Liberties Union. Robert showed Garrison the letter of charges. After Garrison read it, Robert said, "It looks pretty bad, doesn't it?" Garrison replied gravely, "Yes."

Garrison knew they needed to act fast. The first thing they had to do was to get the commission to extend Robert's thirty-day deadline. Garrison rushed to Washington and got the extension granted. Then he began working with Robert to write his response to the charges.

News of the hearing ricocheted across Washington. Vannevar Bush, director of the Office of Scientific Research and Development (OSRD), confronted Strauss in his office. Bush informed him that this was a "great injustice," and that if he pursued the case, he would pay the price. Strauss replied angrily that he "didn't give a damn" and that he wasn't going to be "blackmailed."

Bush's warning aside, Strauss had the upper hand. Every day, the FBI told him where Robert went, whom he spoke to, and what he spoke to them about. They gathered that information from illegal wiretaps of Robert's telephone. Strauss therefore knew in advance what arguments Robert would make, how he would make them, and what strategies he would use to defend himself. Garrison would never see much of the FBI's file against Robert because it was classified—he didn't have the necessary security clearance.

The commission assembled a hearing board. They planned to spend a whole week studying Robert's file so they could build the case against him. Naturally, Garrison believed that he should be allowed to attend so he could see what information would be used against his client. He asked the commission to include him. They refused. Garrison tried to get an emergency clearance to read at least some of the files. Again, the commission refused. Garrison had a "sinking feeling" that after reading so much negative information about Robert over an entire week, the board would become prejudiced against him before the hearing even began.

Because it was a hearing and not a trial in a court of law, Robert's prosecutors didn't have to follow the same rules that a courtroom trial would have demanded. There would be no period of discovery for both sides, no voir dire—no jury selection. Neither Robert nor his lawyer would be able to examine the evidence against them, and there would be no way to really know if the evidence was obtained legally or illegally.

Strauss didn't care if what he was doing might have violated Robert's constitutional right to due process. He knew, but did not care, that the FBI wiretaps were illegal. This angered Harold Green, one of the commission's lawyers, so much that he quit the case in protest. He told Strauss "that the case was not so much an inquiry as a prosecution and that he did not want to have anything to do with it."

Robert knew the FBI was still spying on him. But it wasn't just him—they spied on his friends and family, too. One day, while visiting friends at their home, he made it clear that he thought he was being monitored. "He'd come in the room," recalled his friend Jean Bacher, "and before he'd do anything else, he'd lift the pictures and look under them to see where the recording device was." One night he took down a picture that was hanging on the wall and said, "There it is!"

When Robert's in-laws returned from a trip to Europe, the FBI arranged to have their bags thoroughly searched by U.S. customs agents. They also photographed all the written material they had with them. Kitty's father, who used a wheelchair, and her mother were so unnerved by the treatment that they ended up in the hospital.

Strauss framed the Oppenheimer case as a crusade for America's future. He thundered to a colleague, "If this case is lost, the atomic energy program . . . will fall into the hands of 'left-wingers.' If this occurs, it will mean another Pearl Harbor . . . If Oppenheimer is cleared, then 'anyone' can be cleared regardless of the information against them."

To Strauss, the very future of the United States was at stake. In his mind, the country was fighting a war against a Soviet enemy determined to destroy the American way of life. Left unchecked, they might destroy the free market system, subject Americans to communist rationing and distribution, and send anyone who didn't go along with it to prison camps. To save the United States from such a fate, no matter how much of a fantasy it may have been, Strauss was willing to plow through legal and ethical guardrails that had defined the country since its founding. In cases of national emergency, Strauss reasoned, it was okay to set aside the Constitution and reject trial by jury. It was okay to use evidence that the FBI obtained illegally. It was okay . . . no, it was his *duty*, to assassinate the character of the country's most famous physicist if he was even *suspected* of having ties to the Soviet Union—hard evidence be damned.

Strauss picked Roger Robb to bring the case against Robert. Robb had a well-deserved reputation as an aggressive trial lawyer with seven years of experience as a prosecutor. He had tried twenty-three murder cases and won almost all of them. In 1951, as a court-appointed attorney, he defended CPUSA leader Earl Browder against charges of contempt of Congress. But politically, he was very conservative. In addition to other right-wing clients, he defended controversial columnist and radio broadcaster Fulton Lewis Jr., a friend of Joe McCarthy, and had always cooperated fully with the FBI. Strauss was able to get him a security clearance in just over a week.

Strauss then turned his attention to selecting his judges. He needed three men who knew nothing about Robert, but who would be shocked when they found out about his alleged communist ties. He wanted people he could count on to throw the book at Robert once they found out about his progressive past.

Strauss settled on Gordon Gray to chair the board of three. Gray, the president of the University of North Carolina, was a conservative Democrat who had voted for Eisenhower in the 1952 election. A Southern aristocrat whose family money came from the R. J. Reynolds Tobacco Company, Gray had no idea what he was getting into. He thought the assignment would last a couple of weeks and that Robert would be cleared.

Thomas Morgan, another conservative Democrat and chairman of the Sperry Corporation, would be the second judge. For the third member, Strauss chose a conservative Republican, Ward Evans, whose two major qualifications were his science background—he was a former chemistry professor at Loyola and Northwestern Universities—and his record of taking away security clearances from many other people. The stage was now set for Strauss's kangaroo court.

CHAPTER THIRTY-SIX

"There goes a fool."

One Saturday at midday, after spending hours writing his reply to the commission's charges, Robert emerged from his office in Fuld Hall. As he walked to his car, Albert Einstein appeared. The two men began talking in the parking lot.

Einstein told Robert that he thought the commission's attack on him was outrageous—so outrageous that he should just resign. Why subject himself to such a ridiculous hearing? Perhaps recalling his own experience in Nazi Germany, Einstein told Robert that he "had no obligation to subject himself to the witch hunt, that he had served his country well, and that if this was the reward [America] offered, he should turn his back on her." Einstein had fled his homeland as it was about to be overwhelmed by the Nazis. He refused to ever set foot in Germany again. To Einstein, if a government was coming after you, it didn't make sense to play their game. Was Robert being forced to appear? No. Was he being subpoenaed to testify? No. Would a judge issue an arrest warrant if he didn't appear? There would be no judge—so no.

Robert didn't think Einstein really understood. He told his esteemed colleague that he couldn't just turn his back on America.

He loved America. That love was as deep as his love for science. Of course, Einstein understood that the United States wasn't Nazi Germany, and he didn't think Robert needed to flee. But McCarthyism truly scared him. The attacks on people like Robert, his brother Frank, and so many others reminded Einstein of how the Nazis attacked their opponents as their power became greater and greater.

In 1951, Einstein wrote his friend Queen Elizabeth of Belgium that here in America, "the German calamity of years ago repeats itself: People acquiesce without resistance and align themselves with the forces of evil." He feared that if Robert continued to play the commission's bogus game, he wouldn't just embarrass himself, he would make the whole poisonous process seem legitimate and acceptable.

Einstein's instincts were right—and time would demonstrate that Robert's were wrong. "Oppenheimer is not a gypsy like me," Einstein confided to a close friend. "I was born with the skin of an elephant; there is no one who can hurt me." Robert, he thought, clearly was a man who was easily hurt—and intimidated.

The two men parted ways. Einstein walked back to his office, shaking his head. When he arrived, he looked at his assistant, nodded in Robert's direction, and muttered, "There goes a fool."

Robert Oppenheimer and
Albert Einstein, Princeton, NJ, 1947

CHAPTER THIRTY-SEVEN

He Would Endure the Torture

Robert's hearing took place in Building T-3, a dilapidated two-story temporary structure built on the National Mall during World War II. Room 2022 had become a bare-bones courtroom. The rectangular space was long and dark. Gray, Morgan, and Evans sat at one end, behind a large mahogany table stacked with black binders containing the FBI documents Robert and his lawyer hadn't been allowed to see.

The opposing lawyers sat across from each other at two long tables. On the commission's side was Robb, on Robert's side was Garrison. On the near end of the room was a witness chair, a place Robert would spend twenty-seven hours over the next month. When he wasn't testifying, Robert sat behind the witness chair on a leather couch against the wall, alternately chain-smoking cigarettes and filling the room with the aroma of his walnut pipe tobacco.

The hearing came to order. Gordon Gray read the charges against Robert for all to hear. His alleged crimes: donating money to the Communist Party in San Francisco, being "intimately associated" with known communists including Jean Tatlock and others, and hiring known communists to work at Los Alamos. But the most serious charge was his failure to promptly report his kitchen conversation with Hoke in early 1943 about George Eltenton's attempt to funnel information about the Radiation Laboratory to the Soviet Union.

Robert was the first to admit that he had been friends with Jean Tatlock and other progressives—but he denied that there was anything harmful about those relationships. "I liked the new sense of companionship." He freely admitted donating money to causes he held dear through the Communist Party, but denied that he had given jobs to people he knew were communists. And he admitted that Hoke had come to him with Eltenton's idea, but explained that he shot it down immediately when he heard it: "I made some strong remark to the effect that this sounded terribly wrong to me. The discussion ended there. Nothing in our long-standing friendship would have led me to believe that [Hoke] was actually seeking information; and I was certain that he had no idea of the work on which I was engaged."

But then the commission threw Robert a curveball. They claimed that various Communist Party members made statements saying that Robert, too, was a member—and that he had talked about the atomic bomb with them. But none of those people had ever talked to the FBI. So how did the FBI know? They got the information by illegally wiretapping their phones, offices, or homes. That evidence should, therefore, have been inadmissible.

The large black binders on the table in front of the three judges contained records of those conversations, but Robert's lawyers weren't allowed to see them before the hearing. In an actual court of law, such evidence would be unacceptable and dismissed as hearsay. But this wasn't a trial in a court of law, it was a hearing of the Atomic Energy Commission. Therefore, there were no rules about what "evidence" could be used or disqualified, and no requirement that evidence be shared with the defendant before trial.

At that point, Robert's lawyers should have realized that it would be impossible for him to receive a fair trial. He could have walked out of the hearing room at any time, as Einstein told him to before it began. The commission wouldn't have been able to do anything.

But instead, when Gray asked Robert if he wanted to testify, he said yes. He took the standard oath to tell the truth, the whole truth, and nothing but the truth. The commission had set the trap and, sabotaging himself once more, Robert stepped right into it.

The next morning, a stunning headline shouted from the front page of *The New York Times*:

DR. OPPENHEIMER SUSPENDED BY A.E.C. IN SECURITY REVIEW;
SCIENTIST DEFENDS RECORD; HEARINGS STARTED; ACCESS TO SECRET DATA DENIED
NUCLEAR EXPERT—RED TIES ALLEGED

Newspapers around the world blasted out the story. Millions who had previously considered Robert a genius, celebrity, or hero now looked at him with deep suspicion. The news forced readers to take sides. Liberals like columnist Drew Pearson couldn't believe that the commission would target Robert in such a witch hunt, searching "under the bed of Oppenheimer's past to see whom he was talking to or meeting with in 1939 or 1940." But conservative commentators like Walter Winchill had a field day with the story. Winchell had announced two days before that McCarthy would soon reveal that a "key atomic figure had urged that the H-bomb not be built at all." This famous atomic scientist, Winchell lied, has been "an active Communist Party member" and the "leader of a Red cell including other noted atomic scientists."

When he heard about the *New York Times* story, Einstein said, "The trouble with Oppenheimer is that he loves a woman who doesn't love him—the United States government . . . All [he] needed to do was go to Washington, tell the officials that they were fools, and then go home."

Wednesday, April 14, was one of the most humiliating days of Robert's life. He started the morning in the witness chair.

With no evidence, the commission charged that it might have been Frank who arranged Robert's kitchen conversation with Hoke. Garrison asked Robert directly if Frank was involved. He responded directly, "I am very clear on this. I have a vivid and I think certainly not fallible memory. *He had nothing whatever to do with it.* It would not have made any sense, I may say, since [Hoke] was my friend. I don't mean that my brother did not know him, but this would have been a peculiarly roundabout and unnatural thing" (emphasis added). Strauss, Robb, and Nichols didn't believe him. Without any proof, they insisted he was lying.

Robb stood up at the front of the room. He began to interrogate Robert relentlessly. Robert had never experienced that kind of grilling. He was totally unprepared.

Almost immediately, Robb got Robert to admit that close association with the Communist Party was "inconsistent with work on a secret war project." Robb asked him if he thought it would be appropriate for former party members to work on such a project.

Robert responded: "Are we talking about now or then?"

Robb: "Let us ask you now, and then we will go back to then."

Robert: "I think that depends on . . . what kind of a man he is, whether he is an honest man."

Robb: "Was that your view in 1941, 1942, and 1943?"

Robert: "Essentially."

Robb: "What test do you apply and did you apply in 1941, 1942, and 1943 to satisfy yourself that a former member of the party is no longer dangerous?"

Robert: "As I said, I knew very little about who was a former member of the party. In my wife's case, it was completely clear that she was no longer dangerous. In my brother's case, I had confidence in his decency and straightforwardness and in his loyalty to me."

Robb: "Let us take your brother as an example. Tell us the test that you applied to acquire the confidence that you have spoken of?"

Robert responded, "In the case of a brother you don't make tests."

Robb was just warming up. He produced a transcript of Robert's 1943 interview with Pash, which Robb had listened to prior to the hearing. As Pash quoted the interview, Robert was flummoxed. He had no idea that the conversation had been recorded.

If Robert was being tried in a court of law, his lawyers could have listened to it and discussed it with him ahead of time so that he could have prepared for Robb's questions. Instead Robert, surprised and on the spot, had to rely on his ten-year-old recollection of the conversation, while Robb had been able to listen to it beforehand as many times as he wanted.

Robb got right to the point: "Did you tell Pash the truth about [your kitchen conversation with Hoke]?"

Robert admitted that he hadn't.

Robb asked, "What did you tell Pash that was not true?"

Robert answered, "That Eltenton had attempted to approach members of the project—three members of the project—through intermediaries."

Robb: "Did you tell Pash that [Hoke] had approached three persons on the project?"

Robert hadn't mentioned Hoke's name to Pash at all. But ten years later, he couldn't remember so well. Had he? Hadn't he? Robert responded, "I am not clear . . ."

Robb repeated his question, "Didn't you say that [Hoke] had approached three people?"

Robert responded, "Probably."

Robb: "Why did you do that, Doctor?"

Robert: "Because I was an idiot."

Robert's commitment to ethics, and to his country, had compelled him to tell Pash that the army should keep an eye on Eltenton. But at the same time, he had to walk a delicate line—he didn't want to say anything that could incriminate his friend Hoke. Robert sensed he had to deliberately make the story more confusing. That way, if Pash ever found out it was Hoke who relayed Eltenton's message, the blame wouldn't fall squarely on his friend. So Robert made up a "cock-and-bull story."

Robert was also driven by fear. If he hadn't told the army at the time that the Soviet Union was trying to find out what was going on at the Radiation Laboratory, and the army or the FBI found out, he might have been seen as a traitor—or at least an accomplice to treason. Ultimately, on the spot and against the wall, Robert bent the truth to protect himself and his best friend.

Had Robert told Pash the truth in 1943 about his kitchen conversation with Hoke, he wouldn't be in this mess. He called himself an idiot to try to lighten the mood in a self-deprecatory way. But Robb didn't think it was funny at all.

All he cared about was that Robert had just admitted lying.

Robb went for Robert's throat, pummeling him with questions about every aspect of his conversation with Pash. He knew that the way to destroy Robert was to get people, both in and out of the hearing room, to question his credibility. If Robert was lying about this, what else was he lying about?

Robb had Robert backed into a corner. Robert didn't remember his conversation with Pash well enough to respond to everything Robb threw at him. And Robert's lawyer, Garrison, wasn't experienced enough to properly defend his client. If he had been, he would have insisted that Robert answer no further questions until he had an opportunity to read the transcript or listen to the tape himself.

Every day, Robb updated Strauss on what was happening inside the hearing room. Strauss could barely contain his glee. He wrote President Eisenhower: "On Wednesday, Oppenheimer broke and admitted, under oath, that he had lied." Anticipating victory, he continued, "An extremely bad impression toward Oppenheimer has already developed in the minds of the Board." Ike wrote back, thanked Strauss for his report, and told him that he had burned it. The president didn't want to leave any evidence that he or Strauss were inappropriately monitoring the hearing.

On the morning of April 15, Groves took the stand. Garrison questioned him first. Groves started off by praising Robert's work at Los Alamos. Garrison then asked him if he thought Robert was capable of being disloyal to his country. Groves responded forcefully, "I would be amazed if he [was]." Then Garrison asked Groves if he knew about Robert's kitchen conversation with Hoke. Groves replied that he knew about it because Robert had felt that it was essential to tell him about it.

Groves thought Robert had done the right thing by reporting it rather than keeping it secret. He also knew Robert hadn't been completely honest. But his respect for his co-director ran deep. He testified that Robert's actions were driven by a "typical American schoolboy attitude that there is something wicked about telling on a friend." But then Groves repeated what he had already told the FBI about Frank's involvement: "I always had the impression that Dr. Oppenheimer wanted to protect his friends of long standing, *possibly* his brother, and that his brother *might* be involved in having been in this chain . . ."

Groves had no proof Frank was involved. Maybe he was basing it on things he heard from other people over the years. But by bringing up Frank's name, the board now had even more reason to wonder what else Robert may have been lying about. For if Frank *had* been involved, then not only had Robert lied to Pash in 1943, but he had lied to the FBI in 1946 and was lying again during the hearing in 1954.

Robb then asked Groves point-blank: "Would you clear Dr. Oppenheimer [to work on the Manhattan Project] today?" This was the moment Strauss had been waiting for.

Groves knew the law. The Atomic Energy Act said specifically that people who were thought to be a danger to national security shouldn't be allowed to work on highly secretive projects. Could

Groves prove today that Robert would be a danger? No. But could he be absolutely sure that he *wouldn't* be a danger? He responded to Robb, "It is not a case of proving that a man is a danger. It is a case of thinking, well, he might be a danger." Therefore, "I would not clear Dr. Oppenheimer today if I were a member of the Commission."

That's all Robb needed him to say. In the end, Groves turned against the man he had defended so fiercely for years. He knew that if he didn't, Strauss would destroy him too.

On Friday morning, after nearly five days of grueling questions, Robert took the stand again. He was physically and mentally exhausted. But he wasn't about to let Robb ambush him like he had before. With each question Robb asked him, Robert was getting better at fending them off.

This time, the topic was the hydrogen bomb. Robb asked him if he had opposed the building of the bomb on moral grounds after President Truman announced that it would be built in January 1950. Robert responded, "I could very well have said this is a dreadful weapon, or something like that."

Robb: "Why do you think you could very well have said that?"

Robert: "Because I have always thought it was a dreadful weapon. Even [though] from a technical point of view it was a sweet and lovely and beautiful job, I have still thought it was a dreadful weapon."

Robb: "And have said so?"

Robert: "I would assume that I have said so, yes."

Robb: "You mean you had a moral revulsion against the production of such a dreadful weapon?"

Robert: "This is too strong."

Robb: "Beg pardon?"

Robert: "That is too strong."

Robb: "Which is too strong, the weapon or my expression?"

Robert: "Let us leave the word 'moral' out of it."

Robb: "You had qualms about it."

Robert finally lost his patience. "How could one not have qualms about it? I know no one who doesn't have qualms about it."

By the end of the week it was clear to everyone that Robert and Robb hated each other. "My feeling was," Robb recalled, "that he was just a brain and as cold as a fish, and he had the iciest pair of blue eyes I ever saw."

Robert couldn't stand Robb. During a brief recess, the two men were standing next to each other when Robert suddenly had one of his coughing spells. Robb turned to Robert to express his concern, but Robert cut him off angrily and said something that caused Robb to turn on his heel and walk away.

At the end of each day, Robb met up with Strauss to update him on how the hearing was going. Both men were confident that the board would eventually take away Robert's security clearance. The way things were going, Robert's lawyers thought the same thing. They, too, huddled together each night with Robert to talk strategy and fume at Robb's oppressive questioning. One night, Volpe finally turned to Robert and said, "Robert, tell them to shove it, leave it, don't go on with it because I don't think you can win."

Einstein had told Robert to do that before the hearing even began. Strauss designed the whole thing as a trap, and Robert walked right in. Robert decided he had no choice but to see it through to the end. He would endure the torture just as he had in the camp icehouse so many years before.

After Robert was excused from the stand, he retreated to the leather couch at the back of the room, sighed deeply, and lit a cigarette. Garrison strode to the front of the room. He began calling a parade of witnesses to defend Robert's character and loyalty.

The first was Lieutenant Colonel John Lansdale, the Manhattan Project's former chief of security. Lansdale always had a soft spot for Robert and had defended him multiple times over the years. He told the committee he "strongly" felt that Robert was a loyal citizen.

Then he turned his attention to the committee. Lansdale told them that their whole hearing was just a product of McCarthy-era hysteria. True to character, Robb wasn't about to let that comment pass: "You think this inquiry is a manifestation of hysteria?"

Lansdale began, "I think . . ."

Robb cut him off, "Yes or no?"

Annoyed, Lansdale shot back sharply: "I won't answer that question 'Yes' or 'No.' If you are tending to be that way—if you will let me continue, I will be glad to answer your question."

Robb relented: "All right."

Lansdale continued: "I think the hysteria of the times over communism is extremely dangerous." In his role as an army security officer, Lansdale had denied known communists entry into the army in the past. His supervisors had even belittled him for it. Between 1932 and 1945, he believed that Eleanor Roosevelt, the president's wife, was responsible for allowing communists to easily enter the army. But now he sensed that the pendulum had shifted far to the other extreme, which he believed to be equally dangerous. He understood that times had changed dramatically. In the late 1930s and early 1940s, it hadn't been so unusual for Americans to know communists, be friends with communists, marry communists, or even be communists themselves. But by the early 1950s, so much fear and distrust and anger had built up that it became almost impossible to remember a more tolerant time. With his testimony on record, Lansdale took a seat.

John J. McCloy, chairman of Chase National Bank, took the stand next. He, too, had no doubts at all about Robert's loyalty. Before the hearing, he wrote President Eisenhower: "I am very distressed . . . over the Oppenheimer matter. I feel that it is somewhat like [asking if Newton or Galileo were risks to their countries]." Now he defended Robert to the committee directly: "We are only secure if we have the best brains and the best reach of mind." When it came to quantum mechanics, there were only so many "best brains" out there. America, especially in a time of such great uncertainty, couldn't afford to lose brains like Robert's. But here he was, called before a kangaroo court, blamed for his relationships with others, and accused of being disloyal to the very country he served so expertly.

If America kept persecuting its best and brightest minds, what kind of democracy could it hope to be? How could it remain a world power if it silenced the very people who made it that way? And what about future generations? Would they have to monitor everything they said, everything they did, and every relationship they had, so nothing would come back to haunt them in the future?

Up to the witness chair strode Vannevar Bush. Bush had liked and trusted Robert from the minute he met him at Berkeley. Like

Robert, Bush worried about the future of the world with nuclear weapons in it. He opposed the building of hydrogen bombs and hoped that an international organization could control them before it was too late.

The committee asked him why he thought Robert hadn't wanted the United States to test the hydrogen bomb. Bush told them he agreed with Robert that the United States shouldn't have tested it. Instead, they should have made a pact with the Soviet Union to stop testing bombs entirely.

Bush thought it was absurd that Robert was being accused of disloyalty to the country for speaking his mind. He looked the committee members in the eye and rebuked them: "I [don't think this board, nor any board] should ever sit on a question in this country of whether a man should serve his country or not because he expressed strong opinions. If you want me to try that case, you can try me. I have expressed strong opinions many times, and I intend to do so. They have been unpopular opinions at times. When a man is pilloried for doing that, this country is in a severe state . . . Excuse me, gentlemen, if I become stirred, but I am."

CHAPTER THIRTY-EIGHT

Kitty Didn't Give an Inch

On Monday, April 26, the committee called Kitty to testify. Robert sat right behind her on the couch. Chairman Gray and Dr. Evans immediately started grilling her about her communist past. She answered each of their questions easily and precisely. She was nervous but determined not to show it. As a young girl, her German-born parents trained her to sit still without fidgeting. Now she drew upon this training to put on a performance of tremendous self-control.

Gray asked her if she thought there was a difference between Soviet communism and the Communist Party USA. Kitty answered, "In the days that I was a member of the Communist Party, I thought they were definitely two things. The Soviet Union had its Communist Party, and our country had its Communist Party. I thought that the Communist Party of the United States was concerned with problems internal."

Kitty had only paid dues to the party for less than two years in her early twenties while married to Joe Dallet. She was passionate about social justice but hadn't really cared much about what was going on in the Soviet Union. She certainly wasn't nearly as committed to the party as Joe was and stopped paying dues after he was killed in the Spanish Civil War. But the committee kept grilling her. Gray and Evans wanted to know exactly when she left the party. Kitty responded firmly that she stopped having anything to do with the party after 1936.

Then Gray turned his attention to Robert: "Would it be fair to say that [Robert's] contributions in the years as late as possibly 1942 meant that he had not stopped having anything to do with the Communist Party? I don't insist that you answer that yes or no. You can answer that any way you wish."

Kitty knew darn well she could answer any way she wished. She wasn't about to have this man belittle her or manipulate her into incriminating her husband. Steamed on the inside but cool on the outside, Kitty replied, "I know that. Thank you. I don't think that the question is properly phrased."

Gray responded, "Do you understand what I am trying to get at?"

Kitty: "Yes; I do."

Gray dug in. "Why don't you answer it that way?"

Kitty responded defiantly, "The reason I don't like the phrase 'stopped having anything to do with the 'Communist Party' . . . It is because *I don't think Robert ever had anything to do with the Communist Party*" (emphasis added). Kitty acknowledged that Robert had given money to the party so that they might help people and causes he was passionate about, but he simply hadn't been more involved than that.

Robert's lawyers knew Gray was trying to get Kitty to say things that would make Robert look worse. They wanted the questions to stop, and tried to intervene, but Gray defiantly pressed on. He wanted to know when Robert stopped associating with communists. Kitty thought the question was ridiculous. Robert had known party members at different points in his life, along with all kinds of other people. Some had left the party many years earlier like she and Frank had. Some, like Hoke, were probably still members. What difference did it make? The only thing that mattered was that Robert was loyal and faithful to his country, and that he would never share information about his work with anyone. When Hoke came to him and told him that Eltenton was trying to get information, his first reaction was to tell his best friend that he wouldn't have anything to do with it, because it would be treason.

Gray dug in deeper. He wanted to know how the committee might verify that someone had left the party. Kitty kept her cool. She answered, "I think that varies from person to person, Mr. Gray. Some people [just leave] and even write an article about it. Other people do it quite slowly. I left the Communist Party. I did not leave my past, the friendships, just like that. Some continued for a while. I saw communists after I left the Communist Party."

Evans kept pounding. Kitty remained unflappable. He asked her to tell them the difference between a communist and a fellow traveler. What did that have to do with anything, she asked herself? But she answered the question, "To me, a communist is a member of the Communist Party who does more or less precisely what he is told."

Kitty didn't give an inch. Not even Robb could touch her. Calm and yet wise to the ways the committee was trying to manipulate her, she was a much better witness than the husband she was defending.

CHAPTER THIRTY-NINE

"America must not devour her own children."

The drab hearing room at 16th and Constitution had become the vivid stage for an inquisition right out of a Shakesperean tragedy. Though conducted in secret, it was a lens into the conscience of a troubled nation. Just as in Robert's senior-year ethical studies class with his beloved teacher John Lovejoy Elliott, those present grappled with deep, troubling questions. How should people be judged? By whom they know and spend time with? Or by their own actions? Can people criticize the policies or decisions of their government while still being loyal to their country? Can democracy survive if people are forced to choose their friends based upon whom the government decides is acceptable? And what happens when the government decides they aren't acceptable? Can they take away people's jobs? Their reputations? Their lives?

Garrison stood up to deliver his closing statement. Solemnly, he turned the spotlight on the committee: "There is more than Dr. Oppenheimer on trial in this room . . . The Government of the United States is here on trial also . . . It is behaving like some [massive, immovable] machine that will result in the destruction of great gifts . . . America must not devour her own children." Anticommunist hysteria had caused many Americans to lose sight of the democratic principles that had held the country together for over 175 years. How much longer could it last in such a dire condition?

After testifying in Robert's defense, I. I. Rabi strode out of the hearing room defiantly. He thought the whole thing was ridiculous, sad, and unnecessary. The army was aware that Robert had been friends with known communists before the Manhattan Project even began. They hired him anyway because they knew he was the best man for the job. He performed brilliantly, building what they asked him to build. Rabi lamented, "We have an A-bomb and a whole series of [them] . . . what more [did they] want, mermaids? This is just a tremendous achievement."

The hearing made it plain that the government wanted much more than mermaids. It wanted to keep building bigger and bigger bombs, both atomic and hydrogen, without people like Robert expressing their doubts, fears, or disagreements. Rabi understood all along that Robert was too smart a person, too honest, too empathetic, and too committed to the craft of physics to stop asking the difficult questions about where his life's work would lead. For that, his career was on the line. And so was the future of the human race.

"A BLACK MARK ON THE ESCUTCHEON OF OUR COUNTRY"

*Escutcheon (noun): a shield or emblem bearing a coat
of arms* —Oxford English Dictionary

On May 23, the Gray Board returned its formal verdict. By a vote of
two to one, they ruled that Robert was loyal to his country. But they
also decided he was too risky to trust with America's most sensitive information. Gray and Morgan therefore recommended that
the commission revoke his security clearance, freezing him out of
any future work with the government and eliminating his ability to
influence future decisions.

They didn't accuse him of breaking any rules or laws, because he
hadn't. Instead, they condemned him for associating with people
they didn't trust, including his brother and wife, who were forever
tarred for once being members of the Communist Party. In their
opinion, Gray and Morgan wrote, "Loyalty to one's friends is one of
the noblest of qualities. Being loyal to one's friends above reasonable
obligations to the country . . . however, is not clearly consistent with
the interests of security." For Robert, it had never been an "either-or."
He was just as fiercely loyal to those he loved as he was to his country.
He loved Hoke like a brother but wouldn't budge when Hoke told
him that Eltenton was trying to get information for the Soviets. He
knew it would be treason and told him so immediately.

Gray and Morgan went on. They declared that Robert should
lose his clearance because he had spoken out so strongly against
the building of the hydrogen bomb. To them, disagreement with

government decisions meant that he might *become* disloyal in the future. What if his frustrations boiled over as the government kept building bigger and bigger bombs, or made other decisions he didn't agree with? Would he spill the beans to the Soviet Union or other countries about those plans?

Robert believed he had a duty as a scientist and as a human being to warn the rest of the world about the dangers posed by the weapons he helped birth. His teachers had taught him at the Ethical Culture School so many years ago that it was his duty to speak out against injustices—and speak up for those who couldn't.

To Robert, the hydrogen bomb was an injustice to the entire human race, so he spoke for everyone on Earth and those who came after them. He understood there was no turning back. How many more countries would build nuclear weapons? How many would they build? How powerful might they become? The United States government had already dropped two atomic bombs on cities, killing at least two hundred thousand people. What might happen when enemy countries, armed with hydrogen bombs, pointed them at each other? Could the leaders of either country be trusted not to use them amid the fog and heat of war? It was vitally important to have people like Robert asking these crucial questions of those in power when the future of the human race was at stake. What did it say about American democracy that someone like him was being pushed out of government for doing that? What might happen if all those like him were pushed out? Who would be left to stop the madness?

Evans didn't agree with Gray and Morgan. He didn't believe that any witness had presented new evidence to prove that Robert couldn't be trusted. The army knew about Robert's political views and that he had been associated with members of the Communist Party when they hired him to build the bomb.

"Yet they cleared him," Evans wrote in his passionate dissent. "They took a chance because of his special talents and he continued to do a good job. Now when the job is done, we are asked to investigate him [again]. He did his job in a thorough and painstaking manner. There is not the slightest vestige of information before this Board that would indicate that Dr. Oppenheimer is not a loyal citizen of his country. He hates Russia. He had communistic friends, it is true. He still has some. However, the evidence indicates that he has fewer of them than he had in 1947. He is not as naïve as he was then. He has more judgment; no one on the Board doubts his loyalty—even the witnesses adverse to him admit that—and he is certainly less a security risk than he was in 1947, when he was cleared. To deny him clearance now for what he was cleared for in 1947 . . . seems hardly the procedure to be adopted in a free country . . . *I personally think that our failure to clear Dr. Oppenheimer will be a black mark on the escutcheon of our country*" *(emphasis added).*

CHAPTER FORTY

"It is sad beyond words. They are so wrong, so terribly wrong."

The government revoked Robert's security clearance on June 29, 1954, one day before it was set to expire. The decision sent shock waves across the country. Millions of Americans opened their mailboxes to front-page news that J. Robert Oppenheimer, the physicist whom so many had held in such high regard, had been tossed out of the government on his ear because of his association with known communists. After reading the verdict, David Lilienthal wrote in his diary, "It is sad beyond words. They are so wrong, so terribly wrong."

The consequences for American society were enormous. Just one scientist had been banished. But all scientists were now on notice that if they challenged the government in the future, there could be serious consequences for them too.

Outraged and shocked by the decision, 282 Los Alamos scientists wrote a letter to Strauss defending Robert. Across the country, more than eleven hundred scientists and academics signed another petition protesting the decision. Einstein, disgusted, quipped that henceforth the AEC should be known as the "Atomic Extermination Conspiracy." A television broadcaster declared, "[Oppenheimer] will no longer have access to secrets in government files, and government, presumably, will no longer have access to secrets that may be born in Oppenheimer's brain."

After his long, obsessive campaign to tear Robert down, Strauss sighed with relief and satisfaction. But just beneath the surface, he worried. How would the American public receive the news? Was it possible they might sympathize with Robert? By the time the story broke, Joe McCarthy's anti-communist witch hunt that had consumed and divided the nation for four years was deflating like a popped balloon. McCarthy had made the mistake of picking a fight with the U.S. Army, accusing it of allowing communists to infiltrate the Signal Corps. The army shot back that McCarthy had tried to get them to appoint one of his lawyer's friends to a job without having to follow the same rules as other applicants.

The Senate held a three-month hearing. Networks televised it across the country. While millions of Americans watched in amazement, McCarthy tried to bully the army's lawyer, Joseph Welch, by accusing someone he knew of being connected to a communist organization. Welch wasn't going to let the senator get away with that. He stood up to McCarthy and declared in front of the whole country: "Until this moment, Senator, I think I never really gauged your cruelty or your recklessness . . . You have done enough. Have you no sense of decency, sir? At long last, have you no sense of decency?" With those words, a strong-willed lawyer and the revolutionary new medium of television brought a demagogue to his knees. Almost overnight, McCarthy lost his grip on the American mind. The Senate removed him from his leadership roles and voted to censure him. His party turned its back on him. The press, which had been enthralled by his every word just weeks earlier, ignored him and refused to print what he said.[27]

Feeling the political sands shifting fast beneath his feet, Strauss scurried to have the Government Printing Office publish all three thousand typewritten pages of the hearing. Publishing it violated the Gray Board's promise to the witnesses that their testimony would remain confidential. But Strauss didn't care. He asked commission staff to highlight the parts that made Robert look the worst and send them to friendly reporters who he knew would print them. Salivating for a juicy scoop, some of them obliged. *The American Mercury*, a radically conservative magazine owned by machine-gun salesman and committed antisemite Russell Maguire, hailed the downfall of this "longtime glamour-boy of the atomic scientists" and smeared Robert's supporters as men who would "coddle potential traitors."

Even though McCarthy had nothing to do with Robert's hearing, Robert had become the McCarthy era's most famous victim. Strauss, with the help of his like-minded friends, had succeeded in destroying the reputation of America's most celebrated physicist. But by doing so, he set in motion a chain of events that would destroy his own reputation—and his own career.

Strauss thought that the transcript would only make Robert look worse. But as more people read it, they realized the hearing had been an unfair inquisition—a terrible smear campaign against a man who had always been faithful to his country, and a stain on American democracy. Like McCarthy before him, Strauss had become too cocky. Both men had convinced themselves that nothing could touch them. Like Icarus, they felt as though they couldn't be conquered. But they drifted too close to the sun.

In 1959, Eisenhower nominated Strauss to be his commerce secretary. But the senate had to confirm him first. The battle was as close as it was bitter. It came down to just a few votes. John F. Kennedy, the Democratic senator from Massachusetts, was on the fence. He agonized over which way he would go. It would be politically risky to vote against the wishes of such a popular president. One of Robert's defenders, McGeorge Bundy, tried to convince him that voting against Strauss was the right thing to do. Kennedy protested, "It would require an extreme case to vote against the president." Bundy shot back, "Well, this is an extreme case." He reminded Kennedy how terrible Strauss had behaved during Robert's security hearing. Finally convinced, JFK switched his vote and Strauss lost the confirmation. At long last, the McCarthy era was over.

"IT ACHIEVED WHAT HIS OPPONENTS WANTED TO ACHIEVE; IT DESTROYED HIM."

After the hearing, Robert and Kitty were flooded with letters from admirers, abusive letters from cranks, and anguished letters from close friends. Robert spent a lot of time on the phone with friends and family who were trying to make sense of what had happened. On one call with Frank, he tried to make light of the situation as best he could. Robert told him breezily that he had known "all the time the way the affair would turn out." But then the bitterness would well up in him, and he would make comments like "They paid more to tap my phone than they paid me to run the Los Alamos Project."

The more he tried to put the hearing behind him, the more heavily it weighed on his spirit. Devastated for his friend, Rabi reflected, "I think to a certain extent [the hearing] actually almost killed him, spiritually, yes. It achieved what his opponents wanted to achieve; it destroyed him." The writer John Mason Brown told Robert that his ordeal was like a "dry crucifixion." A thin smile crept across Robert's face: "You know, it wasn't so very dry. I can still feel the warm blood on my hands."

Some of Robert's closest friends thought he began to look a lot older after the hearing. "One day he would indeed look drawn and haggard," said Harold Cherniss. "Another day he was as robust and as beautiful as ever." Always concerned about Robert's emotional well-being, Francis Fergusson was startled by his old friend's appearance. His short-cropped, speckled-gray hair had turned silver white. He had just turned fifty. But now, for the first time in his life, he looked older than his age. "He was like a wounded animal," Francis recalled. "He retreated. And returned to a simpler way of life." Hans Bethe noticed that "much of

his previous spirit and liveliness had left him." Bob Serber lamented that he was "a sad man and his spirit was broken."

The hearing also took a toll on Robert's family. Although Kitty had defended Robert so expertly in the witness chair, her friends noticed how upset she was when they visited her or talked to her on the phone. Nine-year-

J. Robert Oppenheimer, profile view, late 1950s

old Toni seemed to take it all in stride. But Peter, now thirteen, had "a very difficult time in school during Robert's ordeal," according to Harold Cherniss. One day he came home and told Kitty that a classmate had said, "Your father is a communist." A sensitive child, Peter became more withdrawn. One day early that summer, after watching McCarthy's senate hearing on television, Peter went upstairs and wrote on the blackboard mounted in his bedroom: "The American Government is unfair to Accuse Certain People that I know of being unfair to them. Since this [is] true, I think that Certain People, and may I say, only Certain People in the U.S. government, should go to HELL. Yours truly, Certain People."

Just as he had suffered in the camp icehouse so many years ago in stoic silence, Robert refused to protest the commission's verdict. He often passed it off as an absurd accident—something that *happened to him* rather than *was done to him*. "I think of this as a major accident," he told a reporter, "much like a train wreck or the collapse of a building." It was like an out-of-body experience—something he had watched from afar, that had happened to someone else. Such passive reactions left him without the energy and anger that a different kind of man might have used to fight back.

For nearly a decade, Robert had been a household name in America. Now he was suddenly gone—still alive, but disappeared. Robert Coughlan wrote in *Life* magazine, "After the security hearings of 1954, the public character ceased to exist . . . He had been one of the most famous men in the world, one of the most admired, quoted, photographed, consulted, glorified, well-nigh deified as the fabulous and fascinating archetype of a brand new kind of hero, the hero of science and intellect, originator and living symbol of the new atomic age. Then, suddenly, all the glory was gone and he was gone, too . . ."

Since the turn of the twentieth century, Americans had looked to scientists as prophets who held the keys to a brighter, more prosperous, more peaceful future. Not only were they experts in their fields, but some like Robert had become public philosophers. They were lenses into the soul of the nation. They shared the consequences of the technologies they discovered with their fellow citizens, and reflected on how they might impact future generations.

But after the government went after Robert, those discussions gradually came to an end. Scientists could no longer disagree with government decisions if they wanted to keep their jobs.

And as the "Cold War" with the Soviet Union heated up, the government prioritized projects for war over other scientific pursuits. In a few short years, scientists had become mere tools of an ever-expanding American military-industrial complex.

CHAPTER FORTY-ONE

"Operation Oppenheimer"

Robert may have been gone from the public spotlight, but he was able to keep his job at the Institute for Advanced Study. In July 1954, Strauss told the FBI that eight of the institute's thirteen trustees would vote to fire him. But, as the board's chair, Strauss delayed the vote until fall so it wouldn't look like he was throwing salt on Robert's wounds. That was a mistake. The delay gave institute faculty time to write an open letter supporting Robert. Every member signed it. Their bold show of support for Robert forced Strauss to back off. The board eventually voted to keep Robert as the institute's director.

After such a terrible ordeal, Robert thought a long vacation might be good for the whole family. He and Kitty planned a trip to the

Robert, Kitty, Peter, and Toni Oppenheimer at the beach in St. John, Virgin Islands

Virgin Islands in the Caribbean. Kitty made the arrangements. Robert warned her not to send a wire to St. Croix to make reservations because he thought the FBI was still spying on him. Kitty ignored his advice. She sent the cable anyway, reserving a seventy-two-foot two-masted sailboat.

Robert was right. The FBI *was* still spying on him. After the hearing, Strauss convinced them to reinstall illegal taps on his phone. At the same time, the bureau assigned six agents to follow him and monitor his activities from 7:00 a.m. to midnight every day. They thought he might be leaving the country. Both Strauss and Hoover feared he might make a run for it. Strauss's paranoia fueled visions of a submarine surfacing in the warm Caribbean waters and spiriting Robert off to the Soviet Union. Would the Russians kidnap him forcibly? Or would he go willingly?

Robert laughed out loud when he read in *Newsweek* that "key security officials" were worried that communists might try to get him to Europe, then convince him or coerce him to defect to the Soviet Union. They called it "Operation Oppenheimer." "According to the plan," an FBI report read, "Oppenheimer will first travel to England, from England he will travel to France, and while in France he will vanish into Soviet hands."

Herb Marks told Robert that he should write a letter to J. Edgar Hoover to make sure the FBI knew all about his vacation plans and tell them not to worry—everything would be okay. Robert obliged, writing Hoover that he planned to spend three or four weeks sailing in the Virgin Islands. Then they took off for St. John. The FBI followed.

When they got to the island, they hopped in a Jeep taxi, which drove them to an isolated guest house. There were no phones, no electricity, and rooms for no more than a dozen guests. They had sought a solitary refuge and had come to the right place. "It was isolated enough so that people couldn't get at them. They were being careful about who they even talked to . . . Kitty was very protective. She was like a tigress when anybody approached him, because he was willing to talk." For the next five weeks, the Oppenheimers sailed the *Comanche* through the waters around St. John and the neighboring British Virgin Islands.

The FBI tried its hardest to keep Robert under surveillance but found it impossible. So when he finally flew back to New York, FBI agents waited to intercept him at the airport. They accosted him as he and his family stepped off the plane and requested that he go with them to a private room in the airport terminal. Robert agreed but insisted Kitty go with him. When they got in the room, the agents bluntly asked if Soviet agents had approached him in the Virgin Islands and asked him to defect while there. Robert replied that the Russians "were damn fools," but he didn't think they "were foolish enough to approach him with such an offer." He reassured the agents that he would tell them if something like that ever happened in the future.

After the airport interrogation, Robert and his family drove home to Princeton. Agents followed them the whole way. The next day the FBI placed yet another wiretap on their home phone. Incredibly, the bureau then sent another team of agents back down to St. John in March 1955—more than six months after Robert had left—to interview the locals. They couldn't resist. They just had to know who Robert talked to while he was on vacation.

BOMB COUNT
1955

United States: 2,422

Soviet Union: 200

United Kingdom: 10

Estimated Total Destructive Capability:
208,646 "Hiroshimas"

ROBERT WAS DEEPLY TOUCHED

Robert remained a political outcast until January 20, 1961, when President John F. Kennedy took office. Kennedy wasn't about to reinstate his security clearance and bring him back into government, but liberal Democrats now in power thought of him as an honorable man martyred by political extremists like Strauss.

In spring 1963, Robert learned that Kennedy planned to give him the prestigious Enrico Fermi Prize, a $50,000 award and medal for public service. "Disgusting!" cried one senator when he heard the news. Another announced publicly that he would boycott the White House award ceremony. Strauss, of course, was outraged. Other hysterical staffers in the House of Representatives printed out and sent around a summary of the 1954 charges against Robert. On the other hand, veteran CBS broadcaster Eric Severeid described Robert as "the scientist who writes like a poet and speaks like a prophet"—and approvingly suggested that the award signaled Robert's return to the national stage.

On November 22, 1963, Robert was sitting in his office at Fuld Hall, working on his acceptance speech, when he heard knocking on the door to the outer office. It was Peter. He had just heard on his car radio that President Kennedy had been shot in Dallas. Robert looked away. At that moment, his secretary, Verna Hobson, dashed in, exclaiming, "My God, did you hear?" Robert looked at her and said, "Peter just told me." Others began to arrive. Robert turned to his twenty-two-year-old son and asked him if he'd like a drink. Peter nodded, and Robert walked over to Verna's large walk-in closet, where he knew some liquor was kept. But then Peter observed that his father just stood there, "his arm hanging down by his side, fourth finger repetitively rubbing his thumb, gazing downward toward the little collection of liquor bottles." Later, he told his son that "nothing since Roosevelt's death had felt to him like that afternoon."

On December 2, newly sworn-in president Lyndon Johnson went ahead with the Fermi Award ceremony, as scheduled. Standing next to Johnson's hulking figure in the Cabinet Room of the White House, Robert seemed almost tiny. He stood like a "figure of stone, gray, rigid, almost lifeless, tragic in his intensity." With Kitty, Peter, and Toni looking on, Johnson handed Robert a medal, a plaque, and a check for $50,000.

Robert approached the podium. He invoked the words of an earlier president, Thomas Jefferson, who "often wrote of

President Lyndon B. Johnson presents Robert the Enrico Fermi Prize, December 2, 1963.

the 'brotherly spirit of science' . . . We have not, I know, always given evidence of that brotherly spirit of science. This is not because we lack vital common or intersecting scientific interests. It is in part because, with countless other men and women, we are engaged in this great enterprise of our time, testing whether men can both preserve and enlarge life, liberty, and the pursuit of happiness and live without war as the great arbiter of history."

After the speech, JFK's grieving widow, Jacqueline B. Kennedy, sent word that she wanted to see Robert in her private quarters. He and Kitty went to meet her. She told Robert she wanted him to know just how much her late husband had wanted to give him this award. Robert was deeply touched.

BOMB COUNT
1962

United States: 25,540
Soviet Union: 3,346
United Kingdom: 211

Estimated Total Destructive Capability:
974,700 "Hiroshimas"

CHAPTER FORTY-TWO

"That's where he wanted to be."

In the fall of 1965, Robert visited his doctor for a physical checkup. It was not something he did very often, but he came home that day and announced that his doctor had given him a clean bill of health. "I am going to outlive every one of you," he said jokingly. But two months later, those around him noticed that his smoker's cough had gotten worse. That Christmas, he complained to a friend of a "terrible sore throat," and mused, "Maybe I'm smoking too much." Kitty thought he just had a bad cold. Finally, in February 1966, she took him to a doctor in New York. The diagnosis was clear and devastating. Kitty phoned Verna Hobson with the news: "Robert has cancer."

Four decades of heavy tobacco smoke had taken their toll on his throat. When Robert's friend Arthur Schlesinger Jr. heard the "dreadful news," he immediately wrote him, "I can only dimly imagine how hard these next months will be for you. You have faced more terrible things than most men in this terrible age, and you have provided all of us with an example of moral courage, purpose, and discipline."

Though he gave up cigarettes, Robert was still seen puffing on

Robert, pipe in hand, stands behind his desk at the Institute for Advanced Study, Princeton, NJ, 1956.

his pipe. In March, he began radiation therapy for the cancer at the Sloan-Kettering Institute in New York. He talked openly about his cancer with his friends. He told Francis Fergusson that he had a "faint hope that it could be stopped where it was." By late May, however, all could see that he was "wasting away."

On a beautiful spring day in 1966, David Lilienthal went by Robert's house and found Anne Marks, his old Los Alamos secretary, visiting. Robert's appearance shocked him. "For the first time, Robert himself is 'uncertain about the future,' as he says, so white and scared." Walking alone with Kitty in the garden, Lilienthal asked her how he was getting along. Kitty froze, biting her lip; uncharacteristically, she was at a loss for words. When Lilienthal bent down and gently kissed her cheek, she uttered a deep moan and began to cry. A moment later, she straightened up, wiped her tears away, and suggested they go back inside and join Anne and Robert. "I have never admired the strength of a woman more," Lilienthal noted in his diary that evening. "Robert is not only her husband, he is her past, the happy past and the tortured one."

Later that spring, Robert accepted an honorary degree at Princeton's graduation, where he was hailed as a "physicist and sailor, philosopher and horseman, linguist and cook, lover of fine wine and better poetry." But he appeared exhausted and spent; suffering from a pinched nerve, he couldn't walk without a cane and a leg brace.

Frail and battered by his cancer, Robert nevertheless seemed to grow in stature. Freeman Dyson observed that "his spirit grew strong as his bodily powers declined . . . He accepted his fate gracefully; he carried on with his job; he never complained; he became quite suddenly simple and no longer trying to impress anybody . . . he was simple, straightforward, and indomitably courageous."

Robert faced the prospect of death with resignation. His cancer had spread to his mouth. His once brilliant blue eyes now seemed bleary with pain. "The last mile for Robert Oppenheimer," Lilienthal wrote in his diary after visiting in October, "and it may be a very short one . . . Kitty had all she could do to suppress the tears."

In early December, Thomas B. Morgan—a *Look* magazine journalist—dropped by to interview Robert. Morgan found him gazing at the autumn woods and the pond outside his window. On the wall of his office there now hung an old photograph of Kitty jumping her horse gracefully over a fence. Morgan could see that he was dying. "He was very frail and no longer the lean, lank man who impressed you as a cowboy genius. There were deep lines in his face. His hair was hardly more than a white mist. And yet, he prevailed with that grace."

The conversation turned philosophical. Robert told Morgan that even though he had always thought about the ethical dimensions of his work, he was thinking about them more now. He was also thinking about his responsibilities to those he shared the earth with. Throughout his life, he had tried to act ethically and responsibly. But he hadn't always succeeded. He wasn't the greatest husband to Kitty. By his own admission, he wasn't the greatest father to Peter and Toni. He had even reported some of his students to the House Un-American Activities Committee. At times, he was stubborn, arrogant, callous, and disrespectful toward those who loved and respected him. He tried to warn those with more power than he to stop building the weapons that could destroy the world. But did he do enough to contain the fire he had lit?

Forty years earlier in Corsica, he had learned from reading Proust by flashlight that "indifference to the sufferings one causes . . . is the terrible and permanent form of cruelty." Far from being indifferent, Robert was acutely aware of the suffering he had caused others in his life—but he would not allow himself to surrender to guilt. He would accept responsibility; he had never tried to deny it. But since the security hearing, he no longer seemed to have the spark within to fight against the "cruelty" of indifference. In that sense, Rabi had been right: "They achieved their goal. They killed him."

On February 17, 1967, Francis went to visit his old friend whom he had hiked with over the Sangre de Cristos so many years before, whom he had comforted through the deepest depths of depression and consoled after the security hearing that devastated his reputation. Francis could see that his friend was pretty far gone. He could still walk, but he now weighed under a hundred pounds. The two men sat together in the dining room. But after a short time, Francis thought Robert looked so feeble that he ought to take his leave. "I walked him into his bedroom, and there I left him. And the next day I heard that he had died."

Robert died in his sleep at 10:40 p.m. on Saturday, February 18, 1967. He was only sixty-two years old. Two days later his remains were cremated. Newspapers at home and around the world published long, admiring obituaries. *The Times* of London described him as the quintessential "Renaissance man." David Lilienthal told *The New York Times*: "The world has lost a noble spirit—a genius who brought together poetry and science." In Moscow, the Soviet news agency Tass reported the death of an "outstanding American physicist." Senator J. William Fulbright gave a speech on the floor of the Senate, and said of Robert, "Let us remember not only what his special genius did for us; let us also remember what we did to him."

Kitty took Robert's ashes in an urn to Hawksnest Bay in St. John. Then, on a stormy afternoon, she, Toni, and two of her friends motored out toward the tiny island of Carval Rock. When they got to a point in between Carval Rock, Congo Cay, and Lovango Cay, they cut the motor. They were in seventy feet of water. No one spoke, and instead of scattering Robert's ashes into the sea, Kitty simply dropped the urn overboard. It didn't sink instantly, so they circled the boat around the bobbing urn and watched silently until it finally disappeared below the choppy sea. Kitty explained that she and Robert had discussed it, and "that's where he wanted to be."

BOMB COUNT
1967

United States: 31,255

Soviet Union: 8,400

United Kingdom: 355

France: 36

China: 25

Israel: 2

Estimated Total Destructive Capability:
1,203,840 "Hiroshimas"

EPILOGUE

Despite the menacing weather and bitter cold that chilled the Northeast, six hundred friends and colleagues—Nobel laureates, politicians, generals, scientists, poets, novelists, composers, and acquaintances from all walks of life—gathered to recall the life and mourn the death of J. Robert Oppenheimer. Kitty sat in the front row at Princeton University's Alexander Hall alongside Peter, now twenty-five, and Toni, twenty-two. Frank sat next to them.

Strains of Igor Stravinsky's *Requiem Canticles,* a work Robert had heard for the first time and admired in that very hall the previous autumn, filled the auditorium. And then Hans Bethe—who had known Robert for thirty years—gave the first of three eulogies. "[Robert] did more than any other man," Bethe said, "to make American theoretical physics great . . . He was a leader . . . But he was not domineering, he never dictated what should be done. He brought out the best in us . . ." Bethe and other veterans of Los Alamos knew that without Robert the bomb they had built in New Mexico would never have been finished in time for its use in the war.

Henry DeWolf Smyth, a physicist and Princeton neighbor, gave the second eulogy. In 1954, Smyth had witnessed Robert's security hearing and later had become the only one of five commissioners of the Atomic Energy Commission who voted to restore his security clearance. Smyth fully comprehended the travesty that had been committed: "Such a wrong can never be righted; such a blot on our history never erased . . . We regret that his great work for his country was repaid so shabbily . . ."

Finally, George Kennan stepped to the podium to deliver the third eulogy. Kennan, a longtime friend of Robert's and a colleague at the Institute for Advanced Study, ended up becoming the father of America's postwar containment policy against the Soviet Union. No man had influenced Kennan's thinking about the dangers of the nuclear age more than Robert. No man had been a better friend. Kennan said:

"On no one did there ever rest with greater cruelty the dilemmas evoked by the recent conquest by human beings of a power over nature out of all proportion to their moral strength. No one ever saw more clearly the dangers arising for humanity from this mounting disparity. This anxiety never shook his faith in the value of the search for truth in all its forms, scientific and humane. But there was no one who more passionately desired to be useful in averting the catastrophes to which the development of the weapons of mass destruction threatened to lead. It was the interests of mankind that he had in mind here; but it was as an American, and through the medium of this national community to which he belonged, that he saw his greatest possibilities for pursuing these aspirations.

"In the dark days of the early fifties, when troubles crowded in upon him from many sides and when he found himself harassed by his position at the center of controversy, I drew his attention to the fact that he would be welcome in a hundred academic centers abroad and asked him whether he had not thought of taking residence outside this country. His answer, given to me with tears in his eyes: 'Damn it, I happen to love this country.' "

On December 16, 2022, Secretary of Energy Jennifer Granholm signed an order vacating the Atomic Energy Commission's 1954 decision in the matter of J. Robert Oppenheimer. She wrote, "As time has passed, more evidence has come to light of the bias and unfairness of the process that Dr. Oppenheimer was subjected to while the evidence of his loyalty and love of country have only been further affirmed."[28]

At the height of the Cold War, nations on Earth possessed more than seventy thousand nuclear weapons. Since then, the number has dropped considerably to thirteen thousand. Nine countries now possess them. From 1945 to 2017, nuclear-armed nations conducted more than two thousand tests in the atmosphere, underwater, and underground. Some of those tests were much more powerful than the bombs dropped on Hiroshima and Nagasaki. They sickened and uprooted thousands of people around the world. Every person in the continental United States alive since 1951 has been exposed to fallout from nuclear testing. Despite outcry from those most deeply affected by the tests, there are only a few examples of nuclear-armed nations compensating them for detonating the most massive bombs ever made near their homes and communities.[29]

According to the Union of Concerned Scientists, "The warheads on just *one* US nuclear-armed submarine have seven times the destructive power of all the bombs dropped during World War II, including the two atomic bombs dropped on Japan. And the United States usually has ten of those submarines at sea. Moreover, nearly all the major nuclear powers—including the

The Secretary of Energy
Washington, DC 20585

December 16, 2022

SECRETARIAL ORDER

FROM: JENNIFER M. GRANHOLM

SUBJECT: VACATING 1954 ATOMIC ENERGY COMMISSION DECISION: *IN THE MATTER OF J. ROBERT OPPENHEIMER*

BACKGROUND

In June 1954 the Atomic Energy Commission (AEC) revoked Dr. J. Robert Oppenheimer's security clearance. Over the prior decade, Dr. Oppenheimer had served as Director of the Los Alamos National Laboratory and as Chairman of the General Advisory Committee to the AEC. In his years of public service, Dr. Oppenheimer had perhaps more access to information about U.S. nuclear weapons programs than any other individual in the government. And yet, in reaching its decision on his clearance, the AEC did not claim that Dr. Oppenheimer had ever divulged or mishandled classified information. Nor did it question his loyalty to the United States. Rather, the AEC based its decision on the conclusion that there were "fundamental defects" in Dr. Oppenheimer's character.

When informed by the AEC in December 1953 that his eligibility for access to restricted data had been conditionally suspended, Dr. Oppenheimer requested a hearing, no doubt trusting that a fair process would clear his name. Ultimately, the proceeding went through three layers of review within the AEC. First, pursuant to the AEC's security clearance regulations at the time, the AEC convened a three-member Personnel Security Board to adjudicate Dr. Oppenheimer's clearance. On May 27, 1954, by a 2-1 vote, the Personnel Security Board recommended to the General Manager of the AEC that Dr. Oppenheimer's clearance not be reinstated. The Personnel Security Board issued a report outlining the basis for its decision. The Personnel Security Board found "no evidence of disloyalty" and "much responsible and positive evidence of the loyalty and love of country of the individual concerned."[1] Nevertheless, the Personnel Security Board based its recommendation on its appraisal of Dr. Oppenheimer's past associations (which had already been examined when Dr. Oppenheimer's clearance was renewed in 1947) and on a finding that if Dr. Oppenheimer had not opposed the development of the hydrogen bomb, "the project would have been pursued with considerably more vigor, thus increasing the possibility of earlier success in this field."[2]

---

[1] Atomic Energy Commission, In the Matter of J. Robert Oppenheimer: Texts of Principal Documents and Letters of Personnel Security Board, General Manager, and Commissioners, May 27, 1954, through June 29, 1954, at 13 (1954).
[2] *Id.*

United States, Russia, and China—are now significantly increasing their nuclear arsenals in size, capability, or both. The growing new arms race is raising the risk of nuclear war."[30]

But with such peril comes renewed awareness—and hope—that never again will humans or any other species have to experience the unimaginable horrors of those in Hiroshima, Nagasaki, or other bomb-affected parts of the world. On December 10, 2024, the Japan Confederation of Atomic and Hydrogen Bomb Sufferers (Nihon Hidankyo) received the Nobel Peace Prize "for its efforts to achieve a world free of nuclear weapons and for demonstrating through witness testimony that nuclear weapons must never be used again." Their efforts inspire future generations to join them in their call.

BOMB COUNT
2024

Russia: 4,380

United States: 3,708

China: 500

France: 290

United Kingdom: 225

India: 170

Pakistan: 170

Israel: 90

North Korea: 50

**Estimated Total Destructive Capability:
300,000 "Hiroshimas"**

MY LONG RIDE WITH OPPIE

by Martin J. Sherwin

Robert Oppenheimer was an accomplished horseman, and so it was not entirely bizarre that in the summer of 1979 I sought to give new meaning to the scholarly concept of Sitzfleisch (sitting flesh) by starting my research for his biography on horseback. My adventure began at the Los Pinos Ranch, located ten miles above Cowles, New Mexico, from which in the summer of 1922, Oppie had first explored the beautiful Sangre de Cristo Mountains. I had not ridden for decades and, to say the least, the prospect of the long ride ahead—actually and metaphorically—was daunting. My destination, several hours by horseback from Los Pinos, over the ten-thousand-foot summit of Grass Mountain, was the "Oppenheimer ranch," Perro Caliente, the spare cabin on 154 acres of spectacular mountainside that Oppie had leased in the 1930s and purchased in 1947.

Bill McSweeney, the owner of Los Pinos, was our trail guide and local historian. Among other things, he told us (my wife and children were with me) about the tragic death—during a burglary of her Santa Fe home in 1961—of Oppie's good friend Katherine Chaves Page, the ranch's previous owner. Oppie had met Katherine during his first visit to New Mexico and his youthful infatuation with her was one of the strong inducements repeatedly pulling him back to this beautiful country. After purchasing his own ranch, Oppie rented several of Katherine's horses each summer, for himself, his younger brother Frank (and, after 1940, his wife, Kitty), and their stream of guests, mostly physicists who had never mounted anything more independent-minded than a bicycle.

My trip had two purposes. The first was to share in a small way the experience that Oppie had so often shared with his friends, the liberating joy of riding on horseback through this awesome wilderness. The second purpose was to talk with his son, Peter, who was living in the family cabin. As I helped him build a corral, we talked for over an hour about his family and his life. It was a memorable beginning.

A few months earlier, I had signed a contract with the publisher Alfred A. Knopf for a biography of Robert Oppenheimer—physicist, founder in the 1930s of America's leading school of theoretical physics, erstwhile political activist, "father of the atomic bomb," prominent government advisor, director of the Institute for Advanced Study, public intellectual, and the most prominent victim of the McCarthy era. The manuscript would be completed in four or five years, I assured my then editor, Angus Cameron, who is one of the dedicatees of this book.

During the next half dozen years I traveled across the country and abroad, propelled from introduction to introduction, conducting many more interviews with those who had known Oppenheimer than I had imagined possible. I visited scores of archives and libraries, gathered tens of thousands of letters, memoranda, and government documents—ten thousand pages from the FBI alone—and eventually came to understand that any study of Robert Oppenheimer must necessarily encompass far more than his own life. His personal story, with all its public aspects and ramifications, was more complicated, and shed vastly more light on the America of his day, than either Angus or I had anticipated. It is an indication of this complexity, this depth and wider resonance—of Oppenheimer's iconic standing—that since his death, his story has taken on a new life, as books, movies, plays, articles, and now an opera (*Dr. Atomic*), have etched his shadow ever more sharply on the pages of American and world history.

Twenty-five years after I started out on that ride to Perro Caliente, the writing of Oppenheimer's life has given me a new understanding of the complexities of biography. It has been sometimes an arduous journey but always an exhilarating one. Five years ago, soon after my good friend Kai Bird completed *The Color of Truth*, a joint biography of McGeorge and William Bundy, I invited him to join me. Oppenheimer was big enough for both of us and I knew my pace would be quicker with Kai as my partner. Together we have finished what turned out to be a very long ride.

abridged from the original essay

A NOTE FROM THE ADAPTER

In January 1992, I returned to school after a fairly uneventful winter break. Like many other ninth graders, I wasn't particularly excited about it. I went to a large public high school in the suburbs and, many days, struggled to pay attention and even stay awake as the day dragged on. To that point, I didn't quite get how the lessons my exasperated teachers were trying to teach me might help me once I graduated and entered the "real world." But that January day was different.

I walked into my social studies class and fixed my eyes on my teacher, who was smiling like he had won the lottery. That was strange because he hadn't ever really expressed much emotion before. One of my classmates noticed it too. He turned to me and said, "Wow, it looks like *someone's* really happy to be back!"

We sat down at our desks. Our teacher made his way to the front of the room. He surveyed his bleary-eyed students and asked coyly, "So, can anyone tell me how the world is different now from when we last saw each other?"

None of us raised our hands. He persisted, "C'mon, really? *Nobody* can tell me? This is really big!" Finally after realizing none of us were going to supply the answer, he straightened up, took a breath, and energetically declared, "The Soviet Union is history! You all may not realize it, but we're living through an historic time. The world will never be the same."

Our teacher, who was born during World War II and came of age during the Cold War, had never known a time when the United States and the Soviet Union weren't pitted against each other in an ideological battle, bolstered by the terrifying race to build more and more nuclear weapons that Oppenheimer warned against so vociferously.

Unlike us, our teacher remembered ducking under his desk at school during atomic bomb drills and enduring the fear of the 1962 Cuban Missile Crisis, when the United States and the Soviet Union found themselves one false move away from all-out nuclear war. I remember how animated he got when he talked about the McDonald's that had opened in the center of Moscow, and how he marveled at the young Russians who seemed to be embracing American-style democracy and culture. For a time, the future looked bright.

I walked out of class that day motivated to learn more about what my teacher had lived through. But what I learned disturbed me. It disturbed me to think how secretive world governments, particularly those that purported to be democracies, had been as they developed weapons and other technologies in the name of their citizens' collective security. It also disturbed me to realize that, though we often equate progress with positivity, the twentieth century into which I was born is often referred to as the bloodiest in human history.

Today, as was the case when Robert was a young physicist, global empires once again menace each other. War now engulfs Ukraine, Israel, and Palestine as world leaders engage in tough talk. More than thirty-five armed conflicts flare across Africa, and rising political tensions threaten the peace on all continents.[31] The specter of world war is more acute now than at any time since the end of the Cold War.

In an earlier time of turmoil, the United States enlisted Oppenheimer and many others to build the most powerful weapons ever known. The project to build them unfurled in secret, as did the heated debates about whether to build "super" versions—which ended up being made in massive numbers. It makes me wonder as tensions rise once again—are there technologies that governments and corporations are developing right now that might represent similar, or even greater, threats to the world?

I hope that if there are, there are also people working on those projects who will, like Oppenheimer tried to do, ask hard questions and speak up if they realize their work might end up doing more harm than good—without fearing for their jobs or their reputations. Perhaps world leaders will also heed Oppenheimer's call for "candor," especially when it comes to the conflicts that seem most difficult to solve, or problems so great they require the cooperation of the entire world. As Oppenheimer knew so well, secrecy breeds distrust, and distrust can lead to war. Is there another way?

My ninth-grade social studies teacher's name was Tom Hockstra. That day in 1992, he lit a spark that ignited my career as an historian. I express my gratitude to all the teachers and mentors I've had over the years who pushed me to ask "why," and who have given me the tools to hand down their knowledge to others. You all should be paid more! I wish our society prioritized your craft over building bombs.

Peter Kuznick, my teacher, mentor, and great friend: thank you for always believing in me—and in humanity's potential to heal. You are the most positive, encouraging person I've ever met. Without your guidance, encouragement, and so much more, I wouldn't be adapting this book.

As I wrote, I depended upon the guidance and goodwill of great people who helped sharpen the writing, answer sometimes complicated questions, and amass materials that greatly enriched the adaptation. Thank you to James TenCate and the J. Robert Oppenheimer Memorial Committee, Kaysie Kent, Alan Carr and John Moore at the Los Alamos National Lab, the staff of the Niels Bohr Library and Archives, Krista Ahlberg, Emma Martin, Stephen Campanella, Eric Rabin, Vincent Intondi, Alex Wellerstein, Alan Friedman, and Sage Friedman.

Susan Sherwin and Alex Sherwin, Martin J. Sherwin's wife and son: thank you for entrusting me to share with young readers the knowledge Marty amassed over twenty-five incredible years researching the life of J. Robert Oppenheimer. Marty was hugely influential on my career. As one of my most important mentors, he served on my dissertation committee, directly impacting my scholarship, my writing, and my teaching. Marty spent many hours making detailed comments about my arguments, meeting with me to talk through thorny historical questions, and advising me about ways to share my findings with others. Along the way, he acquainted me with the monumental book *American Prometheus*. I wish he was still here to see how his life and work continue to impact so many people. Thanks to both of you for your incredibly important feedback on the manuscript. The book is better for it.

Kai Bird, your encouragement knows no bounds! Thank you for committing to share your remarkable work with the next generation, and for putting your trust and faith in me to adapt it. Thank you also for always responding so quickly and substantially to so many of my emails asking for clarifications, interpretations, and perspectives. I deeply value that collaboration. Your passion for history and your mastery of the art of telling it inspire me and so many others to engage in the craft.

Jill Grinberg, you believed in this project from day one. I so appreciate you deftly helping me jump through the hoops of a complicated publication process and schedule. Your critical feedback on the manuscript helped make this a better and more consequential book. Thank you for always being so positive, encouraging, and realistic.

Rūta Rimas, it has been a real treat to go on this journey with you once more. It is hard to describe how great a feeling it is to work so creatively with an editor of your caliber and positive demeanor. Thank you for believing so deeply in this project, for putting so much of your time and energy into making it happen, for directing the whole process in such an organized way, and for infusing it with such positivity. I am a better writer because of you.

Lastly, to my wife, Rachel, and daughter, Evie: I couldn't have done this without your support. Actually, I don't know what I would do without you. You are the lights in my life. Thank you for putting up with me through those long days of writing, for helping me through the crunch, and for always encouraging me to be my best. I love you.

—Eric S. Singer, 2025

LIST OF HISTORICAL FIGURES, IN ORDER OF APPEARANCE

PART ONE

Julius Oppenheimer: Robert's father and one of the most knowledgeable "fabrics" men in New York City.

Ella Friedman Oppenheimer: Robert's mother and a good enough painter to have her own students and a private rooftop studio in a New York apartment building.

Frank Oppenheimer: American particle physicist and Robert's younger brother.

Benjamin Oppenheimer: Robert's grandfather who lived in Germany. He helped spark his grandson's interest in science by gifting him with a rock collection.

Felix Adler: Founder of the Ethical Culture School, which Robert attended. He encouraged his students to use their talents to create a better world.

Herbert Winslow Smith: Robert's homeroom teacher at the Ethical Culture School, who later became his mentor and friend. Their relationship lasted many years.

Augustus Klock: Robert's first physics teacher at the Ethical Culture School. On many days after school, Klock took Robert on hunts for minerals throughout New York City.

John Lovejoy Elliott: Robert's ethical studies teacher at the Ethical Culture School, who prompted Robert and his classmates to think about how their actions impacted the world around them.

Francis Fergusson: Robert's great friend from the Ethical Culture School who he would turn to in times of need throughout his life.

Paul Horgan: Robert's friend from Albuquerque who also accompanied him on his earlier New Mexico excursions. He would go on to become an American historian and win two Pulitzer Prizes.

Katherine Chaves Page: Katherine ran the Los Pinos ranch where Robert stayed on his early trips to New Mexico. She taught Robert how to ride a horse, motivating him to take risks and become more self-confident.

Frederick Bernheim: Robert's roommate and good friend at Harvard. Along with others, they often took weekend trips together to Cape Ann. Fred went on to become a biochemist and helped found Duke University's medical school.

William Clouser Boyd: Another of Robert's Harvard friends. The two met in chemistry class and had a lot of common interests, including poetry. Robert always called him "Clowser," purposely misspelling his middle name.

Percy Bridgman: Robert's physics tutor at Harvard who went on to win the 1946 Nobel Prize in Physics. He was a wonderful teacher, always thoughtful and willing to think outside the box.

Niels Bohr: The world-famous Danish physicist who visited Harvard at the time Robert attended. Robert looked up to Bohr as a role model and came to speak of him as "his god."

Ernest Rutherford: Eminent physicist and "father of nuclear physics" who developed the first model of the nuclear atom in 1911. Robert applied to study with him at Cambridge's Cavendish Laboratory, but was turned down.

P. M. S. Blackett: Robert's tutor at Cavendish Laboratory. Robert liked Blackett, but their relationship caused him great anxiety. Consumed by feelings of inadequacy and jealousy, Robert poisoned an apple with lab chemicals and put it on Blackett's desk. Luckily, Blackett didn't eat it.

Inez Pollak: One of Robert's classmates at the Ethical Culture School. Robert's parents brought her along when they went to visit him in Cambridge, in hopes that she might help distract him from his depression. They dated for a short while, but it didn't work out.

Albert Einstein: German-born theoretical physicist known for developing the theory of relativity. Widely considered to be the most influential physicist of the twentieth century.

Max Born: Director of University of Göttingen, Born coined the term "quantum mechanics." Born invited Robert to study with him in Göttingen when he finished his studies at Cambridge. The two became close friends and colleagues.

James Franck: One of Robert's professors at Göttingen who won the Nobel Prize for his work on the impact electrons had on atoms. When the Nazis demanded he fire other Jews below him, he refused, quit his job in protest, and fled to the United States.

Ernest Lawrence: Experimental physicist who founded Berkeley's Radiation Laboratory, or "Rad Lab" for short. He built a machine that could accelerate protons back and forth, called an "accelerator," which caused a sensation across the scientific world.

Adolf Hitler: Führer of Germany from 1933 until 1945, obsessed with racial supremacy and territorial expansion. In 1939, he launched an invasion of Poland, starting World War II, then deported to concentration camps and systemically murdered six million Jews and millions of others across Europe.

Bob Serber: Physicist and Oppenheimer's protégé who lived in the garage of Oppenheimer's Berkeley home and who worked under Hans Bethe in the Manhattan Project's theoretical division at Los Alamos.

Mary Ellen and John Washburn: Berkeley couple who cared deeply about the plight of California's workers and believed their bosses had too much power. Their house was a hive of activity day and night, with a who's who of Berkeley professors, students, and others always coming and going.

Franklin Delano Roosevelt (FDR): Thirty-second president of the United States. The only president to be elected four times, he led the country during the Great Depression and World War II. He died in office on April 12, 1945.

Haakon "Hoke" Chevalier: Professor of French literature at Berkeley. Robert met him while forming a union of Berkeley faculty. His friends called him "Hoke." Hoke referred to Robert as his "most intimate friend."

Jean Tatlock: Robert's "truest love," psychiatrist and Communist Party member whose activism helped awaken Robert's sense of social responsibility.

Katherine "Kitty" Oppenheimer: German American botanist, Robert's wife and mother of their two children

Joe Dallet: American communist and volunteer in the Spanish Civil War. He was Kitty's second husband before she married Robert.

Jackie Oppenheimer: Wife of Frank Oppenheimer, civil rights activist, member of the Young Communist League, and later a member of the Communist Party of the United States of America (CPUSA).

Peter Oppenheimer: Son of Robert and Kitty Oppenheimer, who moved with his parents to Los Alamos, then to Princeton, New Jersey, where his father directed the Institute for Advanced Study.

Leo Szilard: Hungarian physicist who imagined the nuclear chain reaction in 1933.

Vannevar Bush: American engineer and science administrator who headed the Office of Scientific Research and Development (OSRD) during World War II.

James Conant: Chemist and Harvard University's twenty-third president

Henry Stimson: United States secretary of war during World War II.

George C. Marshall: American army general and chief of staff of the U.S. Army during World War II. Later he served as secretary of state (1949) and secretary of defense (1950 to 1951). His plan for European recovery became known as the Marshall Plan.

Henry A. Wallace: United States secretary of agriculture from 1933 to 1940, then vice president of the United States under FDR from 1941 to 1945.

J. Edgar Hoover: Director of the Federal Bureau of Investigation (FBI) from 1924 until 1972. He ordered his agents to gather intelligence on Oppenheimer and sent their findings to the White House.

Hans Bethe: German American physicist who fled Europe in 1935 and became the head of the Manhattan Project's theoretical division at Los Alamos.

Edward Teller: Hungarian-born physicist who urged President Harry Truman to develop the hydrogen bomb.

Felix Bloch: Swiss-born American physicist who won the Nobel Prize in 1952 for his work on nuclear magnetic resonance, which made magnetic resonance imaging (MRI) possible.

Emil Konopinski: American theoretical physicist and one of Oppenheimer's "luminaries" who went on to work on the Manhattan Project.

Arthur Holly Compton: University of Chicago physics professor and Nobel laureate who chaired the OSRD's S-1 Uranium Section from 1941 to 1942.

George C. Eltenton: British chemical engineer and Shell Oil Company employee who attempted to get information about the Manhattan Project from Oppenheimer and share it with the Soviet Union.

Joseph Stalin: Premier of the Soviet Union from 1922 to 1953, who ruled the country with an iron fist and transformed it into a global superpower.

Leon Trotsky: Marxist revolutionary and leader of Russia's 1917 October Revolution. He believed that a global communist revolution was possible.

George Placzek: Czech physicist who left Europe with Niels Bohr. He was the only Czech citizen to work on the Manhattan Project.

Victor Weisskopf: Austrian American theoretical physicist whom Oppenheimer recruited to join him at Los Alamos.

PART TWO

Leslie R. Groves: United States Army general in charge of the Manhattan Project, who chose Oppenheimer to direct the Los Alamos laboratory.

I. I. Rabi: Physicist and Nobel laureate known for his work on the magnetic properties of crystals.

Toni Oppenheimer: Daughter of Robert and Kitty Oppenheimer.

Robert Wilson: American physicist, sculptor, and architect whom Oppenheimer recruited to lead the cyclotron group at Los Alamos. He was the youngest group leader at the lab.

Colonel Boris Pash: United States military intelligence officer, chief of West Coast counter-intelligence, who investigated security breaches at the Manhattan Project's Berkeley Radiation Laboratory.

Lieutenant Colonel John Lansdale: United States Army colonel and military intelligence officer who served as security aide to General Groves.

Joseph Rotblat: Polish physicist who became the only scientist to resign from the Manhattan Project for moral reasons.

Harry Truman: Vice president of the United States under FDR from 1944 to 1945, who assumed the presidency upon FDR's death.

James F. Byrnes: Democratic party politician from South Carolina who became secretary of state under President Harry Truman.

Winston Churchill: Prime minister of the United Kingdom from 1940 to 1945, then again from 1951 to 1955, who, together with FDR and Joseph Stalin, shaped Allied strategy during World War II.

Jack Hubbard: American meteorologist, considered one of the best in the world. He was tasked with predicting the weather for the Trinity test.

Richard Feynman: American theoretical physicist and Nobel laureate who became the youngest group leader in the Manhattan Project's theoretical division. There, he came up with the formula to predict how much energy nuclear bombs might release.

Joseph O. Hirschfelder: Theoretical chemist and physicist who led a theoretical physics and ordnance group at Los Alamos, and served as chief phenomenologist at the Bikini atomic bomb tests.

Barbara Kent: Attended Karma Deane's dance camp at age twelve in Ruidoso, New Mexico, where she and her bunkmates were exposed to radioactive fallout from the nearby Trinity atomic bomb test.

Henry Herrera: At age eleven, Henry and his father witnessed the bright light and loud boom of the Trinity atomic bomb test. Radioactive fallout contaminated his home. He later contracted cancer and lost many of his friends and family to the disease.

Harold Cherniss: Oppenheimer's friend from Berkeley who became the country's leading scholar on Plato and Aristotle.

John J. McCloy: Former American diplomat and chairman of Chase National Bank who came to Oppenheimer's defense at his Atomic Energy Commission security hearing.

Dean Acheson: United States under secretary of state from 1945 to 1947, secretary of state and key architect of Cold War foreign policy from 1949 to 1953.

David Lilienthal: First chairman of the United States Atomic Energy Commission.

Bernard Baruch: The Wall Street financier, staunch capitalist, and defender of American power who pushed President Truman to keep atomic energy developments secret from the Soviet Union.

Lewis Strauss: United States Navy officer and Atomic Energy Commission chairman who set out to destroy Oppenheimer's career.

PART THREE

Dwight D. "Ike" Eisenhower: Supreme commander of Allied forces in Europe who later became the thirty-fourth president of the United States, in office from 1953 to 1961

D. M. Ladd: FBI agent and aide to J. Edgar Hoover.

Herbert Marks: Atomic Energy Commission lawyer and Robert's friend. Marks advised Oppenheimer prior to his AEC security hearing.

William Liscum Borden: Legislative secretary to Senator Brien McMahon who later fixated on the idea that Oppenheimer was a Soviet spy and worked with Lewis Strauss to tar his reputation.

Joseph McCarthy: United States senator from Wisconsin who launched a crusade to purge suspected communists and others he deemed "disloyal" from government.

Admiral William "Deke" Parsons: United States Navy officer, leader of the Manhattan Project's ordnance division, and friend of Oppenheimer who died before he could defend him.

Joseph Volpe: Lawyer and friend of Oppenheimer.

PART FOUR

Lloyd K. Garrison: Lawyer and great-grandson of abolitionist William Lloyd Garrison who defended Oppenheimer at his Atomic Energy Commission security hearing.

Roger Robb: Aggressive trial lawyer who prosecuted Oppenheimer at his Atomic Energy Commission security hearing.

Gordon Gray: Democratic politician and president of the University of North Carolina. Lewis Strauss appointed him to chair the Atomic Energy Commission's hearing board that rendered judgment on Oppenheimer's security clearance.

Thomas Morgan: Conservative Democrat and chairman of the Sperry Corporation who served as one of three judges at Oppenheimer's Atomic Energy Commission security hearing.

Ward Evans: Conservative Republican and former chemistry professor who served as one of three judges at Oppenheimer's Atomic Energy Commission security hearing.

John F. Kennedy: Democratic senator from Massachusetts and youngest person ever elected to become president of the United States. Assassinated three years into his term as he rode in a motorcade through Dallas, Texas.

McGeorge Bundy: Intelligence officer during World War II who later became a national security advisor to Presidents Kennedy and Johnson. He helped convince Kennedy to vote against confirming Lewis Strauss as secretary of commerce in 1959.

Jacqueline B. Kennedy: Wife of John F. Kennedy and first lady of the United States during his time in office.

NOTES

EPIGRAPH

1. *Oppenheimer*, directed by Christopher Nolan (Universal Pictures, 2023), 3 hours, imdb.com/title/tt15398776.

PROLOGUE

2. John Hersey, "Hiroshima," *The New Yorker*, August 23, 1946, accessed May 23, 2024, newyorker.com/magazine/1946/08/31/hiroshima.

3. Jim Clash, "Nagasaki A-Bomb Survivor Recounts His Horrific Experiences 73 Years After the Fact," *Forbes*, August 14, 2018, forbes.com/sites/jimclash/2018/08/14/nagasaki-a-bomb-survivor-recounts-his-horrific-experiences-73-years-after-the-fact; "Nagasaki Bomb Horrors 73 Years Later—As Told by Survivor Hiroyasu Tagawa (Part 2)," *Forbes*, August 15, 2018, forbes.com/sites/jimclash/2018/08/15/nagasaki-bomb-horrors-73-years-later-as-told-by-survivor-hiroyasu-tagawa-part-2; "Nagasaki Survivor Recalls Horrors of 1945 WWII A-Bomb Attack (Part 3)," *Forbes*, August 15, 2018, forbes.com/sites/jimclash/2018/08/15/nagasaki-survivor-recalls-horrors-of-1945-wwii-a-bomb-attack.

CHAPTER FOUR

4. Physicist Eric Rabin, email exchange with adapter, January 11, 2024.

CHAPTER NINE

5. Victor G. Devinatz, "Communist Party of the United States of America," *Encyclopedia Britannica*, last updated April 22, 2024, accessed May 23, 2024, britannica.com/topic/Communist-Party-of-the-United-States-of-America.

6. Karl Marx and Friedrich Engels, "Manifesto of the Communist Party," Marxists Internet Archive, accessed May 23, 2024, marxists.org/archive/marx/works/1848/communist-manifesto/index.htm.

7. Dorothy Ray Healey and Maurice Isserman, *California Red: A Life in the American Communist Party* (Urbana: University of Illinois Press, 1993), 40, 59–61, 73.

CHAPTER TWELVE

8. Mark Selden, "Japanese and American War Atrocities, Historical Memory and Reconciliation: World War II to Today," *Asia-Pacific Journal: Japan Focus* 06, no. 4 (April 2008), accessed August 13, 2024, apjjf.org/mark-selden/2724 /article.

9. Jeffrey Hackler, "Japan's Motives for Bombing Pearl Harbor, 1941," *Education About Asia* 06, no. 1 (Spring 2001): 54–58, accessed May 23, 2024, asianstudies.org/publications/eaa/archives/japans-motives-for-bombing -pearl-harbor-1941.

10. "Pearl Harbor attack," *Encyclopedia Britannica*, last updated May 17, 2024, accessed August 13, 2024, britannica.com/event/Pearl-Harbor-attack.

CHAPTER FOURTEEN

11. "Great Purge," *Encyclopedia Britannica*, last updated May 9, 2024, accessed August 13, 2024, britannica.com/event/Great-Purge; Ronald Francis Hingley, "Lenin's successor," *Encyclopedia Britannica*, last updated July 25, 2024, accessed May 23, 2024, britannica.com/biography/Joseph-Stalin /Lenins-successor; Noah Tesch, "The Assassination of Leon Trotsky," *Encyclopedia Britannica*, accessed May 23, 2024, britannica.com/story /the-assassination-of-leon-trotsky.

CHAPTER SIXTEEN

12. Sharon Snyder, "December 1942 War Department Letter Spelled the End for Los Alamos Ranch School," *Los Alamos Daily Post*, January 26, 2019, accessed August 13, 2024, ladailypost.com/december-1942-war-department -letter-spelled-the-end-for-los-alamos-ranch-school.

13. Judith Machen, Ellen D. McGehee, and Dorothy Hoard, *Homesteading on the Pajarito Plateau, 1887–1942* (Los Alamos: Los Alamos National Laboratory: 2012).

14. "Hispanos in Los Alamos," Atomic Heritage Foundation, June 28, 2017, accessed May 23, 2024, ahf.nuclearmuseum.org/ahf/history/hispanos -los-alamos.

CHAPTER NINETEEN

15. "German-Soviet Nonaggression Pact," *Encyclopedia Britannica*, last updated May 31, 2024, accessed May 23, 2024, britannica.com/event/German-Soviet -Nonaggression-Pact.

16. Franklin D. Roosevelt, "Address to the Delegates of the American Youth Congress. Washington, D.C." (speech, Washington, DC, February 10, 1940), UCSB American Presidency Project, accessed May 23, 2024, presidency.ucsb.edu/documents/address-the-delegates-the-american -youth-congress-washington-dc.

17. "U.S.-Soviet Alliance, 1941-1945," U.S. Department of State Archive, accessed May 24, 2024, 2001-2009.state.gov/r/pa/ho/time/wwii/104430.htm.

18. "D. Day and the Normandy Campaign," The National World War II Museum, accessed October 28, 2024, https://www.nationalww2museum.org/war/ topics/d-day-and-normandy-campaign#:~:text=On%20June%206%2C%20 1944%2C%20the,on%20the%20beaches%20of%20Normandy.

CHAPTER TWENTY-THREE

19. Lesley M. M. Blume, "Collateral Damage: American Civilian Survivors of the 1945 Trinity Test," *Bulletin of the Atomic Scientists*, July 17, 2023, accessed May 24, 2024, thebulletin.org/premium/2023-07/collateral-damage-american -civilian-survivors-of-the-1945-trinity-test/; Russell Contreras, "Henry Herrera and the Legacy of the Trinity Test," *Axios*, September 18, 2021, accessed May 24, 2024, axios.com/2021/09/18/hard-truths-deep-dive-environment -trinity-test; Samuel Gilbert, "The Forgotten Victims of the First Atomic Bomb Blast," *Vice*, July 24, 2016, accessed May 24, 2024, vice.com/en/article/gqkgp9 /the-forgotten-victims-of-the-first-atomic-bomb; Barbara Kent's daughter Kaysie Kent, phone conversation with adapter, March 13, 2024.

CHAPTER TWENTY-FOUR

20. Sreejith Sugunan, "The Bhagavad Gita and the Ethics of War," Religion and Humanitarian Principles: Hindu Circles, International Committee of the Red Cross, May 10, 2022, accessed October 28, 2024, blogs.icrc.org

/religion-humanitarianprinciples/bhagavad-gita-ethics-war/; "'Now I Am Become Death, the Destroyer of Worlds'—the Bhagavad Gita Explained," The Conversation, October 24, 2023, accessed October 28, 2024, theconversation.com/now-i-am-become-death-the-destroyer-of-worlds-the -bhagavad-gita-explained-214365.

21. United States "bomb count" figures from 1945 through 1955 in this and subsequent entries are taken from the United States Departments of Defense and Energy chart "Summary of Declassified Nuclear Stockpile Information: Declassified Stockpile Data 1945 to 1994," accessed May 29, 2024, osti.gov/opennet/forms?formurl=https://www.osti.gov/includes/opennet /document/press/pc26tab1.html. Figures from 1962 through 2024 are taken from Hans Kristensen, Matt Korda, Eliana Johns, Mackenzie Knight, and Kate Kohn, "Status of World Nuclear Forces," Federation of American Scientists, March 29, 2024, accessed May 29, 2024, fas.org/initiative/status-world -nuclear-forces. The "number of 'Hiroshimas'" estimates from 1945 through 1967 (and they are certainly just estimates) are derived from the "megatonnage" information on the above-mentioned Departments of Defense and Energy chart. The "number of 'Hiroshimas'" estimate for 2024 is derived from analysis of various data compiled at "FAS Nuclear Notebook: A Deep Dive into the World's Nuclear Arsenals," Federation of American Scientists, March 13, 2023, accessed May 29, 2024, fas.org/initiative/fas-nuclear-notebook. Because the United States is unusual in its level of declassification, to find out how many "Hiroshimas" could have been destroyed in the various years, we divide the estimated megatonnage of the American arsenal by fifteen thousand kilotons, or the estimated explosive yield of the Hiroshima bomb, to arrive at the first figure. Then we add the rest of the estimated total number of nuclear weapons in the world, use American figures to estimate the remaining global megatonnage, divide that number by fifteen thousand kilotons, then add it to the first figure.

CHAPTER TWENTY-SEVEN

22. Jack Niedenthal, *For the Good of Mankind: A History of the People of Bikini and Their Islands* (Majuro: Bravo, 2001), 43–47.

CHAPTER TWENTY-EIGHT

23. Erik Gregersen, "Lewis Strauss," *Encyclopedia Britannica*, accessed May 24, 2024, britannica.com/biography/Lewis-Strauss.

24. Alden Whitman, "Lewis Strauss Dies; Ex-Head of A.E.C.," *The New York Times*, January 22, 1974, 1, accessed March 24, 2024, nytimes .com/1974/01/22/archives/lewis-strauss-dies-exhead-of-aec-lewis-l-strauss -former-chairman-of.html.

CHAPTER THIRTY

25. Richard Rhodes, *Dark Sun: The Making of the Hydrogen Bomb* (New York: Simon & Schuster, 1995), 509, quoted in Tony Reichhardt, "The First Hydrogen Bomb," *Smithsonian Magazine*, November 2, 2017, accessed May 24, 2024, smithsonianmag.com/air-space-magazine/first-hydrogen -bomb-180967074/.

CHAPTER THIRTY-TWO

26. "McCarthyism and the Red Scare," Miller Center, accessed May 24, 2024, millercenter.org/the-presidency/educational-resources/age-of-eisenhower /mcarthyism-red-scare.

CHAPTER FORTY

27. "Have You No Sense of Decency?" United States Senate, accessed May 24, 2024, senate.gov/about/powers-procedures//investigations/mccarthy-hearings /have-you-no-sense-of-decency.htm.

EPILOGUE

28. "Secretary Granholm Statement on DOE Order Vacating 1954 Atomic Energy Commission Decision in the Matter of J. Robert Oppenheimer," United States Department of Energy, December 16, 2022, energy.gov/articles /secretary-granholm-statement-doe-order-vacating-1954-atomic-energy -commission-decision.

29. W. J. Hennigan, "The Toll," *The New York Times*, June 20, 2024, nytimes.com /interactive/2024/06/20/opinion/nuclear-weapons-testing.html.

30. "Nuclear Weapons Worldwide," Union of Concerned Scientists, accessed June 30, 2024, ucsusa.org/nuclear-weapons/worldwide.

A NOTE FROM THE ADAPTER

31. "Today's Armed Conflicts," The Geneva Academy, accessed December 20, 2025, https://geneva-academy.ch/galleries/today-s-armed-conflicts.

PHOTO CREDITS

xiv: United States Department of Energy/courtesy of Niels Bohr Library & Archives, American Institute of Physics; xvii: courtesy of Alex Sherwin; xx, 117, 150–151: National Archives; xxii: Yosuke Yamahata (photographer); © Shogo Yamahata; 3–5, 8, 15, 19–21, 52, 70, 141, 157–158, 265: courtesy of Kitty Oppenheimer and the J. Robert Oppenheimer Memorial Committee; 3 (Robert and father), 4 (sailor): Leo Grubman/courtesy of Kitty Oppenheimer and the J. Robert Oppenheimer Memorial Committee; 5 (music): Wetzel/courtesy of Kitty Oppenheimer and the J. Robert Oppenheimer Memorial Committee; 6: W. Burden Stage/courtesy of Kitty Oppenheimer and the J. Robert Oppenheimer Memorial Committee; 27, 76, 167, 205: Library of Congress, public domain; 47: Frank Oppenheimer/courtesy of AIP Emilio Segrè Visual Archives; 49: courtesy of Kai Bird and the estate of Martin Sherwin; 54: United States Department of Energy/courtesy of NARA; 62: Johan Hagemeyer photograph collection, © The Regents of the University of California, The Bancroft Library, University of California, Berkeley. This work is made available under a Creative Commons Attribution 4.0 license; 64: courtesy of Dr. Hugh Tatlock; 90, 99, 102–103, 104 (Rabi), 106, 108–109, 123: courtesy of the National Security Research Center (NSRC) at Los Alamos National Laboratory; 93, 177–79, 203, 232: Alfred Eisenstaedt/courtesy of *Life* magazine; 95–96: T. Harmon Parkhurst/courtesy of Palace of the Governors Photo Archives (NMHM/DCA) (View/negative 001240, Schoolhouse/negative 001366, Living Quarters/negative 001320); 101: Joseph Gluth/courtesy of Los Alamos Historical Society; 104 (personnel): courtesy of United States Atomic Energy Commission; 104 (physicists), 135: courtesy of United States Department of Energy; 112 (hikers): courtesy of Niels Bohr Library & Archives, American Institute of Physics; 112 (scientists and families), 159: courtesy of Los Alamos National Laboratory; 113: United States Department of Energy/courtesy of AIP Emilio Segrè Visual Archives; 133: Kenneth Bainbridge/courtesy of AIP Emilio Segrè Visual Archives; 144: courtesy of Kaysie Kent; 157 (dignitaries): Paul Southwick/courtesy of Kitty Oppenheimer and the J. Robert Oppenheimer Memorial Committee; 171, 173: United States Department of Defense; 175: Thomas J. O'Halloran/courtesy of Library of Congress, U.S. News and World Report Collection; 192: The Official CTBTO Photostream, Creative Commons Attribution 2.0 Generic License; 258: T. W. Harvey/courtesy of Kitty Oppenheimer and the J. Robert Oppenheimer Memorial Committee; 261: Fritz Henle/courtesy of Kitty Oppenheimer and the J. Robert Oppenheimer Memorial Committee; 268: © Yousuf Karsh; 277: Ulli Steltzer/courtesy of Trustees of the Princeton University Library

INDEX

Page numbers in *italics* refer to illustrations.